# JEWELRY & GEMS
## AT AUCTION

## Books by Antoinette Matlins
*(all GemStone Press)*

### Gem Identification Made Easy
*A Hands-On Guide to More Confident Buying & Selling*
2nd edition

### Colored Gemstones:
### The Antoinette Matlins Buying Guide
*How to Select, Buy, Care for & Enjoy Sapphires, Emeralds, Rubies and Other Colored Gems with Confidence and Knowledge*

### Diamonds: The Antoinette Matlins Buying Guide
*How to Select, Buy, Care for & Enjoy Diamonds with Confidence and Knowledge*

### The Pearl Book: The Definitive Buying Guide
*How to Select, Buy, Care for & Enjoy Pearls*
2nd edition

### Engagement & Wedding Rings
*The Definitive Buying Guide for People in Love*
2nd edition

### Jewelry & Gems: The Buying Guide
*How to Buy Diamonds, Pearls, Colored Gemstones, Gold & Jewelry with Confidence and Knowledge*
5th edition

### Jewelry & Gems at Auction
*The Definitive Guide to Buying & Selling at the Auction House & on Internet Auction Sites*

# Jewelry & Gems at Auction ◆

## The Definitive Guide to Buying & Selling at the Auction House & on Internet Auction Sites

**ANTOINETTE MATLINS, P.G.**
*with contributions by Jill Newman*

**GemStone Press**
Woodstock, Vermont

*Jewelry & Gems at Auction:*
*The Definitive Guide to Buying & Selling*
*at the Auction House & on Internet Auction Sites*

**Library of Congress Cataloging-in-Publication Data**

Matlins, Antoinette Leonard.
Jewelry & gems at auction : the definitive guide to buying and selling at the auction house and on internet auction sites / Antoinette Matlins
with contributions by Jill Newman.
        p. cm.
ISBN 0-943763-29-0
1. Gems—Purchasing. I. Title: Jewelry and gems at auction. II. Newman, Jill. III. Title.
TS756 .M278 2002
739.27'029'7—dc21

                                                                2002001723


10  9  8  7  6  5  4  3  2  1
Manufactured in the United States of America
Text design and composition by Chelsea Cloeter

GemStone Press
A Division of LongHill Partners, Inc.
Sunset Farm Offices, Route 4, P.O. Box 237
Woodstock, VT 05091
Tel: (802) 457-4000    Fax: (802) 457-4004
www.gemstonepress.com

# Contents

## PART I ◆ BUYING AND SELLING AT AUCTION

## PART 2 ◆ BECOMING FAMILIAR WITH GEMS

## PART 3 ◆ DIAMONDS

## PART 4 ♦ COLORED GEMSTONES AND PEARLS

## PART 5 ♦ DESIGN AND STYLE: GREAT JEWELRY

## PART 6 ♦ IMPORTANT ADVICE BEFORE BUYING OR SELLING AT AUCTION

## PRICE GUIDES

## SPECIAL CHARTS AND TABLES

## COLOR PHOTOGRAPH SECTIONS

# Acknowledgments

I WOULD LIKE TO TAKE A MOMENT TO MAKE SPECIAL MENTION OF MY father, Antonio C. Bonanno, who died in 1996. My work would not be what it is today without my having experienced his passion for the field of gemology, his guidance from the time I was a child and throughout my life, and his dedication to the highest professional and ethical standards. Although his name is not on this cover, his knowledge, wisdom, and guidance fill its pages. With each passing year my gratitude only increases.

In the writing of this book there are many people to whom I am grateful—too many to try to mention all of them here. Nonetheless, there are a few people who have been especially influential and supportive of the work I have done, and I would like to acknowledge them.

First I want to thank Jill Newman, whose professionalism made the process a pleasure and the product all the more useful to the reader.

To my brother Kenneth Bonanno, F.G.A., P.G., and my sisters Karen Bonanno DeHaas, F.G.A., P.G., and Kathryn Bonanno Patrizzi, F.G.A., P.G., from whom I continue to learn and with whom I enjoy sharing and debating gemological issues, and my sister Beth Honeycutt, without whose help I would never have met my deadlines, I can only say that I hope you know how much I appreciate your support.

I would like to specially acknowledge C. R. "Cap" Beesley, Director of American Gemological Laboratories in New York City. He has been a great teacher to me personally, and his research and leadership—especially as they pertain to gemstone treatments and disclosure—have had an important impact on the auction as we know it today and have benefited buyers and sellers alike.

I must also specially thank Osvaldo Patrizzi at Antiquorum Auctioneers (who I must point out is my brother-in-law) for his generous sharing of his extensive experience. He opened my eyes to the intricate world of horology and made it possible for me to see some of the world's rarest and most beautiful clocks and watches. Now that I have gained a much broader knowledge about how to judge them and the more modest timepieces, I deeply regret not being able to cover them in more depth here. Perhaps this will be the next book.

I would like to express my thanks also to Hoda Esphahani at Sotheby's, Francois Curiel and Simon Teakle at Christie's, John Block at Phillips, and Joseph DuMouchelle at DuMouchelles, from whom I have gained many insights over the years into buying and selling at auction, and Gail Brett Levine, publisher of *Auction Market Resource,* for helping me gather information on auction houses across the country and tracking the performance of certain types of gems and jewelry.

At GemStone Press, I want to thank the entire staff, with whom it is always a pleasure to work, but especially Polly Mahoney, Emily Wichland, and Bridgett Taylor, whose patience in this effort was sorely tested. Thanks for keeping your sense of humor.

And last, but not least, I want to thank my husband, Stuart Matlins, for his unfailing support and encouragement and for his willingness to spend many lonely nights while I'm traveling around the world to pursue my work.

# Introduction

A NEW SENSATION IS TAKING PLACE—AUCTION FEVER—AND PEOPLE from every walk of life are coming together to participate in the action. Some are vying for the chance to own the world's best, others to find a hidden treasure, and others to find incredible bargains. Some are in it for the pleasure, others for the profit. But whatever the case, the auction market is today's fastest-growing venue for buying and selling gems and jewelry.

Both traditional auction houses and "virtual" internet auctions are increasing in popularity as a source for buying sparkling gems and jewels, and as an exciting way to make a profit on yesterday's treasures. At auction, the opportunity exists for *anyone* to buy or sell, and if you are knowledgeable, astute—and lucky—there is always the possibility of acquiring a rare and valuable treasure at a "bargain" price, or of setting a new world record.

But for me it's the overall experience that draws me again and again. I may not always succeed, but I always have fun and enjoy the people, the rush of adrenaline, the thrill of the moment. I still remember my very first auction experience, over twenty-five years ago, as though it were yesterday. My father and I went to a "Magnificent Jewelry" auction held at one of New York's best-known firms. About two weeks before the auction, we were at the "trade" viewing, which occurs in a private room where knowledgeable professionals carefully examine each lot. We had come to examine several pieces of interest to one of my clients. We took our seats at a long table next to a window, where we would have the benefit of daylight. I pulled out our own gem-testing instruments so we would have whatever we needed within arm's reach as we examined pieces that interested us. I recognized some of the biggest names in the diamond and colored gemstone industry, and swelled with pride when several acknowledged us by name.

Dad and I spotted an exquisite sapphire ring sitting in a dealer's tray. We noted the lot number and opened our auction catalog to read the description and see the estimate. By then, the dealer had finished with it, and we began to examine the sapphire with mounting excitement. It was a "sugar-loaf" cabochon (see chapter 16) weighing over ten carats. The color was an exceptional, rich velvety blue, with a transparency and liveliness without equal (to this day I can't recall a more beautiful sapphire). After carefully examining the stone with the microscope and other instruments, we concluded it was a *natural, Kashmir sapphire,* worth far more than the $15,000 to $20,000 estimate. We couldn't believe our good fortune: to have spotted a rare gem that seemed to have gone undetected. It had no laboratory report and seemed to be regarded as just one of many, many sapphire pieces being offered in the sale.

I established an account with the auction house and registered to bid in the upcoming sale. The day of the auction arrived, I obtained a bidding paddle, and we took seats at the back of the room so we could see who was bidding, and so no one else would see us bidding and possibly figure out that we knew something they didn't. I had always wanted a Kashmir sapphire, and my husband had graciously agreed to let me bid on this piece, up to $60,000. I assured him that, at that price, should we ever fall on difficult times and need the cash, I'd guarantee we'd be able to sell it for a significant profit. The moment was drawing near; my pulse rate was starting to rise. The moment came…and went with amazing speed. There was interest everywhere. Bidding paddles shot into the air. I barely got my paddle up before the price was $75,000, then $80,000, $85,000…and suddenly the hammer sounded, signaling the end of bidding on that lot. The winning bid was $120,000!

I was heartbroken but remained to see what other surprises might occur before the sale's end. Toward the end of the sale, a ring I'd examined came up. I hadn't liked the ring itself and had no interest in the piece until the bidding started. Or, more accurately, didn't start. The auctioneer kept lowering his opening bid request. Finally he asked if anyone would give $12,000 for the piece (the estimate had been $24,000 to $26,000). Before I could think, my paddle was in the air. The next thing, the hammer came down, and the auctioneer congratulated me on the "bargain of the sale." I was nothing short of stunned. And I was very lucky; I had bid without thinking, and impulse bidding can result in costly mistakes. But before I could decide what to do with the ring, a dealer called and made an offer I couldn't refuse.

It was a day to remember, but it was also a day when I learned some important lessons:

- First: you cannot rely on catalog estimates; there are circumstances under which items may sell for much less, or much more, than estimates. The reasons for this are covered in chapters 1 and 2.

- Next: jewelry specialists at auction houses may lack the expertise necessary to recognize rare, valuable gemstones and jewelry. This may provide opportunities for astute buyers to acquire a treasure at a bargain price, but it can put sellers at serious risk of getting much less than the real value of what they are selling. This is covered in chapter 2, along with ways sellers can protect themselves.

- Also: pieces can still be had at bargain prices, even when knowledgeable professionals are in the room. If you are astute enough to thoroughly examine pieces—even those that don't necessarily appeal to you in terms of design and style—and are sure of their identity, quality, and value, you can still get lucky. For whatever reasons, others were not paying attention when I got the "bargain of the sale." Coming at the end of the day probably helped—when people are tired and inattentive—and the unattractive setting might have discouraged closer examination of the gemstones so that even dealers were hesitant to bid when the price was suddenly so low.

- And the biggest lesson of all: auctions are unpredictable…and this just adds to their allure!

Once the exclusive domain of the jewelry trade and affluent consumers, auctions were previously filled with dealers covertly examining items with dead cigars dangling from their lips, and bidding took place in rooms filled with stale smoke. Today this is no longer the case. Today's auction possibilities run the entire gamut of social experience, and offer a wide range of choices for today's auction goer, including the traditional auction house, the country-style auction, and auctions on the internet.

But whatever type of auction interests you, buying and selling at auction presents unique risks as well as opportunities. The key to reducing the risk and increasing success is knowing how to go about it, especially where jewelry and gems are concerned. And yet, as I reviewed what had been written for people interested in buying and selling jewelry and gems at auction, I realized there was nothing that provided what you really need to know. So, here is *Jewelry & Gems at Auction: The Definitive Guide to Buying & Selling at the Auction House & on Internet Auction Sites.*

Here you will find important information about jewelry and many of the gems you will find at auction. But I urge anyone interested in major gems—whether diamonds or colored gemstones—to refer to my comprehensive books *Diamonds: The Antoinette Matlins Buying Guide* and *Colored*

*Gemstones: The Antoinette Matlins Buying Guide* for more in-depth information that it is not possible to provide in a single volume.

In general, this book includes everything you need to know to help you succeed in the auction arena and avoid disappointment:

- What distinguishes auction buying and selling from other methods
- How to buy and sell at auction: the rules of the game
- How to make sure you know what you're really bidding on
- Special concerns when buying and selling on the internet
- What are the pitfalls of auctions...and how to avoid them
- How to determine what to bid
- What auctions do guarantee, and how to protect yourself against what they *don't* guarantee
- And much more....

If you take the time to follow the advice provided here, I think you'll find that the auction venue can be a source of challenge, excitement, pleasure, and, perhaps, even profit. And if you are diligent and astute, you may even find that you are one of the "lucky" ones...that you find that hidden treasure or set a new world record!

*Antoinette Matlins*

## PART I ♦
# BUYING AND SELLING AT AUCTION

# 1 ♦ The Allure of the Auction

Many people seeking to buy or sell fine jewelry or gemstones today are discovering the auction arena. It isn't hard to get caught up in "auction fever" because it is an exciting experience, filled with the thrill of anticipation. Whether buying or selling, whether an experienced veteran or a novice, whether bidding in the auction salon or in a country-style auction, you can't help feeling your heartbeat quicken as "your piece" comes up for bid. A little adrenaline surge will keep you on the edge of your seat until the auctioneer's hammer strikes, signaling the end of the bidding on that lot. And then it is over. But if you are successful, the next sensation you'll feel is a surge of pure delight. If not—well, perhaps you'll be luckier on the next lot that interests you, or the next auction. And so it goes.

The auction arena is like no other environment. Educated buyers can discover treasures—often at bargain prices—while educated sellers may obtain much higher prices for fine, rare gems or jewels sold at auction than they ever dreamed possible. Auctions today provide an international open market, one that facilitates competition and provides an opportunity for virtually anyone interested in a particular item to bid on it if it is within their financial means. Sometimes you win, sometimes you lose, but it's all part of the auction experience.

## Auction Ambiance—Something for Everyone

Once the exclusive domain of gem and jewelry dealers or affluent consumers, auction houses are now attracting a much broader range of buyers and sellers, and a much broader range of jewelry to offer them. Whether you want to buy or sell a modest piece of jewelry worth a few hundred dollars, or a rare jewel worth hundreds of thousands, auctions are gaining the attention of more and more people. And today, depending on what you are seeking, there is also a greater variety of auction venues from which to choose.

## The Country Auction

At one end of the auction phenomenon you'll find the "country auction." Country auctions—distinctive events that often combine a family outing, a social picnic, and treasure-hunting altogether into one big, fun-filled day— have been taking place across America for generations. There is really nothing else like it. It is a very different experience from what one finds at the traditional auction house, and in some ways it is hard to imagine that anything of any value would ever come up for bid in such an environment. But serious auction goers have found important pieces at such auctions. We know of a woman who purchased a brooch at a country auction for under $100. When she took it to her jeweler to find out if the stones were real, she learned it was a rare "Ballerina Brooch" made by the famous French jewelry house of Van Cleef & Arpels. At the time it was worth about $20,000 at a traditional auction house! She was just lucky, but a knowledgeable and astute buyer can still find such treasures at country auctions and have fun doing it.

Summer is a favorite time for country auctions, and you can find one virtually every weekend. In places where the weather is warm year-round, you can also find country auctions regularly. They are usually announced in the local newspaper, but people who have made purchases at previous auctions may also receive a mailing announcing the upcoming auction, highlighting some of the items that will be included in the sale.

Country auctions often take place "on site" at a local home that is being sold (along with all its contents), or in a church, a school auditorium, or on the premises of the auctioneer. It has a very local feeling, with many of the buyers being neighbors or regulars: local dealers and those who just like to come to visit with friends and watch what goes on. The call of the auctioneer is heard amidst the chatter of friends, a glass of homemade lemonade in your hand, and the voices of children playing in the background.

There are usually no catalogs or listing of items to be sold, and no "order" to the auction itself in terms of when a particular piece will come up for bids; the auctioneer usually auctions off each item as it is handed to him. There are also usually no written descriptions of the items to be sold, although the auctioneer will make an effort to describe them to the best of his or her ability. Before the auction, usually on the morning of the sale or on the day prior, you have the opportunity to examine whatever interests you and to ask questions of the auction staff. But keep in mind that they are giving you information to the best of their knowledge, and their knowledge may be very limited at best. Virtually *nothing* is guaranteed. It is whatever it is, the condition is whatever it is, and once you get it, it's yours. Period.

Another important difference between the traditional auction house and the country auction is that there are usually no estimates. This means that you have nothing that provides any indication of the value of an item; at the traditional auction house, many participants use the estimates as a guide, and are lost without one. Without any value indicator, *you* must have sufficient knowledge to know what something is worth, or risk overpaying for it. On the other hand, there is often no "reserve" (the price, agreed to in advance by the seller and auctioneer, below which the piece cannot be sold). This can work to the advantage of someone knowledgeable because it means that the item will be sold for whatever the high bid is, even if it is ridiculously low.

The country auction can be fast paced and intense, or almost unbearably slow, depending on the auctioneer. It is also somewhat chaotic compared with the traditional auction house, and occasionally you may find that you were not bidding on what you thought you were bidding. If you find out soon enough, and call it to the auctioneer's attention, it may be possible to re-auction the item, but you must be much more attentive to what is really going on and to what is actually being sold. You pay that day, and take it away.

The country auction can be more fun than other types of auctions, but it also presents a higher risk where jewelry is concerned because there is seldom anyone available with gemological training who can provide reliable information about the jewelry being sold. And the environment in which such auctions usually take place often makes it much more difficult, even for those with gemological skills and gem-testing instruments, to conduct a proper examination (there is often no electricity for instruments that might be needed, or proper lighting, and so on). Knowledgeable buyers will know their limitations, and bid conservatively or not at all.

Never assume, just because you are buying at a country auction, that you're getting a bargain. Many people pay more at such auctions than they would pay at the local retail jewelry store for something of the same quality. More than in any other auction environment, the key to getting a good deal at a country auction is knowledge. But with it, bargains can be found. Many years ago my young daughter had learned that a piano was going to be auctioned off at a country auction a few miles from our home. She begged me to go so that she could bid on the piano. We went and had a great day. She succeeded in getting her piano for $75 (plus the $200 I incurred in getting it moved to our home), and I found a wonderful handmade ring that contained a rare, natural, fiery orange garnet, for which I paid $35. I have no idea what the piano was worth, but my daughter practiced on it for the next four years. The ring, however, was then worth about $600. While it was not exactly a rare treasure worth thousands of dollars, I still have it and enjoy wearing it.

## The Auction Salon

At the opposite end of the auction phenomenon you will find the auction "salon." This is the domain of the educated and successful, of collectors and connoisseurs, of the rich and famous. Today, the pillars of industry, the patrons of the arts and sciences, the grande dames of society plan their calendars around the dates of those special events known as the "Magnificent" and "Important" auctions. Here limousines descend upon the scene, lining the streets outside prestigious addresses in New York, Geneva, London, and Hong Kong. Their elegant passengers alight to attend the exhibitions, parties, and other special events occurring during the week of the auctions. While socializing in the lobby over tea or champagne and canapés, an international roster of "Who's Who" casually discusses the current exhibition, hoping to entice a well-known expert to join the conversation. Here you are in a world where international commerce merges with haute couture, where people in sleek cars and dazzling jewels, serious collectors, and even the novice mingle with the most respected experts in the field, all brought together by their passion for whatever is coming onto the auction block.

But what is it that draws such people to the auction? After all, they can afford to buy whatever they want, wherever they want. Part of the allure is the glamour, but the glamour itself is connected to the realization that here is where one can find a greater variety—assembled together in one amazing exhibition—of the best of virtually anything one could possibly want. Whether one's passion is antique jewelry, jewelry from a particular period, diamonds in rare colors such as blue, pink, or red, or an exotic gemstone, you will find it at the fine auction salon. In a world where mass production and mediocrity have become the norm, the auction salon offers the loveliest and most distinctive objects ever produced, including those from the greatest masters of the past. And sometimes, as we saw when the estate of the Duchess of

Windsor came to Sotheby's, the provenance can be as exciting as the objects themselves, allowing us to be part of the romance or history of a bygone era.

The finest auction salons have also unveiled collections containing treasures rarely seen outside of museums. There is a striking difference, however, between viewing rarities in a museum and viewing them in a fine auction salon. While both venues provide an opportunity to see and learn, museums keep their treasures *beyond* our reach, whereas the auction salon places them *directly within* it. The auction salon creates a unique opportunity not only to see, but to *touch*, to *feel*, to *examine* closely and carefully, and even to *try on*. But above all, the greatest allure is that the auction provides the opportunity for us to acquire a treasure and make it our very own.

The auction salon may be intimidating—certainly its ambiance can be—and most of us cannot afford to bid on the rarest pieces, but the auction salon still has something to offer to everyone. Attend the exhibitions to see and examine the best; this will help you develop your eye to appreciate subtle quality differences in gemstones and recognize the fine workmanship and artistry that separate fine jewelry from the common. Attend the auctions, and note the prices at which items actually sell. By seeing and examining the finest gems and jewels, and gaining an appreciation of their value, you'll be building the expertise you need to spot a hidden treasure that might come up for auction elsewhere. And at worst, you'll be able to share in the thrill and drama of it all, if only vicariously.

We will discuss the ins and outs of buying and selling at the auction salon in chapter 2.

## The Regional Auction House

In between the country auction and the major international salons you will find the regional auction house. There are many fine, reputable regional auction houses today. Some have been around for decades, some are relative newcomers, and others are making their mark by specializing in particular types or styles of jewelry. They may lack the glamour of the large international salons, but they are not lacking in excitement. They may offer fewer rare and exotic treasures, but rare and exceptional pieces have been bought at bargain prices in small, little-known auction houses. And you can often succeed in acquiring beautiful, distinctive, well-made jewelry, and fine diamonds and gemstones, at very attractive prices.

One of my loveliest pieces—a beautiful *natural pearl* necklace—was acquired from a small regional auction house in the South. It was dirty, needed restringing, lacked a clasp, and was described as a "cultured pearl necklace." As I examined it I began to suspect from various characteristics that the pearls might not be cultured but natural (see chapter 20). I decided to bid up to an amount consistent with their description as cultured pearls and succeeded in getting them, after which I confirmed that they were indeed natural. After cleaning and restringing, they are beautiful. Their value is about twenty times what I paid for them. And what a beautiful "heirloom" to pass on to my daughter and granddaughter.

Some regional auction houses have on-staff gemologists or use the services of an outside gemologist to more accurately identify and describe the jewelry and gemstones they offer, but many regional houses do not have access to experienced gemologists. Be sure to ask. Where gems and jewelry are concerned, the lack of gemological expertise at an auction house increases the risk, especially to novices or lay people interested in jewelry. On the other hand, as illustrated above, it can increase the opportunity for those who are knowledgeable.

Buying and selling at regional auction houses will be discussed in chapter 2.

## Internet Auction Sites

Last, but far from least, is the internet auction phenomenon. First, by providing online catalogs and descriptions of items to be sold, the internet provides greater convenience for buyers at traditional auction houses. One international firm, Antiquorum Auctioneers (which specializes in fine watches), also provides *online bidding* during *live auctions,* providing greater convenience and wider participation. There are also internet sites such as eBay and Yahoo!, where viewing, bidding, and all administrative details, including payment and shipping, are handled on-line; here buyers are buying sight unseen, which greatly increases the risk where gems and jewelry are concerned, and requires greater diligence on the part of buyers. Finally, several traditional auction houses such as Sotheby's have created new business ventures—online auction sites modeled similarly to eBay—but with the added advantage of providing live viewing in their showrooms for a limited time before or during the auction. Information about viewing is provided on the website.

The rise of the internet, and its impact on our ability to link globally with a speed and economy never before imaginable, has also had its impact on the auction market. It has created greater interest and participation in auctions held at traditional auction houses by providing up-to-the-minute information about what is coming up, what has been auctioned previously, and prices at which pieces sold. It has also created the new online auction venue and companies such as eBay are becoming increasingly popular (see chapter 3).

Many traditional auction houses such as Christie's, Sotheby's, and Phillips provide online access to their catalogs to make it easier for people to preview what is coming up. While nothing can replace the need to see and evaluate gems and jewelry firsthand, the online catalogs provide a quick and easy way for people to see whether or not there is anything that *might* be of interest. If there is nothing of interest, you've saved the time and expense involved in going to the live exhibition. On the other hand, if you see something in which you do have interest, in addition to a description of the piece, the website will provide information about where and when the pieces will be on exhibition, so you can arrange to see and examine the pieces carefully.

Should you decide to bid, the internet also makes this part of the process easier. While it's always more fun to be present while the action is taking place, if you cannot be present you can submit written bids via the website or make an online request to have someone telephone you so you can bid by phone during the live auction. And, as mentioned above, firms such as Antiquorum are taking advantage of new technology to provide clients with the capability to bid on-line while a live auction is actually taking place, from virtually anywhere. In short, the internet now enables you to do a lot of the legwork right in your own home.

The internet is also becoming an important educational tool, providing access to numerous sites that offer information about gemstones and jewelry to help consumers become more knowledgeable, and bolstering their confidence in their own ability to buy or sell in the auction arena. You must keep in mind, however, that information provided on-line is not always reliable or complete. You need more than basic gemstone facts—such as where particular gems come from, myths surrounding them, colors in which they occur, their hardness or chemical composition—to make sound buying decisions. For those who love gems and jewelry, the best education comes from firsthand experience looking at pieces, handling them, and comparing them side by side with the help of someone knowledgeable. This, combined with the advice you will find in the following chapters, will start you on an exciting journey into the unique auction world, and help ensure your success as a buyer or seller.

Buying and selling at auctions on the internet is different from buying and selling at the traditional auction house, and will be covered in chapter 3.

## Auction Exhibitions Offer a Unique Learning Opportunity

The auction arena provides a unique opportunity to learn about jewelry and gems. Many auction firms have exhibitions that are open to the public, at which you can view the jewelry before the sale. Often exhibitions are also scheduled in other cities, and important pieces may go on international tour. At the exhibitions you can learn a tremendous amount simply by looking at, comparing, examining—and even trying on—hundreds of diverse designs, including antiques, Art Nouveau, Art Deco, Retro, and modern jewelry (see chapter 23 for definitions of various jewelry periods). You can see and examine diamonds and colored gemstones that satisfy a wide range of tastes and budgets. You can see differences in design, workmanship, and the artistry associated with a particular period. The experience of seeing some of the finest and rarest gemstones provides an excellent opportunity to develop an eye for important quality differences, and to begin to appreciate how subtleties can affect value.

Many auction houses produce beautiful color catalogs that can be purchased or, as mentioned above, viewed on-line (although the detail in the online photographs is usually not comparable to that in the printed catalogs). The catalogs themselves can be important educational references. They include photos and descriptions, and they usually include estimates of the price each piece is expected to bring. They often include valuable information about various jewelry periods or artists, or what makes certain pieces unusual or exceptional. Post-sale price sheets are sent to those who subscribe to the jewelry catalogs, but they can also be requested or viewed on-line. The post-sale price sheets are very important because they show whether or not an item sold and, if so, at what price. One note of caution here: pre-sale estimates are often not reliable indicators of the true value of a piece or the price it will actually bring. Many variables can affect these estimates, so whether buying or selling, you must be sure you understand how they are determined (see chapter 2).

You can learn invaluable lessons by examining the jewelry, reviewing the estimates, and keeping track of the actual prices at which they sold. You can also begin to notice trends and see whether particular jewelry styles or gemstones are increasing or decreasing in value. By tracking certain styles and gemstones sold at auction over a period of time, you can begin to sense which of today's bargains might be tomorrow's treasures.

## THE ALLURE OF AUCTIONS FOR THOSE WHO WANT TO *BUY* JEWELRY AND GEMS

There is no question that ever-increasing numbers of people from the world over are getting on the auction bandwagon. And there are some very good reasons why people who love gems and jewelry are buying at auction.

**Great prices.** Price is certainly one of the primary reasons why people are turning to the auction arena. Buyers believe they can buy jewelry for less than they would pay from traditional retail jewelry stores, and often this is the case. For the knowledgeable buyer, prices can be as low as one-half to one-fourth the price of comparable pieces from a jewelry store. In some cases, items come to the auction block to settle estates, or as a means to dispose of unclaimed property, and may need to be sold at whatever the highest bid may be, regardless of value. While this is no guarantee that you'll get a bargain, a knowledgeable buyer may recognize a treasure that others have missed, and pay very little. And sometimes such pieces sell at very low prices because no one obtained proper certification and they are overlooked, even by the pros. (There is more on this in later chapters.)

For sellers, it is often true that fine jewelry and gems will bring more at auction than from any other source. Educated sellers often succeed in getting a much higher price for a fine, rare gem or jewel sold at auction than they ever dreamed possible, because the fine auction house can deliver an international clientele that includes collectors from the world over, along with great publicity.

**Huge diversity.** Auctions provide a huge diversity of jewelry styles and gemstone choices—from basic, everyday designs to rare, period pieces with historical significance. Most traditional jewelers will not have access to such a broad range of products and prices at one time. The auction houses strive to offer diversity so that each sale will attract a wide audience of potential buyers and sellers.

Art Deco brooch (sold: $8,800)

Modern gold and gemstone ring (sold: $700)

Charming Retro brooch (sold: $5,500)

*One-of-a-kind jewelry with distinctive workmanship from bygone days.* Auctions offer some of the finest examples of jewelry from collectible periods. These pieces often exhibit elaborate workmanship that cannot be duplicated today except by the most extraordinary artists, at prices much higher than what such pieces bring at auction. The intricate platinum work seen in Edwardian or Belle Epoque pieces, for example, is often so delicate that it resembles fine lace. You cannot find such intricate workmanship in new jewelry, nor can you find anyone willing to attempt to duplicate it. As more and more people seek jewelry that is unique or distinctive in some way, they are discovering antique jewelry (jewelry over one hundred years old) and jewelry from the Belle Epoque, Edwardian, Art Nouveau, Art Deco, Retro, or other collectible periods (see chapter 23 for definitions of jewelry periods). And, they are discovering the auction house as a primary source from which to acquire it. While some

Intricate Belle Epoque brooch (sold: $94,000)

Diamond and sapphire floral brooch, circa 1950 (sold: $4,600)

of the masterpieces of these periods can fetch stellar prices among collectors and connoisseurs, lovely pieces often sell at auction for very modest prices. The very astute buyer who seeks even more affordable one-of-a-kind pieces—without sacrificing interesting detailing and beautiful workmanship—can pay special attention to jewelry made in the 1950s and 1960s. Many pieces from those decades, not yet regarded as collectible period jewelry sought after by collectors, can still be had at unbelievably low prices.

***Historically important gems and jewels.*** At the other extreme, the auction arena is one of the few places where you can actually acquire museum-quality jewelry and gems, including pieces of historic importance. One finds many examples of this at auction, such as La Peregrina, a famous natural pearl that is one of the largest and most beautiful ever found, which can be traced all the way back to 1554, when King Philip II of Spain gave it to his wife, Mary Tudor, on their wedding day. La Peregrina was purchased at Sotheby's auction house by the Welsh actor Richard Burton for his wife, American movie star Elizabeth Taylor. Burton then commissioned Cartier to design a magnificent necklace in

La Pelegrina
(sold: $463,800)

which to hold this historic pearl. Ms. Taylor permitted her necklace to be placed on display as one of the highlights of the massive "Pearls" exhibition that ran at the American Museum of Natural History in New York City and the Field Museum in Chicago in 2001–2002.

***Major source of masterpieces by great artists and the greatest jewelry houses.*** Whether you are searching for an exquisite Etruscan revival masterpiece by a nineteenth-century master such as Giuliano or Castellani, or a flowing Art Nouveau creation by Lalique or Fouquet, or a fanciful jewel from the famous workshops of Fabergé or Cartier, beautiful examples can be found at a fine auction salon. The finest pieces from these earlier periods are also becoming more and more rare, and signed jewels such as those created in the Art Deco period by Cartier, or those from the Art Nouveau period signed by Lalique or Fouquet, are especially sought after today. While collectors pay top dollar at the major auction houses for the right piece (and if you want to *sell* such

Rare Mauboussin Art Deco
carved emerald necklace
(sold: $167,500)

a piece, I recommend only the biggest and best-known houses), they still slip through at affordable prices at some of the lesser-known auction firms.

*Fine timepieces at timely prices.* Watches—old and new, for him and for her, and by every major manufacturer—can be found at auction at bargain prices or at prices that set new world records. You will often find very fine watches in "like new" condition, by firms such as Piaget, Cartier, or Tiffany & Company, at prices much lower than what they would cost if purchased new. Women seeking fashionable watches in eighteen-karat gold, perhaps with diamonds or gemstones, will find some great values at auction. My favorite watch is an eighteen-karat gold watch I succeeded in getting at auction for $350. I'm sure that one reason I got it for so little was that it wasn't running during the exhibition. I had removed the back to examine it and saw that it was terribly dirty, but I didn't notice any broken parts. I decided to bid on it because I thought it was really beautiful and worth the risk at the price I bid. Once cleaned, it kept perfect time. For those especially interested in clocks and watches, it is worth noting here that Antiquorum Auctioneers—a firm specializing in fine timepieces—is the only auction firm that provides in-depth "condition reports" and *guarantees* that all timepieces they sell are in working condition.

Chronograph Amalfi watch by International Watch Company (estimate: $8,500–$9,500)

Ladies gold Retro watch (estimate: $4,500–$5,000)

For those interested in selling, a fine watch or a rare watch with an intricate movement may fetch a much higher price at auction than anywhere else—perhaps a figure well into the seven digits. A Patek Philippe wristwatch sold by Antiquorum was the first to cross the seven-digit threshold when it set a world record at $1,100,000.

*Fine auction houses are now the primary source of the finest and rarest natural gemstones.* Today, connoisseurs and collectors of the finest natural gemstones are turning to the auction house for the gems they seek because natural gems of fine quality are rarer than ever before, and increasingly difficult to find in the traditional jewelry marketplace. Each year it becomes more difficult, and many of nature's most spectacular gemstones have all but disappeared, forcing those who seek them to turn elsewhere. The legendary Kashmir sapphire, for example, has not been mined for almost seventy-five years, and ruby sources in Burma are no longer producing gems in the size and quality for which they were known for centuries. So those seeking these fabled gemstones are turning to the fine auction salon, where such gems can still be found in the magnificent old jewels they adorn. Rare gems may fetch handsome prices, and sometimes the price brought at auction sets a new world record. Such was the case when the Rockefeller sapphire—a rich, deep blue, rectangular-cut Burmese stone weighing over 60 carats and thought to

The Rockefeller sapphire (62.02 carats) by Tiffany & Company (sold: $3,636,000)

be the finest sapphire in the world—set a new world auction record in June 2001, at $3.6 million.

***Jewels of famous people and famous moments.*** At auction you can discover jewels from some of the world's renowned royal families, socialites, and celebrities, as well as pieces with historical significance or connected to a historic moment, because sellers are more likely to offer such jewels at auction, where publicity and an international marketplace can result in the highest price.

For some, the attraction is the thrill of owning a piece of history, to connect personally to a significant historical event, person, or jewel. This was clearly the case for a lucky bidder who leaped for joy after succeeding in acquiring *the* red, white, and blue "patriotic" watch always worn by American comedy legend Bob Hope during his Christmas tours to American troops abroad. The watch was a common, inexpensive watch (it was base metal, not even gold), but to the war veteran who purchased it, its value lay in its historic significance and to the much-loved celebrity behind it. In another auction, a woman fell in love with a piece from the estate of Jacqueline Kennedy Onassis and was the successful bidder on it. She paid far more

Bob Hope's patriotic watch. Antiquorum, NY (sold: $4,000)

than it was worth but explained that although she had never known Jackie personally, she'd been an important figure in her life and a great inspiration.

For her, the value of what she acquired lay not so much in the piece itself but in the feeling she knew she would get when she wore it: the feeling of being connected in a small but very personal way to this remarkable woman.

Historic jewels and gems are often consigned to an auction house in order to ensure worldwide visibility and bidding on an international scope, adding further to the excitement of the auction floor. When the jewels of the Duchess of Windsor went on the auction block at Sotheby's, the auction room might as easily have been the location for an episode of *The Lifestyles of the Rich and Famous.*

You must be very careful, however, before letting "provenance" dictate the price you are willing to pay for an item, especially if there is any possibility you may resell it at some future time. You must first ask yourself whether or not you will be able to definitively prove the connection to the famous person at some future time. For example, how can anyone prove that a strand of imitation pearls is *the* strand that belonged to Jackie Kennedy or the Duchess of Windsor? One imitation pearl necklace looks like the next, and there is nothing to distinguish one from another. On the other hand, when a fine gem or jewel is accompanied by laboratory documentation or is signed and numbered by the house that created it (where there will be documentation pertaining not only to the design but also to the stones used), you will have the documentation necessary to prove the provenance of a particular piece at a future time.

***Easy access.*** The auction process allows you to participate in a way that is very easy and convenient. You can participate in a "live" auction via phone, by a written bid, or through a live webcast. Bidders from all over the world can participate in the process without ever leaving their homes or offices.

## THE ALLURE OF THE AUCTION FOR THOSE WHO WANT TO *SELL* JEWELRY AND GEMS

There are many reasons people today are considering the auction arena when they want to sell gems or jewelry. When estates are being settled, auctions provide a quick way to turn assets into cash—a useful option when estates must be divided among several heirs. In some cases people sell jewelry they don't like, or pieces they no longer wear, in order to get cash to buy something they would like better, or to use for some other purpose altogether. In such cases, people often have more confidence turning to a respected auction house than to a jeweler or dealer. Sometimes pieces are sold because one is in need of money but wants to handle the disposal of valuable items discreetly. In these cases, selling at auction is attractive because it provides anonymity. Whatever the reason, selling at auction can be attractive for several reasons:

***Rare gems and jewelry can command the highest prices at auction.*** While many people turn to the auction hoping to find a bargain, bargain hunters aren't the only people accounting for the increased auction activity. The auction arena has also become the primary market for gem and jewelry connoisseurs and for collectors seeking rare gems and jewels that are virtually impossible to find today, even in the finest jewelry stores. Antique jewels in pristine condition and exceptionally fine natural gems have become so rare that when collectors or connoisseurs find what they want, they are willing to pay whatever it takes to get it. And the auction houses take advantage of such pieces to obtain even greater publicity than usual, creating even greater visibility. So if you have a piece that is rare, distinctive, or collectible, it will probably fetch a higher price at auction than from other sources because of the overall visibility provided through media and the auction house's own clientele of collectors and connoisseurs. Very rare pieces may fetch startling amounts, sometimes setting new records, because of the clientele fine auction houses attract and the great publicity they provide, so an educated seller can get a higher price for a fine, rare gem or jewel sold at auction than he or she ever dreamed possible.

***Prices brought at auction often exceed offers from jewelers or estate dealers.*** Even pieces that are not rare or unusual may bring a higher price at auction than from other sources. As a general rule, a jeweler or estate dealer who buys from a private seller must pay for it immediately. In such cases, there is always an element of risk for the jeweler or dealer; it could be stolen merchandise, or the item might not sell for a long time, and so on. Furthermore, if the piece is something that can be easily obtained through wholesale sources (from which people in the trade can obtain merchandise "on memo," that is, without paying for a period of time or until the item is sold), why tie up cash buying from someone outside the trade? The only incentive is being able to buy it for much less, so the offer will reflect this. The amount usually offered is approximately half the current wholesale value. This is also the formula usually used to establish auction estimates, so one usually won't get less at a well-attended auction than from another source. On the other hand, there is always the possibility that you could get more at auction. Someone outside the trade, for example, who likes the piece and compares it with other items at a local jewelry store, may be willing to bid much more than the auction house estimated. A consumer who bids up to the full wholesale value would make a good buy—even though they might pay almost double what a jeweler or estate dealer might pay. And if the piece is especially beautiful or desirable, and not something one can easily find or duplicate at a jewelry store, two consumers interested in the piece might bid much more than wholesale.

*Visibility to a much larger audience increases the chance of finding a buyer.* Major auction firms provide live exhibitions, special events, online information, and media coverage that reaches a diverse, international audience unrivaled by any jeweler or estate dealer. Well-known auction firms have established a large, international clientele to whom catalogs are sent before each auction. Any of their clients are potential buyers for your piece. The catalog, combined with the pre-sale exhibitions where pieces may be seen, examined, and discussed with the auction house gemologist, can elevate interest. Further interest is generated through information provided on websites. Important pieces may also go on tour to cities around the world, and special events—such as lectures or social events and VIP previews—increase attendance and visibility. Large firms have aggressive public relations departments that get publicity on television and in magazines and newspapers. Beautiful pieces will receive high visibility and generate lots of interest, and this usually translates to very active, fast-paced bidding.

*The seller can remain anonymous.* As mentioned earlier, for a variety of reasons the seller may prefer to remain anonymous. The auction house does not normally disclose the name of a consignor unless the piece carries with it a "provenance" that might increase attention and interest, and result in more competitive bidding. Yet, even if the name carries significance, it will not be disclosed if the consignor requests anonymity.

## A GOOD TIME FOR *INFORMED* BUYERS AND SELLERS TO CONSIDER THE AUCTION ARENA

Today there are many enticing and wonderful opportunities in the auction arena for both buyers and sellers. And as competition heats up among auction houses, both on-line and off-line, customer services are being increased to entice newcomers and build relationships with current clients. The most prestigious auction houses often find themselves competing with one another for the most important and beautiful jewels or important estates—these will command top dollar, media attention, and higher revenues. As a result of this increased competition, buyers are finding that there is a wider range of gemstones and jewelry styles coming to the auction block than ever before, and potential sellers are finding that they have greater leverage in negotiating specific consignment terms. But to take advantage of the numerous opportunities and avoid costly mistakes, you must first educate yourself about the risks, and how to protect yourself from disappointment.

The auction arena is not one that should be entered casually. For the inexperienced and uneducated, there are hidden risks that greatly increase the possibility of being disappointed or buying something that is not what it appears to be. But with some basic knowledge, the auction market can be a great source of some of the world's finest gems and jewelry, record-setting treasures, and great bargains, too.

# 2 ♦ The Traditional Auction House: How to Be a Successful Buyer or Seller

AS YOU WILL SEE THROUGHOUT THIS BOOK, NO ONE CAN PROPERLY judge any fine gem or piece of jewelry without seeing it firsthand and examining it with proper gem-testing equipment. Where auctions are concerned, proper examination is even more critical because the auction house has limited liability. Where gems and jewelry are concerned, we cannot recommend buying blind—that is, bidding on something you have not seen and examined carefully. For this reason, we will focus primarily on buying through the traditional auction house, possibly *bidding* on-line, but having had the benefit of viewing the pieces and speaking with a gemologist expert.

Being a player at a traditional auction is an exciting and thrilling experience. The ambiance, mystique, and unpredictability create a unique mood and feeling within the room, an unparalleled experience for everyone present. But it is not for everyone, nor is everyone a winner.

Success requires knowledge—knowledge about the auction process itself and about the product that interests you. Costly mistakes can be made if you don't take time to be an observer and learn as much as possible *before* you take an active part. But don't let this discourage you. While knowledge doesn't come overnight, learning can be a lot of fun and reveal a much wider range of choices than you ever imagined. Once you have a general understanding of some of the basics, you can start exploring catalogs of upcoming auctions, viewing interesting pieces at the exhibitions, and attending live auctions to see the action. You'll find it an entertaining and exhilarating way to start your in-depth education and to prepare yourself to become a participant.

One important thing to keep in mind when considering the auction venue is that some product categories are more risky than others. Buying a dress that belonged to Princess Diana, for example, is fairly straightforward: it was designed for her alone; it is the only one that exists; either it fits or it doesn't;

it is in good condition or it isn't; and so on. By contrast, you'll find that buying any gem or jewelry at auction lies on the opposite end of the risk scale: it may be a ruby or it may be a red spinel; it may be a naturally occurring gemstone or it may be synthetic; its color may be natural or it may be artificially enhanced; and so on. Gems and jewelry top the list of products in the "very high risk" category.

Buying or selling gems and jewelry at auction is very different from buying or selling through the traditional jewelry retailer. Understanding how it all works—the ground rules and the ins and outs of the actual auction process—is just the first step. While beautiful, distinctive jewelry can be acquired at auction at very attractive prices, and rare treasures can set new records, these are not the only possible scenarios. All too often a lovely gem is *not* what it is represented to be. All too often an antique jewel is *not* a true antique. All too often, a "signed" piece is *not* made by the famous house whose signature it bears. Whatever the case, buyers of such pieces usually overpay. There are even more serious risks for someone who wants to sell something at auction. While it is possible for a rare piece to exceed your highest expectation, or perhaps even set a new record, all too often inexperienced sellers consign something rare and valuable without knowing what they really have and permit it to be sold for a fraction of its real value.

The key to enjoying the auction arena and to experiencing the excitement, anticipation, and thrill—and to being pleased with the outcome—requires a two-step process. The first step is learning how to go about it. This will be covered in this chapter and the next. But where jewelry and gems are concerned, the real key to avoiding the pitfalls and being successful—whether buying or selling—is having an in-depth knowledge about the gemstones themselves and the lovely jewelry they adorn. This will be covered in the remaining chapters.

With the information provided in the following pages, and by watching and exploring this fascinating arena, you will gain the knowledge, expertise, and experience that will enable you to enjoy many sparkling purchases…or profitable sales.

## Getting Ready to Buy or Sell at the Traditional Auction House

Most auction houses operate generally in the same way, whether they are huge international companies or small regional firms. Internet auctions, however, require a different approach to buying and selling and will be covered separately in the next chapter.

Be sure you check the reputation of the firm, regardless of its size. Check the gemological credentials and expertise of the staff as well as the terms and conditions under which they operate. If you are thinking about consigning a piece to sell, check to see that auction houses are adequately insured to cover any unforeseen damage or loss to your property while in their possession. If they plan to conduct exhibitions in numerous locations, be sure that their insurance provides coverage in all locations.

Be sure to check with the Better Business Bureau to see whether or not there have been any complaints, especially related to paying consignors or delivering merchandise. If there is a knowledgeable gemologist-appraiser in the city where the auction house is located, I strongly recommend checking with that person; gemologists can often provide important information about the firm and its reliability (see chapter 25 to locate a gemologist-appraiser with reliable credentials).

Within the United States, the large international houses such as Christie's, Phillips, and Sotheby's are among the best known, but there are many regional firms that should not be overlooked. We provide a list of some of the best known in the appendix. Some auction houses specialize in certain types of jewelry. Antiquorum Auctioneers, for example, specializes in timepieces. If you are interested in a particular type of jewelry or particular style or period, dealing with a firm that specializes in that particular genre can increase the likelihood of your finding exactly what you want. And for sellers, specialist firms attract a higher percentage of collectors and connoisseurs who will appreciate and recognize the value of rare and unusual pieces, assuring a strong price.

You will also find that some of Europe's most prestigious small auction houses, such as Antiquorum, now have offices in the United States. Antiquorum, headquartered in Geneva, Switzerland, has an office in New York City and holds auctions in New York City as well as Geneva. Antiquorum's policy, regardless of the location of the auction itself, is to provide a full exhibition of all lots in both cities, so that prospective buyers can carefully inspect each piece before the sale. This is not always the case. Some international firms, including Christie's, Sotheby's, and Phillips, exhibit only a small selection of lots coming up at future sales in other cities—generally the highlights of the sale—which are usually available for examination during exhibitions for the

New York sales. You can view the entire sale in the printed catalog or on-line, but unless you plan to be present in the city where the sale is taking place, it is not possible to view many of the pieces firsthand. As you will better understand in later chapters, we strongly recommend against bidding on any gem or jewelry piece unless you have had an opportunity to examine it carefully.

As you can see, there are many auction houses, here and abroad, offering beautiful jewelry and competing to attract more and more buyers and sellers. The thrill and excitement of the experience is just waiting for you. And you're almost ready to begin. But before getting started, let's make sure you understand some of the terms you'll see and hear:

**Lot:** Each piece sold at auction is called a "lot." A lot may be a single piece, or it may contain several pieces that are being sold together. When you bid, you are bidding on the entire lot, unless otherwise stated by the auctioneer. If a lot contains five items, for example, and your bid is $300, you get all five pieces for a total of $300 (plus the buyer's premium).

**Lot number:** Each lot is assigned a number, and the lots are listed numerically by that number in the catalog. This makes it easy to locate the lot in the catalog so that you can read the description and learn what the estimate is. When you bid by fax or phone, it is essential that you know the exact lot number so that you are bidding on the correct lot.

**Estimate:** An estimate of the price range within which a particular lot is expected to sell. Estimates are not "the price" of the lot and are not wholly reliable—lots often sell for much *more* than the estimates, and sometimes for *less*—but they can provide an indicator of value that can be useful to beginners.

**Reserve:** The lowest price a consignor is willing to accept for a particular lot, and below which it cannot be sold by the auction house. At most auction houses there will be a reserve on each lot unless otherwise indicated (by a mark designated in the catalog). When a lot fails to meet the reserve and goes unsold, the auctioneer will use the term *pass* or *bought in* or something similar. (According to United States law, the reserve must be *within* the estimate or below it; it cannot exceed the estimate. Therefore, if you are the high bidder, and your bid is an amount equal to the high estimate, the lot will be yours. This is not the case in other countries, such as France, for example. In France, the reserve can be above the estimate, so if you had the highest bid, and it was at the high end of the estimate, you still might not have met the reserve and fail to obtain it.)

*Without reserve:* A term indicating that the lot will be sold to the highest bidder regardless of the amount of that bid. For example, if a lot is being sold "without reserve," it could be sold to a bidder for $250 if that is the highest bid, even if the estimate was $2,000–$2,500.

*Bought in:* A term used by auctioneers to indicate a lot failed to sell.

*Passed:* A term used by auctioneers to indicate a lot failed to sell.

*Returned to owner:* A term used by auctioneers to indicate a lot failed to sell.

*Withdrawn:* Lots are usually not withdrawn before a sale, but it happens occasionally. The lot numbers of withdrawn lots are announced before the start of the auction session, and again when that lot number comes up within the auction sequence.

*Bid:* The act of raising your paddle to indicate agreement to pay the amount being asked by the auctioneer (verb); the amount you have agreed to pay for a particular lot (noun). When a lot is being auctioned, the auctioneer asks the room whether or not someone is willing to give a specific amount for that lot. For example, "Who will give me $500? Do I hear $500?" If you raise your paddle, you are saying, "Yes, I'll give you $500." You bid $500, and if that is the highest bid, and it is sold to you, then the winning bid is $500.

*Bidder:* A person who has registered with the auction house and obtained a bidding paddle with which to place bids during an auction.

*Bidding paddle:* A plastic, cardboard, or wooden sign upon which a number has been printed. The number is assigned to the bidder when the bidder registers. The auctioneer calls out the number of your paddle each time you are the winning bidder on any given lot, and the lot number is then listed as having been purchased by the person to whom the paddle number has been registered.

*Absentee bidder:* A person who is not present during an auction but who has placed a bid by fax, e-mail, or telephone. In such cases, the house will bid on their behalf, up to the maximum authorized. Should the absentee bidder be the winner, the price paid will be the next increment over the highest bid on the floor, which may be an amount less than the authorized maximum bid. When sold to someone not present, the auctioneer will indicate that the lot was sold to the "absentee bidder."

*Hammer price:* The amount of the highest bid. When the bidding comes to a halt and no one is willing to go any higher, the auctioneer announces that he is going to let it "go"; you may recall seeing an auctioneer in a movie or on television say "Going once, going twice, sold!" As he says "sold," he strikes the hammer against the wooden block at the podium. This signals that the bidding is over. Immediately following the strike of the hammer, the auctioneer restates the amount at which he has "knocked down" the lot. If the bid was sufficient to allow the lot to be sold, he will also state the paddle number of the high bidder along with the "hammer price."

When a particular lot sells, it is on this amount (the hammer price) that the buyer's premium and the seller's commission are calculated. When a piece does not sell, this is the amount on which the house calculates what the seller owes them.

***Buyer's premium:*** A designated percentage that is added to the price bid on any lot and paid to the auction house by the successful bidder. The percentage varies among auction houses, but it normally runs between 10 and 20 percent. At some auction houses, the percentage drops on bids that exceed a certain amount. For example, at this time Christie's charges a premium of 17½ percent on any amount up to and including $80,000, and 10 percent on the amount above $80,000. The buyer's premium is subject to change, so be sure to check; the amount is always stated in the auction catalog.

***Seller's commission:*** A commission paid by a consignor, in this case the seller, to the auction house, based on a fixed scale, on all sold lots that were consigned. The amount of the seller's commission is indicated in the auction catalog and in the contract between the consignor and auction house. Typically it ranges from 10 to 20 percent. On unsold lots, there is also a fee, which varies between auction houses but is significantly less than the fee paid on sold lots.

***Unsold:*** If a lot does not reach the reserve, it remains unsold and is returned to the consignor.

## BUYING AT AUCTION—HOW TO BE SUCCESSFUL

We cannot overemphasize the importance of taking time to understand what you are doing and, if possible, to participate as an observer at least several times before taking an active part.

Recently a very successful-looking couple wandered into a well-known auction salon while an important jewelry sale was in progress. They took seats next to me. They didn't have a catalog. It soon became clear to me that their knowledge about each piece was restricted to what they were seeing on the slides appearing on the screen at the front of the room. After a while, a pair of earrings by a well-known designer appeared on the screen, and the woman suddenly got excited because she knew the designer and thought the price was so low that her husband should bid on them. He did, and he got them. Later, a pair of diamond earrings appeared on the screen, and the man commented to the woman that the price sounded very cheap and perhaps he should bid on them. I couldn't help overhearing them, nor could I resist asking if he had examined them. "Oh no," he said, "we just happened to be in the neighborhood and noticed that a jewelry sale was taking place and thought it would be fun!" I told him that I had examined them, and they were very, very tinted in color (not nearly as "white" as they appeared on the slide) and that they also had visible black inclusions. "Oh my," he said. "We wouldn't want anything like that." He thanked me and decided against bidding on them. We met again later, just after they picked up the earrings, and they were very upset. While they had really gotten a very good buy, they were disappointed because the finish on the gold was worn, along with some of the detailing. I explained that the designer could easily restore the finish, and tried to reassure them that they had done well on their purchase, but they were still angry. As far as they were concerned, the photo was "misleading," and the auction house, having such a fine reputation, should have been willing to stand behind "their product" and refund the money.

This is a perfect example of what can happen if you just jump in cold. This couple did not understand what they were doing nor did they understand that the auction house didn't "own" the earrings and was not liable in any way. Luckily, their "mistake" was not compounded by having added the diamond earrings to their purchase that day, which would certainly have been a disappointment. In any case, this is not the way to begin.

## Purchase Catalog Subscriptions and Track Sales

The best way to get started is to subscribe to the jewelry auction catalogs. You can purchase a domestic subscription for auctions taking place in the United States, or an international subscription for jewelry auctions worldwide. Take the time to carefully review the catalogs. Then, with catalog in hand, attend several exhibitions to examine pieces you like, comparing them with what is shown in the catalogs, and then track sales performance. By noting the prices at which comparable pieces sell in a particular sale, or by tracking prices over a period of time or from previous sales, you can get a sense of what it will cost to get what you want. You may also be able to spot trends or see whether or not prices seem to be strengthening or declining.

Today most of the important auction houses publish extensive catalogs—some are beautifully bound books—and many firms now have websites on which you can also view the items shown in the catalogs. The catalogs provide images and descriptions of each lot (and each lot is assigned a lot number). Typically there will also be an estimate alongside each lot. The estimate is usually shown as a price range within which the piece is expected to sell. For example, a brooch might show an estimate of $2,000 to $2,500, suggesting that the piece will probably bring at least $2,000 but could fetch as much as $2,500.

Viewing the catalog is the first step and will make it easier to accomplish the second step: viewing the actual piece. It is best to review the catalogs before the exhibitions so you will know exactly which lots are of interest. This will save you lots of time. The exhibitions are organized in numerical order, so it is usually easy to find the particular lots you need to see. It is essential to view each piece carefully. You cannot depend upon photographs—many pieces look better in the photograph than in reality, while other pieces look worse. You will find, for example, that emeralds often look much worse in the photographs, and rubies often look much better.

Compare the pieces you like side by side, and don't be afraid to seek guidance from the jewelry expert to help you better understand how they may differ from one another. In cases where there are significant price differences for items that seem similar at first glance, ask why. Make notes in your catalog that will remind you of things that might not be obvious from the photos or information that may have been left out of the description.

When you are first getting started, we recommend that you take time to participate only as a spectator for the first few times. If this isn't possible, or if there is a particular lot in which you are especially interested in a current sale, then we strongly recommend you request several catalogs from previous sales and the price sheets for each, so you will know which lots actually sold, and at what price. Study them carefully. While the catalog may not reveal unusual factors affecting the price at which something may have sold, or that would explain why something didn't sell, generally speaking you can still gain some valuable insights. And the jewelry expert at the auction house might also be able to explain why something in a previous sale might have sold for an exceptionally high price, or why it didn't sell at all.

## The Importance of Tracking Auction Performance Before You Enter the Game

Whether you take time to be a spectator at several auctions or invest time in carefully studying previous catalogs, it will be time well spent. First, you'll be able to see whether or not particular gemstones, styles of jewelry, or jewelry firms and designers are selling well, or if they are showing an upward or downward trend. For example, if something seems to sell consistently within the estimate, this would suggest that performance is steady. On the other hand, if something consistently sells for more than the estimate, this would suggest that the market might be strengthening. This could be a good time to buy if the upward trend is just starting. If something fails to sell consistently, or sells at the low end of the estimate or below, this would suggest that interest is declining. If the decline is just starting, you might want to wait to see if the decline continues, and buy when interest is lowest.

If you were to take time to track the sale of pieces containing important rubies, sapphires, and emeralds over the past two years, you would see that prices have been strengthening steadily for natural gemstones—that is, gemstones that have not been subjected to any enhancement. On the other hand, you would also see a steady decline in prices for treated gemstones. In terms of jewelry, you would note that pieces made by David Webb were not selling as well as in the past, and when they did sell, they sold at lower prices, while Cartier and Tiffany pieces were continuing to fetch strong prices. And so on.

This type of information should be factored into determining the bid you might want to make on a particular piece in a current or upcoming sale. It can also be fun to try to predict what various pieces that interest you might bring—based on what you've learned from the prior catalogs or from attending several live auctions—before you take part in your first auction. Take the current catalog, view the pieces, and then pencil in what you think they will actually bring. If you do well, you may be ready to take an active part; if you don't do well, perhaps you should wait.

By viewing the catalogs, going to exhibitions to carefully examine pieces, asking good questions, and attending several sales, you'll know when you are ready to take an active part, and you'll have the confidence to succeed.

## BEFORE YOU BUY

Once you have had a chance to review several auction catalogs, attend a few exhibitions, and experience the pace of the live auction, it's time to get down to specifics. The following advice can help you avoid costly mistakes, whether you are buying or selling.

## Read the Capitalized Headings Carefully

It may surprise you to know that the auction house stands behind the description of an item only as it is described in the capitalized headings in the catalog. This means the auction house is *not* responsible for what is stated in the paragraph beneath the heading, which provides the more complete description of the piece. While fine auction firms may do their best to accurately and fairly describe the jewelry, this is not always the case, nor is it a guarantee, and anything stated in the small print is only *an opinion*.

In one case, a beautiful "pink" topaz necklace came up for sale at a respected auction house. It was described in the capitalized heading as "an antique topaz and seed pearl necklace, circa 1820." It was purchased by a woman who immediately took the necklace to my father to verify that the stones were pink topaz. She learned that the stones were topaz, but not pink topaz. They were colorless topaz behind which *pink foil* had been placed to create the impression that they were pink. Pink topaz is rare and is much more valuable than colorless topaz. The woman telephoned the auction house to advise them of the problem and to say that she would be returning the necklace for a refund. She was quickly informed that the auction house could not accept the necklace back or refund the money. Despite the representation of the stones as "pink" topaz in the full description, they were described only as "topaz" in the capitalized heading, and this was accurate. The woman was informed that the auction firm was not liable for any other representations. Furthermore, the woman was chastised for not having been aware that foil-backing was common in necklaces such as the one she had bought, and that the presence of colored foil was "obvious" to anyone who knew jewelry. The purchaser then asked why, if it was so obvious, had the description not mentioned that the necklace contained foil-backed pink topaz, in which case she would have asked the auction house expert to explain what that meant. Acknowledging that she had a valid criticism, she was offered a free year's subscription to their catalog, which she declined. She had no interest in ever buying at that auction firm again.

Pay attention to what is printed in the catalog, but also pay attention to what is *not* printed in the catalog, to what is *not* stated in the capitalized headings. *Ask* questions, and most of all, don't *assume* anything.

Keep in mind that there are numerous representations made in the descriptive paragraphs on which you *cannot* rely. Unless stated in the capitalized heading, the following information does not come under the representations that are "warranted" or "guaranteed" by the auction house:

- *Information contained in accompanying documentation such as Gemological Institute of America (GIA) diamond grading reports.* Often the capitalized headings state only that the piece contains a genuine diamond, and there is no description of quality or condition. Therefore, the only thing *guaranteed* is that the stone is a genuine diamond, and nothing more. Even if the fuller description says that the diamond is accompanied by a diamond grading report describing the stone as having a particular quality, the auction firm is not guaranteeing this. It is possible that the diamond was damaged since the report was issued and is no longer the quality stated on the report. It is also possible that the report is fraudulent.

- *The jewelry period.* Jewelry made in certain styles, during certain time periods, is known as "period jewelry." Certain periods have become very collectible, including Edwardian and Belle Epoque (circa 1900–1915), Art Nouveau (circa 1885–1915), Art Deco (circa 1920–1935), and Retro (circa 1940s). When a piece is described in the capitalized headings as Art Deco, for example, the auction house is guaranteeing the piece to be of that period, made between 1920 and 1935. However, if this is not stated in the capitalized headings, and the item turns out to be a reproduction, the auction firm is not liable. Jewelry described as being in the "style of" a particular period, such as "Art Deco Style," means that the piece was definitely *not* made during the period but only resembles jewelry of that period in its design.

- *Provenance.* If a piece of jewelry is described in the capitalized headings as being created by a particular house, such as Cartier or Harry Winston, then the auction house is guaranteeing that the piece was produced by the company stated. Also implicit in the capitalized heading attribution is that the piece is essentially in the original condition and contains the original gemstones. If you learn that this is not the case, the auction house would be liable. For example, if a piece is represented to be by Cartier in the capitalized headings, but you learn that it no longer contains the original stone shown in the records of Cartier, it cannot be represented as a Cartier piece, and you would be entitled to a refund. The auction house would also be liable if the piece turned out to have been seriously damaged and repaired so that it was no longer "essentially as made by Cartier."

*Any reference to a particular jeweler or jewelry house made in the small print only is not a guarantee.* The piece may be a fake, a "marriage piece" (something reconstructed from one or more pieces, one of which may contain a famous mark) or a mounting only, in which the original stones have been replaced.

## Examine the Jewelry Firsthand

As a general rule, always view each lot personally. Don't rely on catalog pictures, which can be misleading in terms of size, color, and the general condition of a gemstone or jewelry piece. Even in high-resolution images, you can't count on pictures to capture the true color and character of a gem, or the feel and movement in a piece of jewelry. Furthermore, catalog descriptions do not always capture the subtleties of a piece.

Several years ago one of my father's students purchased a kunzite ring—without having seen it personally—from a respected auction gallery. She had seen the photo in an auction catalog, but since the firm was located on the West Coast and she lived on the East Coast, it was not convenient or practical for her to personally view the piece. The color as it appeared in the catalog was very rich, so she called the gallery's jewelry specialist on the phone to try to get a reliable estimate of the color. Based on the description provided, she placed a bid and succeeded in buying the ring. When she received the ring, she was shocked; it was very pale, much paler than in the photograph, and she had paid much more than such a pale kunzite was worth. The jewelry specialist had described the stone as having "very fine color, for kunzite." One can only conclude that this person had never seen a fine kunzite. Whatever the case, she was stuck with it. Eventually she sold the ring at a loss by consigning it to a local jeweler.

In short, if you want to avoid disappointment, ***do not rely on photographs or subjective descriptions by other people. You must see gems and jewelry*** *pieces firsthand.* Remember, once you have purchased the item at auction, you have little or no recourse if the piece is not what you expected based on the catalog image.

Most firms, both large and small, put the pieces coming up for sale on exhibition for public viewing. Some permit viewing only on the day of the sale; others have viewing over several days. Important houses such as Sotheby's, Christie's, Phillips, and Antiquorum Auctioneers also offer private viewing rooms and provide gemological equipment for the convenience of those who know how to use it. For very important auctions, such firms often arrange exhibitions in several cities, and in some cases, the exhibitions tour internationally.

You can find out when and where public viewing will take place by contacting the auction house. Private appointments can also be scheduled.

*Get a loupe—and use it* (see chapter 5). While you won't see what the professional will see, you will be amazed by how much you will see. It can be an invaluable tool in spotting makers' marks and hallmarks; in seeing traces of solder that indicate repair or alterations of some sort; in spotting chips, nicks, and scratches; and so on. It can be especially useful in seeing surface-reaching cracks in gemstones, and it is particularly useful in checking opals for crazing (a web of small cracks, which, if extensive, can increase fragility). I recall examining what appeared to be a beautiful opal at first glance, especially in the exhibition room with all the bright lights. However, when I held the opal on top of my small light (I always carry a mini maglite) and examined it quickly with the loupe, it revealed crazing across the entire opal, with some very deep cracks. Minor crazing is normally not a serious problem, but this was not minor. And even a novice could have spotted it by using a loupe.

## Check Accompanying Documentation

Fine diamonds and colored gemstones are often accompanied by a laboratory report from a respected laboratory (see appendix) documenting the identity and quality of the stone, and indicating whether or not the stone has been subjected to any treatment (see chapter 17). Not all gemstones have such reports, but when they do, be sure to ask to see the report and read it carefully (see chapter 16). Also, be sure to ask the jewelry specialist or gemologist if he or she has examined the piece carefully to make sure that the stone actually matches the report. In some cases, or if the auction house lacks a gemologist, it may be worthwhile to retain a gemologist consultant to confirm the reliability of accompanying documentation. Sometimes a gemstone has been damaged since the report was issued; in rare instances, documentation does not match the gem at all. And in any event, the auction house does not guarantee representations made in accompanying documents. *Remember: information provided in accompanying documentation is not guaranteed by the auction house.*

## Check the Condition Report

Many auction firms issue condition reports for each lot, which you can request. These generally describe the overall condition of a piece of jewelry, the mounting, the number of stones, and the approximate weights. It may also indicate missing stones or damage to stones, settings, or enamel. Where diamonds are concerned, it may also provide an estimate of quality in lots without accompanying laboratory documentation. Once again, while efforts may be made to accurately describe the gems and jewelry, these descriptions do not constitute guarantees, and the auction house cannot be held liable for errors in condition reports.

## IMPORTANT QUESTIONS TO ASK

There is a lot to learn. Don't be afraid to ask questions of the jewelry specialist or house gemologist. If there is something you don't understand, ask. This is the only way you will learn. Here are some specific areas where asking good questions can be very useful:

*Ask about estimates.* If you examine lots carefully, you may notice pieces that appear similar but whose estimates are very dissimilar. Ask for the jewelry specialist, and ask why. Often this will help you notice details in the way a piece is made, or the impact of a particular "name" on value. Sometimes, an evasive answer can suggest that one estimate is abnormally high (possibly because it was consigned by someone in the trade) or abnormally low (which may be the case, for example, if it was consigned to settle an estate).

On pieces that interest you, or about which you would like to know more, ask explicitly whether the specialist thinks the lot will sell below, within, or above the estimate, and why. At first you will lack sufficient experience to judge the reliability of the specialist. But by watching what happens on the day of the sale, and by tracking what happens on the lots that interest you, over time you will begin to see how reliable that advice was, and decide whether or not to rely upon it in the future.

*Ask why lots sell or don't sell.* This may seem silly at first, since there are many factors that can affect whether or not a particular lot sells, but you will be surprised at how much you can learn from asking why. If you don't understand why something doesn't sell, asking why might reveal that it had something to do with the piece itself (such as a forged mark; a piece with a well-known name that has been reconstructed with another piece, called a marriage piece; and so on). If something sells for three times the estimate, asking why can help you understand the influence of a particular design and style, or how some particular detail makes it rare, or the impact of a particular provenance, and much more. It may also help you to understand when it has nothing to do with the piece but rather with an unrealistically low estimate.

*Ask about jewelry marks.* Where fine jewelry is concerned, you will often find jewelry marks indicating the firm that made the piece. You may not recognize the mark, and the specialist may not recognize it either, but often this can provide important information that should be factored into the price you are willing to pay. There are several excellent reference books on marks (see "Selected Readings" in the appendix) and I highly recommend them to anyone serious about obtaining fine jewelry at auction. Sometimes, your ability to spot a mark that others have missed may result in your getting a beauty at a bargain price.

Where the capitalized headings in the catalog indicate a jewelry house, such as Cartier or Van Cleef & Arpels, there *must* be a mark. Ask the jewelry expert to show you where the mark is. By examining marks yourself, you will learn where various houses may place their marks and what they look like. Being familiar with legitimate marks, and where they are normally placed, can help you spot fake marks.

*Ask about the gemstones.* You will hear about rare gemstones such as Burmese or Kashmir sapphires and Colombian emeralds, but they are not all rare and precious. Compare gemstones side by side, and ask the specialist to help you see and understand differences. Ask why certain gemstones are more desirable than others.

You must assume, unless it is otherwise stated, that all gemstones have been treated, but not all gemstones are treated. In cases where it is assumed a gem is treated, ask the expert if he or she knows for sure that it is treated;

there may be documentation of treatment, or the staff gemologist may have confirmed treatment through gemological examination. But sometimes, especially with smaller stones (under three carats), no one bothers to obtain documentation, and natural gemstones can slip through the cracks.

Antique and estate jewelry can also be an excellent source of *natural* pearls. On lots represented to be *cultured* pearls, be sure to ask the specialist or gemologist if they know for sure that they are cultured. Often they do, but sometimes they do not. In the absence of laboratory documentation to the contrary, the pearls must be represented as cultured—but laboratory examination has shown that sometimes pearls sold as cultured are natural.

By viewing the catalogs, going to exhibitions to carefully examine pieces, asking good questions, and attending several sales, you'll know when you are ready to take an active part, and you'll have the confidence to succeed.

## DECIDING WHAT TO BID: ESTIMATES ARE NOT A RELIABLE GUIDE

Estimates are often used as a guide to what something is worth and what you should bid, but they are not always reliable guides. It is very important to understand how a reserve is established, and how it affects estimates. By having a more realistic understanding of how these figures are determined, you can better understand why some lots seem to bring so much more than the estimates, spot estimates that are unrealistically low (or high), and better gauge what a realistic bid might be if you really want a particular lot.

### What Every Buyer and Seller Needs to Know about Reserves and Estimates

Low reserves are good for the auction business. The reserve is the price agreed to by the auction house and the seller in advance, below which a piece will not be sold. A reserve is set for most lots consigned to an auction house. Often, new jewelry is consigned by gem dealers or manufacturers in an effort to sell certain pieces to "privates" (people not in the jewelry trade). These pieces often have a higher reserve than comparable pieces from other sources. On the other hand, jewelry on consignment from an estate may have a very low reserve or, in some cases, no reserve. In the case of private estates, it's easy for the auction house to set low reserves because sellers are usually not knowledgeable about the value of their jewelry and they look to the auction house's own jewelry specialist for counsel.

If a reserve is not set, or if it is set too low, a fine piece can sell for much less than its true value. Unfortunately, this happens much more often than people realize, especially when jewelry pieces are consigned to the auction house by people who don't know the true value of what they have and rely on the auction house for guidance. The most important thing for any seller to understand is that it is generally in the auction firm's business interests to obtain pieces at prices that will ensure they sell. The best way to do this is to get sellers to consign pieces at the lowest possible reserve. At first glance this might not appear to make sense, because on the surface it would seem that the higher the price, the more the auction house will make. But this is not really how it works. This is true only if bidding is strong on the day of a particular sale, and the piece sells. A closer examination of how it all really works will make it easier to understand.

On all pieces that are actually "sold" at auction—those for which bidding reaches or exceeds the reserve price—the auction house collects a commission (normally 10 to 20 percent) from both the buyer and the seller. In other words, for each *sold* item, they typically earn between 20 and 40 percent (the exact details are provided in the consignment agreement between the auction house and the seller). But if an item does *not* sell, the auction house collects only one fee: from the seller only. Furthermore, when an item fails to sell, the fee paid by the seller is much less than what it would have been had the item sold. On an unsold item, the house typically collects a fee of 5 percent of the reserve price, or some very low percentage on the hammer price.

If an auction house succeeds in getting a seller to consign a piece with a reserve price that is *one-quarter* what it should bring under normal circumstances, the auction house will be in a stronger position financially than it will be with a higher reserve. Let's look at the numbers and you will see how. Let's imagine you have a piece that should bring $1,000 at auction, but the auction house recommends a $250 reserve (one-quarter what it would be expected to bring under normal circumstances). This means the auction house can sell it for as little as $250, a price so low that there is bound to be someone who will buy it, regardless of unforeseen events that might cause weak bidding. In the worst-case scenario, let's say that on the day of the sale there is a disaster of some sort and bidding is weak, resulting in the sale of the piece at the low reserve, $250. At 15 percent from buyer and seller, the house will earn 30 percent on the $250 purchase price, for a total of $75. On the other hand, had the reserve been set at $1,000, and the piece brought only $250, the auction firm would earn only one fee, from the seller only—a fee of $50 (5 percent of the $1,000 reserve). Even if the higher estimate resulted in a higher bid, say $900, the piece would still go unsold; the fee would still be only $50. As you can quickly see, this is *less than they would have earned if the piece had sold for $250 with a $250 reserve;* with the higher reserve, the house would have lost $25.

Such extreme situations don't occur often, but they can happen. Such was the case on "Black Monday," a day in October 1987 when the New York stock market crashed on the first day of a two-day jewelry auction taking place at Sotheby's. Similarly, auction performance at the "Magnificent Jewelry" sales that took place in October 2001, following the World Trade Center tragedy, set an all-time record low.

Understanding the true value of any item, whether you are buying or selling, is the key to recognizing opportunities and to protecting yourself from risk. For buyers, low reserves can work to your advantage if bidding is off and if you know the real value of what you are bidding on. But for sellers, low reserves increase your risk. Sellers must keep in mind that the auction house is usually ahead when pieces sell—*even at a fraction of their true value*—but the seller won't be.

As you can see, the experts at the auction houses have an incentive to acquire pieces with the lowest possible reserve, at a price that will virtually guarantee that they sell. When they succeed in doing this, they also succeed in guaranteeing that they have a good sale, that most of the lots will sell. It is also important to understand that selling a high percentage of the total number of jewelry lots consigned to an auction house makes news, and the subsequent media coverage creates a very good image for the firm. When a good percentage of those lots also sell for more than the pre-sale estimate, it makes very good public relations and provides a strong incentive for people to consider that firm when they are thinking of selling their own jewelry or gems.

Sellers should always seek the counsel of an outside gemologist consultant or gemologist-appraiser regarding what they have, and the identity, quality, and value of their pieces, *before going to the auction house.* Only by knowing in advance what you have and what it's worth can you protect yourself from consigning something for less than its true value.

Fortunately, unforeseen circumstances that may cause negative results in the auction room are rare. Normally the auction room will be filled with knowledgeable people who will recognize the true value of each lot and bid accordingly. If something is really worth $1,000, bidding will usually reach this amount or exceed it. The auction house will do well, the buyer usually pays a fair price, and the seller will be ecstatic, believing that he or she received much more than the piece was really worth. But as a seller, you need to protect yourself from the unforeseen "off day" and be sure to establish a fair reserve price to protect your own interests.

## How Estimates Can Be Misleading—Lots from Private Estates Often Have Low Estimates That Do Not Reflect True Value

The auction catalog explains that estimates are typically determined by calculating the value of the stones, whether the piece is signed or has a known provenance, the overall condition and desirability, and the performance of comparable pieces at previous auctions. This is often the case, but not always. And where private estates are concerned, unrealistically low reserves are often established, in which case the estimates will also be unrealistically low.

The estimates that are printed in the catalog are directly tied to the reserves that have been established by the seller at the time of consignment. Theoretically they represent the price range within which the auction firm believes the piece will sell, and normally they are set at an amount only slightly higher than the reserve. If the reserves always reflected the true value of a piece, estimates could provide a reliable guide to what one should expect to pay at auction. But this is not the case.

As we have already seen, when pieces are consigned by people who do not know the true value of what they have—which often applies to people consigning a piece of personal jewelry, or executors' consigning estates for liquidation—they may agree to a very low reserve. When this happens, they have usually agreed to allow something to be sold for too little because they are under the impression that the reserve actually reflects what the item is worth, or an amount just slightly less. In such cases, the estimates will also be low for obvious reasons: if the house shows a much higher estimate in the printed catalog, the consignor would have to wonder why they were advised to allow the piece to be sold for so much less.

Low estimates often accompany pieces from private estates and this can create a problem for the novice who relies on them as a guide to what to bid. So if you are interested in a lot consigned from a private estate, you must realize that the estimates can be very low and be prepared to pay a price that reflects the true value, a price possibly much higher than indicated by the estimate.

By paying close attention to the catalogs, attending exhibitions, asking the right questions, and watching the live action as an observer several times—especially noticing who bids, and how much—you'll soon start to get a sense of which lots come from private estates and are accompanied by unrealistically low estimates. Then, if you are interested in bidding on a particular "undervalued" lot, you'll know that you will have to be prepared to pay much more for it if you want to succeed in getting it, and that the higher price is still a "fair price."

## Gems and Jewelry Consigned by the Gem and Jewelry Trade

Today a very large percentage of jewelry sold at auction is consigned not from private estates but by people in the gem and jewelry trade, who are also important buyers of jewelry at auction. Auctions provide a means by which dealers can convert old inventory into cash and also reach collectors and connoisseurs directly with their rarer and finer gems and jewelry pieces. Dealers, however, know the value of what they have and can negotiate a reserve price that protects their financial interest, usually not less than two-thirds of the current wholesale value, that is, the price a retailer might pay a dealer for something comparable. These pieces normally also sell above the estimate on a good day and bring prices equal to wholesale or more, but the higher reserves still protect them from a serious loss on a bad day. Items consigned by the trade are usually priced so that they are still of interest to others in the trade, and they provide very good value to people outside the trade. And the rarest and finest jewelry pieces might surprise even the dealer and fetch a record-setting high.

Reserves and estimates can also be set unusually high on some jewelry consigned by gem and jewelry dealers because they don't really need to sell the piece and want to ensure they will get more than they would normally get within the trade. Here, the reserve price is usually slightly higher than the wholesale value to ensure that the dealer doesn't net less than wholesale on the transaction. These items are intended to attract private buyers and, regardless of the higher estimates, may still offer a good value.

Another situation in which an estimate may be high is when there are no "comparables"—that is, the auction house has never auctioned off anything like it before, or at least not recently, and there is nothing in the wholesale marketplace to establish a benchmark. In such cases, there is no way to predict how the market will react and what buyers will be willing to pay. Depending on the piece, the house may set a very high estimate in an effort to create greater interest. Sometimes it works, and sometimes it doesn't. Sometimes there is a lot of interest, but not enough to reach the reserve.

## DECIDING WHAT TO BID

While this is rapidly changing, most jewelry sold at auction today is still purchased by people in the trade. But for dealers, it doesn't take many gem or jewelry purchases to tie up a tremendous amount of capital. Thus, the incentive to tie up valuable working capital is price, and where auctions are concerned, an attractive price is one that is well below the cost of something comparable in the wholesale market.

As a rule, the economic incentive for the trade equates to approximately one-half to two-thirds of the current wholesale cost of a comparable item. If you can determine what the wholesale cost of a gem or jewel would be in the current market—one of the primary reasons people interested in buying gems or jewelry work with a gemologist consultant—you can determine approximately how much the trade will be willing to pay. Then it is just a matter of deciding the price at which it will be of interest to you, and bidding accordingly. If you are lucky, you may succeed in getting a lovely piece at a price just above what the trade is willing to bid, which is often still significantly below the wholesale cost and way below the retail value. Just be careful not to get carried away bidding against someone who lacks knowledge or professional guidance; they often bid too much because they think the quality is better than it really is, or they are comparing their bids with retail prices. Unless the piece is rare or one-of-a-kind, there will always be another opportunity. Furthermore, if you are working with a gemologist consultant, why pay more than wholesale for something your consultant could easily acquire for you through normal wholesale channels?

If you are not in the trade, you can afford to bid more than the dealers because you do not have to be concerned about reselling what you buy and making a fair profit on it. But people outside the trade often bid much more because they lack the expertise to know the true value of what they are purchasing, and if several people outside the trade are bidding against one another on the same lot, bidding sometimes becomes an emotional bidding war. We've witnessed people caught up in trying to outbid one another, and they end up paying more than retail. You can guard against this if you have been attending auctions and paying attention to the bidders; you can often figure out who are the dealers and who are the private buyers. Some words of advice: if you are not working with an independent expert, beware of pieces in which there is no interest shown by any dealer—they may know something you don't.

Typically, if you are bidding against a room that is filled primarily with people in the trade, you can get some excellent buys if you know what to avoid. Even if you go several bids above the point where dealers stop bidding—perhaps because you are bidding against another private buyer—you may still be paying a price comparable to wholesale, or below, and much less than retail. We are starting to see this on engagement-type rings. About-to-be-engaged couples are discovering the auction arena as a source for getting good value on an engagement ring.

On any lot in which you have interest, if you aren't sure of the value, it is sometimes helpful to speak to the jewelry specialist and ask explicitly whether or not the specialist thinks the estimate is realistic. While you can't always rely on what the specialist tells you, he or she may indicate that there has been a lot of interest and that the estimate is on the low side; this often suggests an unusually low estimate. And if you've spent some time as a spectator, you may also be able to identify the dealers in the room. If you keep bidding as long as several dealers are bidding against each other, there's a good chance you won't make a mistake. You probably can go a few bids higher. If the bidding continues at an energetic pace, you may want to slow down, or let it pass to another bidder. There may be something that makes it worth the extra money, but if you lack the expertise to know for sure, you may overpay if you end up caught up in an emotional bidding war.

After all is said and done, the bottom line is this: while estimates may provide a guide, you cannot rely on them as an indicator of what any particular lot will bring at auction or of its true value. Your best protection is knowledge about the piece and sufficient expertise and experience to know its true value. Sometimes reserves and estimates are unrealistically low. Sometimes they are unrealistically high. Sometimes auction activity is buoyant and perfectly predictable, and other times unforeseen events result in weak bidding. And in good times or bad, sometimes the winning bidder is simply someone with more money than knowledge...or brains...and when that happens, hopefully he won't be bidding against you, but on something consigned by you.

## A New Trend—Using a Gemologist Consultant

Today you don't have to take unnecessary risks. If you lack the expertise to know what you are buying, an independent gemologist consultant can provide the expertise you lack and can look out for your best interests. An independent gemologist consultant works for you, not for the auction house. The consultant can confirm the identity and quality of gemstones (or advise you if important facts cannot be verified for whatever reason); evaluate quality and condition; estimate true value; help you compare other lots of interest, including lots at other auction houses; and determine realistic bids.

Whether your interest is diamonds, colored gemstones, or pearls, working with a gemologist consultant can protect you from costly mistakes and help you spot opportunities others may miss. A gemologist can also be a wonderful teacher, sharing expertise not only about gemstones and jewelry but about auctions as well. And in cases where you acquire a lovely gem but want to dispose of its setting and recreate a new one, the gemologist can also provide invaluable help in finding the right designer and goldsmith, overseeing production, and confirming that the stones in the new creation are in fact yours, and in original condition. The gemologist can also help you get laboratory documentation that can add value.

Here is a case in point. Several years ago, a young man who was searching for a 1½- to 2-carat diamond engagement ring, on a very limited budget, sought my help. He had heard about an upcoming auction and had gone to see several diamond rings that sounded attractive. But he became confused and began to question whether or not everything was as it appeared, since several pieces had extremely low reserves, even those with diamond grading reports issued by GIA, so I agreed to examine them for him. After looking carefully at the rings he was considering, I was confident that the rings with the GIA reports were going to be long shots because the estimates were unrealistically low, and there would be lots of interest from other about-to-become-engaged couples. Nonetheless, it can't hurt to hope, so we determined what he could bid, and marked our catalogs. I then began to examine other diamonds for him—in other types of rings, in pendants, and at other auction houses—as a back-up. I finally spotted an interesting diamond mounted in a very unattractive yellow gold necklace (which worked in our favor because there would be less interest in it as a piece of jewelry). But between the yellow gold mounting and years of caked-on dirt and grime, it was very difficult to grade the diamond precisely. It looked very tinted, but I suspected that this was to a large extent the reflection of the yellow mounting and the greasy dirt. My worst-case estimate of the quality was acceptable to the young man. He decided he wanted me to bid on the lot if we weren't successful on two other rings—both of which came up before our "safety" ring—and we decided what the maximum bid should be, based on a worst-case quality estimate. On the day of the sale, we watched how the bidding was going. The first two rings sold for way above the estimates, and way above what he could afford to pay. But we succeeded in getting our back-up lot. After the diamond was removed from its setting and cleaned up, it turned out to be a much finer quality than we had dared to hope. We obtained a GIA diamond grading report on the stone and mounted it in a lovely ring. What he paid in total, including the GIA report and making the ring, was about one-fourth what he would have paid at a retail jewelry store for the diamond alone.

Private individuals tend to bid on stones accompanied by laboratory reports because they are afraid to bid on any stones without them; they know they lack the expertise to be certain of the quality. Private individuals are usually also prepared to bid more than dealers because they are not concerned about having to resell the piece and make a profit. So when individuals work with a gemologist consultant, they can consider stones without reports and can often succeed in getting what they want at a better price, because normally they will be competing against the trade only. On this particular acquisition, the young man was thrilled, and to this day we have lots of fun at auctions. We aren't always successful, but we always have fun.

While this is a relatively new trend, many gemologists now offer consulting services for auction enthusiasts. They can provide an invaluable service. But it is important to retain someone with reliable, respected credentials. To locate someone with reliable credentials in your area, information in chapter 25 on selecting a gemologist-*appraiser* may be helpful. But keep in mind that many skilled gemologists—and excellent consultants—are often not "appraisers" and may lack some of the credentials suggested in this chapter.

## THE DAY HAS COME—YOU'RE READY TO BE PART

You've taken a lot of time to do your homework. You've followed all the advice in the preceding pages—and in the subsequent chapters—and you're ready to get in on the action. But before you begin to bid, be sure you have read the entire catalog very carefully, especially the front matter and back matter, and understand everything it tells you. Here's a final checklist:

- *Do you understand the "terms and conditions"?* The auction catalog provides all of the terms and conditions by which you will be bound when you bid. Make sure you understand them; if not, have a specialist explain them so you won't be disappointed later.

- *Do you understand the "terms of guarantee"?* The terms of guarantee are also explained explicitly in the auction catalog. Make sure you understand them; if not, have a specialist explain them. If you do not understand what is guaranteed, you may be disappointed later; more importantly, you may not realize the situations in which you *do* have recourse if something guaranteed has been misrepresented. While the auction venue is very much one of "caveat emptor," there are, nonetheless, situations for which the auction house can be held liable.

- *Do you understand the "buyer's premium" and all other charges that will be added to the hammer price? Have you factored all additional charges into what you plan to bid, so you know what the total will be?* The catalog will state the amount of the buyer's premium (the commission the buyer is expected to pay the auction house, usually 10 to 20 percent of the hammer price).

  As you bid, keep in mind that you will be paying not only the hammer price—the amount you bid in the auction room—but also the additional commission, plus sales tax where applicable. If you have made a purchase outside the United States, you will also be responsible for customs duty, where applicable, and shipping and insurance. Be sure you have factored in *all* of the costs; they can add a substantial amount to the hammer price. You don't want any unpleasant surprises or to find out that with all the added charges to what you paid, your purchase might not have been such a bargain after all.

- *Do you understand what the "bidding increments" are?* This is the amount by which the bidding will be advanced. For example, if the bid is at \$2,000, the next increment would normally be \$250, so the next bid would have to be $2,250; then $2,500, and so on. The catalog normally explains what the bidding increments are, so you can plan your bidding accordingly.

- *Do you understand the auction house's position regarding "gemstone enhancements"?* Unless a colored gemstone is listed in capitalized headings as *natural or untreated,* assume that it has been treated. (Gemstone treatments and enhancements are covered in chapter 17.)

- *If you cannot be present to bid in person, do you clearly understand the bidding options?* The catalog explains the various ways in which you can bid—telephone, fax, and so on—but make sure you understand the procedure clearly. If two bids of the same amount are faxed, for example, and the winning bid is that amount, the bidder whose fax was received first will be the winning bidder. Sometimes you can protect yourself by placing a "bid, plus one." This means your maximum bid is X, but if another bidder bids X ahead of you, you will go one more increment.

- *Have you selected the lots on which you are going to bid, and decided what your maximum bids will be?* Don't allow yourself to get carried away by auction fever and bid impulsively. Set a realistic bid price—based on how much you like the piece, what comparable items have brought in previous sales, whether or not it is rare, irreplaceable, or difficult to find—and stick to it.

## Establish an Account

If you can answer yes to all of the above, then you are ready to experience the thrill of it all. The auction catalogs will explain what you need to do to be a buyer or seller, but the basics are really quite simple.

For first-time buyers, the most important thing to do before the sale is to become qualified as a bidder. This will require stopping by the auction house several days before the sale, or contacting the jewelry specialist and requesting a form that you can complete and return to the auction house. Make sure you allow sufficient time for the accounting department to check your bank references. Sometimes personal as well as financial references may be required in addition to banking information.

Once you have supplied the necessary credit information, and it has been established that it meets the requirements of the auction house, you will be "qualified" to bid, and you will be assigned an account number which will enable you to bid. You can obtain a bidding paddle on the day of the sale, with which to bid during the live auction, or you can submit a bid by whatever other means designated by the auction house you find most convenient.

## Time to Bid

This is the moment you've been waiting for. There are several ways in which the auction house makes it convenient to bid. Generally, you can bid in person, bid on the phone during the live auction, or fax or e-mail bids to the auction house in advance, which will be noted and carried out by the auction house on your behalf. Currently, you can bid on-line during the live auction only at Antiquorum, but other houses may offer this capability in the future.

We prefer to bid in person and to position ourselves at the back of the room so we can see the bidding taking place: who is bidding, and how much. Sometimes when you lose to another bidder, the winning bidder will be willing to let you have the piece at a modest profit after the sale. For the inexperienced auction goer, paying attention to who is bidding and what they are bidding on can provide clues to whether or not they are in the trade. And if so, watching them can often provide insights into the value of certain types of jewelry, along with what's hot and what's not.

When your lot comes up, you may feel a bit breathless—perhaps somewhat nervous—but focus on what you are doing, and pay attention to the bidding. You will signal the auctioneer that you are bidding by thrusting your paddle into the air. You may want to be among the first bidders, getting in early and hanging in till the end, or you may want to wait until the bidding slows or comes to a stop, and then raise your paddle if you are prepared to bid more. Determining the pace at which you want to bid takes experience and practice; it can vary from lot to lot, depending upon how aggressive the bidding is and how many people are actively bidding. There are different theories about how to bid, and no one can say which is the best way. It is something you will decide for yourself over time and with experience. But regardless of how you go about it, the bidding will be over before you know it. Suddenly the next lot is up. You were either successful or not. If not, maybe next time.

We recommend keeping a record of each lot on which you are the successful bidder, along with the amount of the hammer price. You will have a certain amount of time to pay for and pick up merchandise (which is stated in the catalog), but we prefer to confirm purchases immediately following the sale. While errors seldom occur, they are not impossible, and in the event that a lot you purchased has been omitted from your account, or a lot you didn't buy has been placed on your account, the sooner you discover the mistake, the more likely it will be resolved satisfactorily.

**Proceed with caution.** Remember, auctions are very different from traditional jewelry retailers. You cannot exchange or return your purchase.

Once you have a basic understanding of how auctions work and are ready to try buying some jewelry pieces, the most important requirement is knowledge. You must know what to look for, and perhaps even more important, you must know what to look out for. This is not an arena one should enter casually. But people who are astute and take time to learn about the gems and jewelry that interest them, or time to find a knowledgeable professional with whom to work, will find auctions exciting, educational, and profitable.

## SELLING AT AUCTION—HOW TO BE SUCCESSFUL

The most important thing for sellers to remember is not to turn to the auction house to find out what you have and what it's worth. As we explained in the section about how reserves and estimates are determined, relying on the auction house can result in your getting less than the true value of what you are selling. If you follow these steps, however, you should be able to consign pieces to auction houses with confidence:

1. **Consult an independent gemologist-appraiser or consultant before going to the auction house.** Retail jewelers, gem dealers, and auction house specialists may not be the best source of reliable information about what you have. Many lack the necessary skills to do a reliable evaluation, and all have a vested interest; they are all potential buyers and, as such, have an interest in not revealing all the facts or the true value. Your best source of reliable information is an independent expert.

   As we mentioned earlier in this chapter, it is very important to select an independent gemologist-appraiser or consultant with respected credentials in order to obtain reliable information to confirm the identity, quality, condition, and value of what you have. Once you know what you have and what it's worth, *then* you can go to the auction house with whatever you wish to consign.

   In some cases, the gemologist might recommend getting laboratory documentation. This would be appropriate for a fine-quality diamond weighing one carat or more, or for any fine-quality colored gemstone, especially if the appraiser believes it to be *natural* (that is, unenhanced in any way).

2. ***Establish a realistic reserve that protects you.*** Once you know the true value of your piece, you can work with an auction house to set a reserve that is realistic and acceptable. You must find the right balance between a reserve that is too low and one that is too high. If it is too low, your piece could slip away at a price much less than its true value, but if it is too high, it might fail to sell altogether. As we explained earlier, it is usually in the best interest of the auction house to set as low a reserve as possible, but when you have taken the time to get an independent expert evaluation and know the true value of what you want to sell, you can come to an agreement that makes sense for both parties.

3. ***Establish a realistic estimate.*** The estimate is normally somewhat higher than the reserve. It usually reflects the reserve price to some degree, and in the United States it cannot legally be lower than the reserve price. Try to get the auction house to agree to as high an estimate as possible, however, because while you don't want it to be so high that it discourages bidders, buyers often look at the estimate as a guide to the value. But auction firms sometimes feel that lower estimates might be an enticement to prospective buyers, and great publicity sometimes results when pieces sell for prices way beyond the estimate. Here again, when the true value of the piece is known, it's easier to come to a meeting of the minds. You both really want the piece to sell. But as the seller, your primary concern must always be doing whatever you can to ensure you get a fair price.

   You may want to consider having the gemologist consultant accompany you when you are meeting with auction houses, to help you negotiate the best possible reserve and estimate.

4. ***Compare offers from several auction houses.*** Don't assume that all auction houses operate the same way or will offer the same deal. Sometimes you will find that one firm will agree to a higher reserve and estimate than another, especially if the auction house is relatively new and is trying to encourage sellers to consign to them rather than to one of the better-known houses. But before making a final decision, consider the audience that the house will deliver; will it attract as many bidders? Will it attract the right kind of bidders for the type of jewelry you plan to consign? For example, a small auction firm that specializes in your particular type of jewelry may not deliver as large an audience but may deliver

a larger audience of prospective bidders for your particular piece, and those bidders may be more knowledgeable about your type of jewelry, better qualified to judge it, and willing to pay more for it. And in this case, the house may also be willing to agree to a higher reserve and estimate. But if the firm is new or has no special niche or established audience, you may be better off going with a better-known firm, even if the consignment terms are not as attractive.

5. ***Get laboratory documentation on important gemstones.*** Important gemstones are usually accompanied by laboratory documentation today, so any gemstone that lacks documentation is considered less important and thus less valuable. The seller must incur the expense of getting the documentation, but it is money well spent when you consider how much it can add to the price that prospective buyers are willing to bid as a result of the increased confidence it instills. Furthermore, major collectors and connoisseurs will not be interested in gemstones without laboratory documentation from a respected laboratory (see chapter 16 for important information pertaining to what should be included in the documentation). A list of internationally recognized laboratories that issue reports on diamonds and colored gemstones is provided in the appendix. Take extra precautions to confirm documentation accompanying gemstones; if documentation was issued by a laboratory not included on this list, ask the auction specialist to confirm that the laboratory is reliable. If he or she is unable to do this, do not rely on the information.

6. ***Read the fine print in the catalog.*** In addition to the terms stated in the consignment agreement between the auction house and consignor, be sure to read the fine print in the auction catalog, especially as it relates to fees when the consigned lot sells and—equally important—when it does not sell. Be sure to ask explicitly about all costs, including insurance and catalog photography as well as commissions or other fees for services provided by the auction firm "on your behalf."

# 3 ◆ What to Expect at Internet Auctions

THE INTERNET HAS CHANGED MANY ASPECTS OF OUR LIVES, BUT PER-
haps none so much as how we buy and sell a wide range of products. It offers
unparalleled selection, information, and convenience. And for anyone interested in buying or selling almost anything imaginable, one of the fastest-growing
internet services is the online auction, offering a virtual flea market of merchandise from around the world.

For buyers or sellers, the online auction arena offers an unprecedented marketplace. For buyers, there are seemingly limitless choices in variety and, of
course, the promise of bargain prices; for sellers, there is an opportunity to reach
a vast international audience that was inconceivable before the internet age.

Online auction fever is growing at a rapid pace. For some people, browsing the auction sites, bidding, and buying have become favorite pastimes—
instantly accessible forms of shopping and entertainment. These auction
junkies are enthusiasts of specific collectibles, bargain hunters, and those who
simply relish the thrill of winning at auction.

The internet auction business was started in 1995 and is still considered
a relatively new, evolving arena. At first glance, it appears as though there are
endless choices and bargains to be found on-line, and many people have
succeeded in getting lovely gems and jewelry at very attractive prices. But a
closer look reveals that the risks of buying and selling jewelry and gems on
an auction website are *far greater* than the risks of buying from the traditional auction house, where you have the benefit of examining pieces firsthand, often with the aid of an expert consultant. You must take much greater
precautions if you are to succeed and avoid costly, frustrating mistakes.

## Why People Are Turning to the Internet

For many, the major attraction of shopping on-line is convenience. It is fast,
easy, and private, enabling you to make decisions without feeling pressured or

intimidated by salespeople. For many buyers who live in remote areas far from fine jewelry stores, it provides an opportunity to see what is available, view what's new and exciting, and keep current about everything from gemstones to the latest award-winning designers. For many online vendors such as new jewelry designers whose work may not yet be available in jewelry stores, it provides opportunities to showcase their work to a much wider audience than would otherwise be possible. Some also find the online educational sites to be very helpful, especially since they can take advantage of the information provided at whatever time works best for them. And for people who leave important gifts to the last minute, the internet can bring the world of jewelry directly to the screen in time to be a real lifesaver.

Any avid internet user will gladly rattle off the numerous advantages of shopping on-line in today's harried, fast-paced society:

**Selection.** First and foremost, the internet provides consumers with the greatest assortment of merchandise, in every category, instantly at your fingertips. With a few simple clicks of a button, you'll find jewelry and gemstones in all qualities and prices; a broad selection of antique, estate, and vintage designs; and new products.

**It puts buyers in the driver's seat.** You have the unique ability to search through thousands of items using various keywords such as a designer name, a specific period, or a precise material like gold, ruby, or diamond. And a buyer can also limit selection and save lots of time by indicating a specific price range as a search criterion. The internet clearly puts you in the driver's seat when it comes to selecting merchandise to meet your own unique specifications.

**Great bargains.** There are some great buys to be found on-line. Some major jewelry retailers use online auctions as a vehicle to liquidate the previous season's stock. Private sellers might not know the real value of their gems and offer them at considerably lower prices. And, with such a vast assortment, you are more likely to find a wider selection within your price range faster and more easily on-line than through a traditional auction or retailer.

**Easy access.** Easy access is another factor driving consumers to the internet. People who live in remote places, far from jewelry stores or live auctions, can view a wide selection of jewels and gems. Others prefer the convenience of shopping at home in their pajamas into the wee hours of the night. Still others like the idea of browsing, shopping, and bidding without the added pressure of dealing with salespeople.

*A source of information about products that interest you.* The internet can also help make you a smarter shopper and seller. The vast assortment gives you the ability to easily compare the quality and prices of gems and jewelry. It certainly beats going from store to store in the shopping mall. Many online vendors provide educational information to help you understand more about what you are buying. And, established industry organizations have informational sites to help you be a smarter shopper.

## SOME FACTS THAT MAY DISCOURAGE BUYING AND SELLING ON INTERNET AUCTIONS

It is easy to see the allure of internet shopping, but in all too many cases it is not all that it appears to be—especially where auction sites are concerned—and the disadvantages may quickly outweigh the advantages when the product you are buying happens to be jewelry and gems.

According to a survey commissioned by the National Consumers League, approximately one-third of Americans who spend time on-line have participated in an internet auction; of those, over 40 percent have reported having a problem, including merchandise that never arrived.

### Nothing to Touch and Feel

A major concern is not having the ability to examine the quality, condition, and overall desirability of the jewelry before making a purchase. It is impossible to accurately judge these characteristics from a static photo. Buyers are dependent on the seller's information, description, and pictures. But this information can be incomplete, inaccurate, and misleading.

In general, everything we warn about later in this book is even more so when purchasing from an online auction. We cannot overemphasize the importance of being able to carefully examine any gem or jewelry piece *before* purchase and, whenever possible, to seek expert counsel. Even when dealing with an honest and experienced seller, a buyer can be unintentionally misled by a description or photograph, and ultimately be disappointed with his or her purchase.

### Information Provided Is Often Unreliable

Another serious problem is that many people purchasing jewelry from online auction sites also rely on the internet for information about gems and jewelry—

information they then use to make choices and decisions about what they are buying and what they are paying. But there is no screening mechanism to help you determine the reliability of information provided. Product information provided by vendors pertaining to gems or jewelry being sold is often incomplete and inaccurate, and many "educational" sites are also filled with inaccurate, incomplete, or misleading information. A buyer who relies on incorrect information will make serious mistakes.

## Difficult to Check Out Sellers

It is difficult to find reliable information about the competence or trustworthiness of many online vendors, especially those selling gems and jewelry on auction sites. Many internet companies and individual vendors are unknown entities, without reliable track records or well-established reputations. This makes it more difficult, or impossible, to resolve problems satisfactorily, regardless of "guarantees" made before purchase. You must also remember that it may be difficult or impossible to find the seller "off-line," and you cannot rely completely on vendor ratings because they can be easily rigged by the unscrupulous.

## Representations May Be Worthless

Representations may be meaningless. Unless you can figure out a way to verify facts before making payment to the vendor, you may find yourself a victim, with no recourse. Factors affecting quality and value cannot be accurately judged without gemological training, experience, and proper equipment, and many online vendors lack the requisite knowledge and skill to provide reliable representations or descriptions. Appraisals and other documentation should always be suspect as well.

## Appraisals and Laboratory Reports May Provide a False Sense of Security

Appraisals and gem-testing laboratory reports are being used increasingly by online sellers to increase confidence among prospective buyers. Unfortunately, they are also being used increasingly by the unscrupulous. We are seeing an increase in bogus appraisals and fraudulent lab reports that have duped unsuspecting buyers into purchasing something that has been misrepresented. We have also seen diamonds accompanied by reports from highly respected labs, where the quality of the stone does not match the description on the report. Be sure to get independent verification of any documentation provided by the seller (see chapter 25)—before payment, if possible.

Remember also that you cannot properly judge a gem on the basis of a lab report or appraisal alone. We've seen many diamonds with "great reports" that were not beautiful (and should sell for less than one might surmise from the report alone), and others with "questionable" reports that were exceptionally beautiful (and should cost more than the report would indicate). In other words, you really must see the stone along with the report.

## Protection May Be Illusion

Where some online auction sites are concerned, you may be under the impression that you are protected against misrepresentation and have recourse should there be a problem, but this may be just an illusion. Never forget that in situations where proper examination is not possible, the risk is dramatically increased: you are bidding on a blind item, from a blind source. Be sure to read the "terms and conditions" very carefully, especially the fine print pertaining to "representations, warranties, and limits of liability." As we stress throughout this book, no one can properly judge any fine gem without seeing it firsthand. When you purchase gems and jewelry sight unseen, more than anything else, success is dependent upon having incredible luck.

Problems are not uncommon. One of my own clients had two separate experiences that illustrate the risks for buyers. In the first instance she had a very good experience. She purchased a diamond through an internet auction, and she was able to arrange for us to confirm that the diamond was properly represented *before paying for it.* She obtained a very nice diamond at a price that was less than half of what she would have paid at a retail jewelry store. What she paid was comparable to wholesale, that is, the price a retailer might pay to a diamond dealer for a stone of similar quality. She was very happy.

On her next auction purchase, however, she ran into a problem. She thought she was purchasing a diamond at a bargain price, and she expected to be able to confirm the quality before paying for it, as she had in the earlier case. The diamond was described by the seller to be a certain color, clarity, and weight, but, as in the first case, it was not accompanied by any lab report or appraisal. My client, the buyer, was aware of this when she bid, but she had been told by the seller that she could have it verified by a third party. She was the winning bidder. She became alarmed and suspicious when the seller would not agree to ship the stone for verification before payment. The seller was adamant about receiving payment before shipping the stone anywhere. My client suggested setting up an escrow arrangement, and she was willing to pay the extra costs. The seller would not agree.

While the seller had agreed that my client could send the stone to a third party for verification, it had never been made clear before bidding that the seller would send the stone to a third party only *after* receiving full payment. So, my client did not want to continue with the transaction because she thought she had been subtly misled. The seller expected payment, but my client now refused to pay for the stone. In a final effort to resolve the problem, my client asked if I would be willing to speak with the seller to try to arrange a mutually acceptable course of action—one in which the interests of both parties would be protected.

The seller called me with only one goal: to get paid immediately. I asked how she was able to provide such a precise description of the diamond without any appraisal or lab report, and she responded that she knew "by looking." I then tried to discreetly explain why she could not know the precise quality of any diamond without proper tools and training, and that there were ways differences could be concealed. As a specific example, I mentioned that cracks could be concealed in diamonds, but before I could finish explaining about new methods, she cut me off and stated that she had "looked at hundreds of diamonds" and that the diamond "wasn't *fracture-filled*"—a term normally used only by people inside the jewelry trade.

At this point, alarm bells sounded. I suspected the seller was very knowledgeable and knew both the true quality and the value of the diamond she had sold. The conversation became increasingly futile, and in light of her unwillingness to consider reasonable ways to proceed to bring it all to conclusion, I became increasingly convinced that the seller knew the diamond was not the quality she had represented it to be, nor the bid price a bargain. In fact, I suspected the reverse was probably true. She then tried intimidation tactics, stating that she was a lawyer and that the buyer had entered into a legally binding contract, knowing at the time that the description was only her "opinion." With this, the conversation ended. My client decided on her own not to pay for the stone, and filed a complaint with the auction site against the seller. The seller was unable to pursue it further because she did not know how to reach the buyer, who happened to live outside the United States.

This unfortunate scenario provides lessons for buyers and sellers alike. First, buyers bid a certain amount on an item based on information provided by the seller, but buyers usually lack the expertise to judge the reliability of online sellers and the reliability of the information they provide. They often do not know the identity of the seller. Furthermore, how do buyers protect themselves from situations like this one, in which the seller was clearly a "pro" who knew how to legally exploit the inexperienced? By using the "terms and conditions, warranty and limits of liability" clauses established by the auction site, the seller knew it would be difficult to hold her liable for any description she provided; she knew that the representations she made were not guarantees. Once payment had been received, she would not have been required to make any refund regardless of independent documentation that the quality was lower than represented, nor would she have been legally liable to do so—unless the buyer could have proved that she was knowledgeable and that there had been calculated misrepresentation. Litigation is expensive.

From a seller's perspective, how can you be assured of payment from online buyers? In this example, clearly the seller was a "pro," and yet, she was unable to get payment from this buyer. While I can sympathize with my client, the reality is that the legal issues here are very murky, and while she might have been able to prove that something fraudulent was going on, she never pursued it. Technically, she was in the wrong.

From the seller's perspective, this experience illustrates another point. The online seller is just as much in the dark as the online buyer in terms of the integrity of the party with whom they are doing business. When an item has been sold but not yet delivered, the seller has only e-mail contact information about the buyer; the seller has no physical address or telephone number. Should the buyer subsequently decide not to pay for an item, the seller's options are very limited. It may be very difficult, sometimes impossible, to bring any action against a buyer for nonpayment. In some cases, as you saw above, the seller was in the United States and the buyer was abroad, so litigation would have entered the realm of international law, which is time-consuming and costly. While there are systems in place to try to prevent such things from occurring, they may be difficult to monitor, and there are many ways that both buyers and sellers can create new identities on-line to avoid detection.

Some auction websites, including amazon.com and eBay.com, are now offering free insurance coverage to protect registered users against loss and fraud. There are also independent companies that provide insurance coverage for online auction transactions. But the fact that they are doing this is further evidence that such problems are not infrequent.

## REGARDLESS OF RISK, SAVVY BUYERS CAN FIND GREAT JEWELRY AND GREAT VALUE

Today there are numerous internet auction websites where you can buy and sell jewelry. They include auction-specific sites, traditional auction houses with online services, and conventional jewelry retailers. Each site has its own specific rules and guidelines, and there isn't room here to go into all of them.

As we've emphasized, when buying gemstones and jewelry at auction, being sure about the gemstones is where the biggest challenge exists, and the biggest risk. When you combine the complexities of judging gems with the limited liability of the online auction world, we cannot recommend buying blind—that is, bidding on something you have not seen and examined carefully. Not all web-based auction sites and vendors are of the same quality, and we hesitate to recommend the online auction venue as a source for gems and jewelry *unless you can find the means to arrange for viewing and gemological testing before making payment.* Fortunately, online auction firms are also beginning to realize the necessity of viewing gems and jewelry before purchasing, and we are now seeing some interesting new services.

Some auction websites combine the benefits of the auction house with the convenience of the internet: online catalogs provide convenient viewing, exhibitions provide potential buyers the opportunity to examine pieces carefully and discuss them with experts, and buyers can *bid online during the actual "live" auction.*

Sothebys.com now provides two auction venues: traditional live auctions, which take place

Sotheby's online auctions started out focusing on antique and estate (used) jewelry, such as these pieces. They have now added contemporary jewelry manufacturers and designers as vendors on their site.

at the auction house, and online auctions, which take place on-line. At sothe-bys.com, one can view pieces that will be sold in either venue. One can go on-line to view the catalog of jewelry to be sold at the live auction, and learn about exhibitions where these items can be examined, but online bidding during live sales at the auction house is not available. Sotheby's online auctions are alto-gether different. They operate like other online auctions but with one impor-tant difference: there is sometimes an exhibition of the pieces being sold, so interested buyers have the opportunity to see and examine whatever inter-ests them. By clicking onto sothebys.com and then going to "online auctions," you can learn about upcoming auctions. For example, last year "Jewels Online: The Holiday Gift Collection" took place on-line November 15 through December 6; the exhibition of all the pieces in this auction took place Decem-ber 1 through December 5 at Sotheby's New York location. For people who are able to actually attend the exhibitions, this combines the benefits of the traditional auction house with the convenience and fun of the online auction.

## How the Internet Auction Works

Generally, anyone can list just about any jewelry item or gemstone on-line for a nominal fee through an auction site. For instance, at eBay.com, one of the largest online auction destinations, the seller pays between 30 cents and $3.50 to list an item depending on the value of the opening bid. While auction sites typically have guidelines about how to list, describe, and show an item on-line, it is entirely up to the seller's discretion how much information to list.

Most online auction sites provide thorough how-to information and tuto-rials to help both buyers and sellers operate successfully. Remember, these auc-tion sites make their profit by having as many transactions as possible; each time a seller lists an item, he or she pays a fee. But if sellers don't sell what they list, they'll stop coming back. And if buyers are not happy with their purchases or have a bad experience, they will stop coming back. So online auction com-panies try to create sites that will provide buyers and sellers with an easy, con-venient, and positive experience, so they will return again and again.

A seller can set a reserve or minimum bid: a hidden or exposed preset price that must be met in order for the piece to be sold. Again, this is the only protection a seller has to ensure the piece will not sell for less than its true value. This is why it is so important for private sellers—people who are not in the jewelry business—to know what they themselves really have and what it's worth. Without that knowledge, an astute buyer might find a real treasure, at a steal price. That might be great for the buyer (and one reason knowledgeable buyers spend hours surfing auction sites) but very sad for the seller.

Buyers should also keep in mind that a large percentage of sellers participating in online auction sites are jewelry designers, manufacturers, and used-jewelry and gemstone dealers, not private individuals. While this is no different from what you find in most traditional auction houses, online buyers may have more limited recourse in the event of misrepresentation if they deal with a vendor whose real identity and location may be unknown. On the other hand, depending on the vendor, buying from a vendor in the jewelry business can also be a benefit. They are normally more knowledgeable about what they are selling than people who are not in the business, and they should be able to provide accurate descriptions of what they are selling. Many online buyers have purchased very lovely pieces from these vendors at very good prices. Others have paid more than they would have paid at a retail jewelry store. So don't delude yourself into thinking you will always get a "steal" or a really great bargain, or that you are paying wholesale prices. You must always check it out, as we have already recommended. And some of the best values, along with the highest risk, are found in jewelry sold by people who are not in the trade and don't know the value of what they have.

Each item is listed for a predetermined amount of time, which can range from a few days up to ten days. Many sites offer sellers the opportunity to list a "buy it now" price, allowing buyers to pay a preset price that overrides the current auction, and purchase that piece immediately.

In order to place a bid, most sites require that buyers pre-register with a *user name.* This provides the buyer anonymity but still permits the auction sites to track their business dealings. If there are complaints about deceitful business dealings in regard to a specific buyer or seller, some auction sites will bar the registered user from operating again. However, there are ways that the unscrupulous can obtain new identities and return repeatedly.

Buyers usually bid in preset increments based on the general value of an item being sold. Typically, they can bid an unlimited amount of times on a piece right up until the auction closes: the time and date that are clearly identified on each lot. Astute buyers may wait until the very last moment, and jump in at the end to place the winning bid just seconds from the closing (this is called *sniping*). To eliminate sniping, some online auction sites such as sothebys.com and dickeranddicker.com have adopted a method whereby the auction will continue for ten minutes *beyond the last bid.* Just as at the live auction, where bidding continues for as long as bidding continues, the ten-minute rule adds the drama and excitement of the auction floor and eliminates sniping. Of course, you must also "stay tuned," and you don't know how long those "last few minutes" will actually take, but the bidding typically ends within a reasonable amount of time.

Both buyers and sellers can keep their true identities concealed and operate under user names. Undoubtedly, this has advantages and disadvantages. Some people prefer anonymity during business dealings. On the other hand, if you are not satisfied with your purchase, this system presents obvious problems in tracking down a vendor.

The seller will set all the terms of the transaction, including who pays for shipping, insurance, and handling; a return policy; and the acceptable form of payment. In essence, each seller operates as an independent vendor; the auction site is not responsible or liable for whatever transpires.

Once a buyer has made a successful final bid, it is up to the buyer and seller to promptly contact each other to arrange for payment and delivery. Remember, a successful bid is a legally binding agreement. The buyer is obligated to complete the transaction and pay the vendor, just as the seller is required to deliver the merchandise in a timely fashion.

Ice.com, an online merchant of new jewelry, also uses yahoo.com and ebay.com to sell older jewelry items in the auction venue. Dicker & Dicker Jewelers auction both old jewelry and designer jewelry from smaller or less well-known designers that don't have their own websites.

Increasingly, buyers and sellers are arranging for online payment through services such as Paypal (www. paypal.com) or BillPoint (www. billpoint.com), which set up electronic transfers for greater security and convenience. Some vendors will accept major credit cards, bank transfers, checks, and money orders. (Some payment options are riskier than others; see below.)

The seller typically pays a commission fee to the auction site based on a percentage of the final sale price of each item, which varies on average between 2 and 5 percent.

Many online auction sites include vendors who are brick-and-mortar retailers, designers, manufacturers, and private individuals who have developed a healthy income from online sales. These seasoned sellers, who are likely looking for return business, can make the shopping, payment, and delivery a pleasurable experience. But regardless of the source, whether buying from someone in the jewelry business or from private individuals, you cannot generalize: there are people who are knowledgeable and honest, and those who are not. Always find a reliable gemologist-appraiser to check it out (see chapter 25 for more on where and why).

## HOW TO GET STARTED

Just as with traditional auctions, it's essential to get to know the marketplace before you start buying or selling on-line. Visit the various auction sites and investigate how the different ones operate. The important sites offer step-by-step tutorials that take potential buyers and sellers through the process. Review the jewelry and gemstones listed on the sites, the prices, the bidding activity, and the final sale prices.

Remember, anyone can start a website. Make sure you buy and sell at auction from a reputable online business. While this may be difficult to ascertain, there are new websites that monitor various sites and list companies about which there have been complaints. While you can fall victim to unscrupulous buyers and sellers on any site, you are more likely to have a positive experience. You may even find additional services such as insurance to help you along the way.

## HOW TO BE A SMART BUYER

Once you have selected an established website where you feel comfortable, browse the site, compare prices, and be aware of the time limitations for the item that interests you. Remember, new merchandise is coming on-line all the time.

## Know What You Are Buying

As we mentioned earlier, some products are in a higher risk category in an auction than others. Buying used books, garden equipment, or camera parts on eBay will carry a much lower risk than buying gemstones or jewelry. As we have stressed repeatedly, it's critical to see the jewelry or gemstone before making a purchase. Do not rely only on descriptions, lab reports, or pictures to accurately identify the piece. Many factors that affect the quality and value of a piece cannot be judged without gemological training, experience, and the proper equipment. Some online vendors lack the requisite knowledge and skill, so their representations may be unreliable. If you can make arrangements whereby the seller will agree to allow a gemologist acceptable to both parties to examine the item to verify quality, authenticity, and value, then you greatly the reduce risk and increase the fun. But some vendors will not agree to this, and then your risk is greatly increased. Unless you can view the item before paying for it, my advice is simple: find another vendor.

Online sellers are increasingly using appraisals and gem-testing laboratory reports to instill confidence in buyers. Unfortunately, as we've already explained, some bogus appraisals and lab reports have duped unsuspecting buyers into purchasing something that has been misrepresented. We have also seen diamonds accompanied by reports from highly respected labs, where the quality of the stone does not match the description on the report. In other words, sometimes a different stone accompanies the report. Be sure to get independent verification of any documentation provided by the seller before payment.

## Don't Assume It's a Good Deal

Prices run the gamut at auction, so don't assume that because you're buying a piece from a woman living in some small town, you are getting a bargain. Checking prices before purchase is virtually impossible unless you have seen the piece and know the true quality. Normally, if you are permitted to examine it before payment, you will be obligated to honor the transaction as long as the quality representations are verified. However, after purchase, it can still be useful to compare the price of what you bought with the prices of comparable pieces being sold at jewelry stores or from online retailers. If you've overpaid, you'll know better next time. If you got a good deal, you might want to consider future purchases from that vendor.

Before deciding whether or not you're getting a good deal, here are some other things to ask about:

- Is the item new and unused?
- If new, does it come in the original box?
- Does it come with original paper guaranteeing its authenticity?
- Is there an identifiable signature or stamp that is visible?
- Who pays for shipping and handling, and how much will it cost?
- Will it be insured when shipped?
- How soon can I expect to receive it?
- Can I return it? If yes, for refund or for credit? Within what time frame?

## Read Terms and Conditions Carefully

As with any auction house, if you are going to play, know the ground rules. Carefully read the auction site's terms and conditions, and the seller's own terms and conditions. Ask questions, and if you are not satisfied with the answers, be prepared to walk away from the sale. If the sale does not feel right, then it probably is not.

## Check the Seller's History

Whenever possible, check out the seller's history. Some auction sites post feedback ratings of sellers based on comments by other buyers. If the seller has more than one negative rating, you may want to reconsider your purchase. But remember, it's easy to fake "positive" ratings and comments. And don't assume that the absence of "negative" ratings means you're dealing with someone trustworthy—victims may not have discovered they've been had.

Before you bid, find out what form of payment the seller will accept. If the seller accepts only cashier's checks or money orders, decide whether you are willing to take the risk of sending payment before you receive the item. If the seller is not willing to consider Paypal or BillPoint, or establish an escrow arrangement (see below), you may want to think twice.

## GET READY, GET SET, BID!

Once you have selected the piece and the terms and conditions meet your expectations, it's time to make a bid. Remember, a bid is a legally binding offer to buy the item at any price up to your maximum bid amount.

Be prepared to watch your lot until the final hour. Take note of the day, hour, and minute that bidding will close on your lot. Other bidders can enter the game at any moment and drive up the price, even if you've been the lead bidder for one full week.

Decide in advance how high you will go on a specific bid, and don't get caught up in auction fever, which can lead to overpaying. If there is a lot of action on your item of interest, you may want to wait until close to the end before you bid up the price. However, others may be thinking the same way, so be prepared to move fast.

## Payment—Doing It Right Is Key to Avoiding Fraud

Once you have won a successful bid, contact the seller immediately via e-mail to arrange for payment and shipping. This may be the most critical part of the entire online experience: the step that can protect you, or signal you that there is a risk. According to the National Consumers League Internet Fraud Watch, online auctions are the most likely place for consumers to become the victim of fraud, and those who have been victims have usually paid by check, cashier's check, or money order (about 70 percent). There is an equal risk to buyers and sellers—by the time a buyer discovers there is a problem, the check or money order has already been cashed; if a seller has shipped merchandise before a check clears the bank, there may be no easy way to get it back.

There are several payment options that might provide some protection. Credit cards offer the most consumer protection because consumers have the right under federal law to dispute charges in cases of misrepresentation, or if a purchase is not delivered. This includes the right to seek a credit from the credit card issuer. New services handling online payment, known as Paypal or BillPoint, are also worth considering; they are becoming more widely used among both buyers and sellers. It's a quick and convenient way to complete a transaction and, like credit cards, may provide some protection.

Another option is an escrow service, where a buyer can place money in the custody of a third party, and the money is then paid to the seller once certain conditions have been met. An escrow account generally costs 5 percent of the value of the item.

You can select a payment option that best meets your needs, but beware of any buyer or seller who insists upon a check or money order.

## How to Be a Savvy Seller

### Sellers Should Shop Around

Explore the various internet auction sites and select the site most likely to attract the best audience for your specific product. One of the best parts of internet shopping is that nearly everything is transparent, which means you have the unique ability to shop and compare the types of gems and jewelry being sold, the price range of items offered, the presentation, and more.

### Presentation Is Key

With so many options at auction, it's essential to present your jewelry or gemstones in a professional, attractive, and easy-to-shop format. A good presentation not only attracts more potential buyers but can also help you command a greater price for your product.

Take advantage of what the internet auction sites provide to help sellers make a good presentation. Bear in mind that you are acting as a virtual store. Consider yourself a retailer: how can you attract customers, and what can you do to provide the most value and service to your customer?

Here is some advice that might make your efforts yield more sparkling results:

- *For private sellers, get documentation from a reliable, respected gemologist-appraiser.* (See appendix.) This will be especially useful for several reasons: (1) You need to know what you have, and what it's worth, *before* you sell. (2) A gemologist can help you write a reliable and thorough description. (3) A gemologist may have photographic services to aid in getting good images. (4) A gemologist can help you establish a realistic reserve to protect you from consigning something at too low a price and not getting its true value. (5) Documentation provided by a reliable gemologist—which a prospective buyer can document by contacting the lab—will increase credibility and encourage bidding.
- *A picture is worth a thousand words.* Invest the time to get good images of your jewelry, showing the piece from various angles. Be sure to show any identifying marks, stamp, signature, or serial number, which will add credibility and value to the product. There are many places to visit on-line to learn how to obtain good images. If you don't

have a good digital camera, now may be a good time to invest in one.

- *Provide detailed, accurate descriptions.* Try to be straightforward and avoid exaggeration. Try to anticipate what questions a buyer might have, and provide information that covers them in your description.

- *List your lot in bold type.* Make your item stand out by listing it in bold type and showing a banner or other visual enhancement. There is a nominal fee for banners and other visuals, but they will attract greater attention.

- *Explain your terms and conditions carefully.* Reasonable terms are likely to increase credibility and encourage a buyer to invest in a big-ticket item. For instance, a short-term return policy might encourage cautious buyers to take a risk—but realize that it also increases your own risk. Proceed carefully and cautiously.

- *Outline the shipping and handling costs, and who is responsible for the cost.* Indicate whether or not you are willing to ship internation-ally. Keep in mind that shipping and insuring gems and jewelry can be very expensive, and international shipping can cost even more.

## Set a Reasonable Reserve

Just as you would at a traditional auction house, you must first learn the value of what you have before you can establish a reasonable reserve. Your best bet is to consult a gemologist-appraiser, but if this is not possible, check with a variety of sources: local jewelers, designers, or estate dealers (keep in mind that their valuations may be low, and that they may have a vested interest in what you are selling). Once you know what you have, and its quality, you may be able to identify comparable items on-line and use the prices at which they are selling as a guide to establishing your reserve.

Once you know the true value of your piece, set a reserve that is comfort-able for you. Keep in mind that a low reserve means your piece may sell for less than its true value, and a high reserve can prevent your piece from selling.

Remember, an auction is a legal commitment to sell your item to the high-est bidder; if you receive one bid at or above your reserve, you are obligated to complete the transaction.

## Payment

Accept secure forms of payment: credit cards or online payment services such as Paypal or BillPoint. If you accept personal checks or money orders, make sure the payment is in full, and make sure any check has cleared the bank before you release the merchandise. If a party insists on seeing the merchandise before buying, for a nominal fee you can set up an escrow service with a third party.

## Closing a Deal

After the auction closes, sellers are required to deliver the merchandise within the time frame designated during the auction or, if no time frame is specified, within thirty days. A seller who does not ship within the time period is required by law to give the buyer an opportunity to cancel the order for a full refund or mutually agree to a new shipping date.

## Fees

The seller pays a *listing fee* or *insertion fee* to place an item on an auction site. The fee structure is different on every site but ranges from a low of 30 cents to $10, depending on your opening bid amount or reserve price. If your item sells, you'll be charged a fee or commission based on the final sale price, which ranges anywhere from 1.25 percent to as high as 20 percent.

## WINNERS AND LOSERS

Despite all the warnings about fraud on-line, there are numerous successful transactions. One buyer we know bid on an exceptional six-carat star sapphire ring with diamond accents, set in platinum, circa 1920s. She requested more information and wanted to see the ring. The private seller, a woman from the Midwest, was cooperative, and they spoke on three different occasions. Ultimately, the buyer purchased the ring without seeing it. After talking on the phone with the seller, and seeing detailed photos, she felt confident in her purchase. She paid $850 for a beautiful ring. The sapphire was genuine, the ring was a beautiful Art Deco piece, and the appraiser said it would cost $4,000 in a retail store.

The trick is knowing where and how to have such wonderful experiences.

Keep in mind that there *are* many positive transactions on-line from which both buyers and sellers leave satisfied.

But you cannot ignore the other side. As you have seen, the risk is greater, and the incidence of misrepresentation is higher, when one turns to online auctions for gems and jewelry. In general, according to the Federal Trade

Commission (FTC), internet auction fraud has become a significant problem. Most consumer complaints center on sellers who:

- Don't deliver the advertised goods.
- Deliver something far less valuable than was advertised.
- Don't deliver in a timely way.
- Fail to disclose all the relevant information about the product or terms of the sale.
- Fail to comply with FTC guidelines, most notably by omitting critical information pertaining to quality factors, exact weight, and treatments used on diamonds, colored gemstones, and pearls.
- Represent themselves to be wholesalers but are not bona fide wholesalers.

To sum up, when buying or selling on-line, whether from e-tailers, auction sites, or individuals, the rewards may be great, but the risks are much higher than when buying from traditional sources.

Only you can decide whether online auction sites are for you. If they are, take appropriate steps to reduce your risk, and then be sure to verify all the facts. If you do, the good experiences may outweigh the bad. Keep in mind the importance of finding ways to see whatever you are buying before making payment, and when you do pay, pay by credit card or through an escrow arrangement or one of the new services such as Paypal or BillPoint. And always verify your purchase. If everything checks out, great! And you'll have a basis on which to begin placing your trust and confidence in the seller. If it doesn't, hopefully you will not have paid, or if you have, you will have used a credit card. And you'll know for next time.

If you have a problem, the auction websites suggest that you first try and work it out directly with the seller, then turn to the auction firm for advice. If that fails, you can file a complaint with the FTC by calling toll free 1-877-FTC-HELP (382-4357) or by visiting its website at www.ftc.gov. The FTC does not resolve individual problems for consumers, but it may act against a company if it sees a pattern of possible law violations.

Visit the FTC website to also learn about the more common fraudulent practices and possible ways to protect your interests on-line.

## BEWARE OF ONLINE APPRAISAL SERVICES

As this book was going to press, the *Wall Street Journal* announced that eBay was considering a new service—online appraisals—to give buyers and sellers more reliable guidelines as to the value of items being offered on their website. Online appraisals may be reliable for some products, but particular caution must be used when dealing with gems and jewelry, especially antique or period jewelry, and jewelry containing diamonds, gemstones, or pearls. There are two separate issues: (1) Is the piece properly identified and of the quality represented? (2) If it is as represented, what is its value? As you will see throughout the following chapters, an accurate appraisal of any gemstone or piece of jewelry to determine its true identity and quality requires testing with scientific equipment, and this cannot be done sight-unseen. Even gold jewelry must be tested to ensure the gold content, regardless of any mark that might be present. Thus, online appraisals are usually not reliable, and anyone proceeding on the basis of an online appraisal may make a costly mistake. However, if you follow our earlier suggestions about verifying representations made about the piece and its quality prior to making payment, then guidelines as to value may be useful.

# 4 ♦ Opportunities Exist, but Not without Risk: What to Watch Out for When Buying or Selling at Auction

THERE IS NO QUESTION THAT BUYING AND SELLING GEMS OR JEWELRY at auction can be exciting, fun, and profitable. But the auction arena is not for everyone, and not every purchase is a bargain. Keep in mind that even at the best firms there is an element of risk.

You have seen how alluring the auction venue can be, and there are certainly many reasons to pursue the auction market seriously. But in addition to the finest and rarest gems and jewelry, and good values to be found, you must not ignore factors that might discourage buying at auction.

The auction arena is not one that should be entered casually. For the inexperienced and uneducated, there are hidden risks that greatly increase the possibility of being disappointed or of buying something that is not what it appears to be. But with some basic knowledge, the auction market can be a great source of some of the world's finest gems and jewelry, record-setting treasures, and great bargains, too.

## RISKS TO BUYERS

Depending on whether you are buying or selling, the risks are somewhat different. We will start with a discussion of some of the risks faced by those interested in buying at auction:

- *No returns or exchanges are possible, and often there is no recourse.* Generally speaking there are no returns, exchanges, or recourse when you are buying at auction. At the auction house, bidding takes place in a matter of minutes, and you cannot change your mind afterwards (unless you can prove that something guaranteed by the house has been misrepresented). Unlike a traditional retailer, auctions offer consigned jewelry from a variety of sources, and returns and exchanges are rare. It is *your* responsibility to view the piece before the sale, to understand the limitations of the house (especially in terms of the descriptions and guarantees), and to decide what you want to pay, *before* you start bidding.

- **Liability is limited.** Descriptions of items sold at auction are not guaranteed. Auction houses, as a rule, guarantee only what is stated in the *capitalized headings* in the catalog. The full description of any piece—the information provided in the text below the heading—is provided to assist buyers, but the auction house cannot be held liable for any errors provided in the descriptions. The catalog provides explicit and detailed information about where their liability stops. Be sure you read it carefully. In most cases, should you later discover that the description was inaccurate, you may have no recourse. Where online sellers are concerned, the liability may be even more limited and the risk much greater.

- **Descriptions are not guarantees and may confuse or mislead buyers.** While auction houses may make an effort to provide accurate information, some auction houses have well-trained gemologists on staff whereas others do not. In either case, they may make mistakes or omit important information. So remember that if information is not stated in the capitalized headings, there is always a degree of risk.

  Auction firms are not required to supply documentation on a stone or even to stand behind certificates accompanying items they are selling. In short, you cannot rely on the descriptions or on accompanying documentation, and if they prove to have been inaccurate, it will be your loss. For instance, if a ring is described in the capitalized heading as "An Important Diamond Ring," the only guarantee being made is that the stone is a genuine diamond. The quality of the diamond is not guaranteed. Even if the description includes reference to a diamond grading report accompanying the stone, the quality is not guaranteed. Most auction houses don't have a large enough staff to be able to precisely grade every diamond or confirm that documentation is accurate, and in some cases a diamond grading report accompanying a diamond sold at auction has not matched the diamond it accompanied.

  Where colored gemstones are concerned, if a gemstone is not described as *natural* in the capitalized headings, it should be assumed that it is treated or enhanced in some way. It might be natural, but without documentation, you must assume it is not, and bid accordingly. On the other hand, when it is accompanied by a laboratory report you cannot assume that the report matches the stone; if it does not, the auction house is not liable. As with diamonds, even where there is documentation, the auction house does not guarantee anything stated on the accompanying documents.

Where diamonds and colored gemstones are concerned, some auction houses will be happy to estimate the quality of a diamond or other stone for you, in the absence of documentation, or will provide an estimate of quality in a *condition report* (see chapter 2). Just remember, these are estimates only and not representations for which the auction house can be held liable.

It's important to look carefully at the fine print, examine the jewelry, and ask questions. Where major gems are concerned, you might want to retain an independent gemologist to examine pieces for you, confirm documentation, advise you on whether or not to bid, and if so, what amount.

- *Misrepresentation of "facts"—the representations stated in capitalized headings—often go undetected.* Auction firms may try to provide accurate representations in the capitalized headings, but here again, they make mistakes. While the auction house *is* responsible if they have misrepresented any fact stated in the capitalized heading, few people ever discover what has happened because they never ask an independent gemologist-appraiser to determine whether or not a piece is what it was represented to be. Most people assume that whatever is stated in the capitalized heading *must* be so. However, this is not always the case. For whatever reasons, we've seen many pieces acquired from reputable auction firms that are not what the capitalized headings stated them to be. We've seen pieces represented to contain genuine sapphires, rubies, or emeralds that contained synthetic stones; we've seen antique pieces described as containing "diamonds" when the stones were common colorless sapphire. And so on.

  There are also several treatments, such as fracture filling diamonds and diffusion-treatment of sapphires (see chapters 9 and 17), that must be disclosed by jewelers or other retailers before sale. However, this is not always the case at auction, and we've seen such stones sold at auction without disclosure. There is a lot to know—a lot to *look for* and a lot to *look out for*—if you want to keep the "sparkle" in your auction experience. (These details will be covered in later chapters.)

- *Buying sight unseen may lead to disappointment.* It is virtually impossible to judge gems and jewelry from a picture in a catalog or on-line, and even more difficult to make a decision based on someone's verbal descriptions. Even among legitimate sources, not seeing the gem or piece of jewelry before acquiring it can lead to disappointment upon receipt of the merchandise. Even if all of the representations are accurate, the piece may not have the look or feel that you expected, or the personality and overall appearance of the stone may not be what you envisioned. But like it or not, you may be stuck with it. Where internet auctions are concerned, the risk is even greater if you cannot examine the stone or jewelry in person before bidding. Be sure to read the terms and conditions very carefully before bidding online, especially the fine print pertaining to representations, warranties, and limits of liability.

- *Emotions can lead to overbidding.* Live auctions can generate excitement and exhilaration, and this can lead to getting caught up in the passion of the moment. It's important not to get carried away in a bidding war and end up exceeding your budget or, even worse, overpaying for the jewelry. Decide in advance the maximum amount of money you are willing to pay for an item, and don't exceed that amount.

## RISKS FACED BY SELLERS

While people can do very well selling gems and jewelry at auction, uneducated sellers can be easily exploited, often without ever realizing it. In order to do well selling at auction, you need to be aware of how to avoid some of these pitfalls.

- *You may receive less than the true value if bidding is weak during auction.* As we discussed in chapter 2, if a reserve—the pre-established price set by the auction house, beneath which a piece cannot be sold—has not been established, or if the reserve is too low, a seller risks getting less than the true value of the jewelry at auction. Remember that the auction firm's first consideration is obtaining pieces at prices that will ensure the auction house doesn't lose, even if the seller does. This means with a low reserve. Whenever you consign jewelry to the auction house without first knowing what it is worth, you are vulnerable to being exploited. An auction house will be financially ahead when pieces sell, even at a fraction of their true value, but the seller won't be. Always remember: the lower the reserve, the greater the potential revenue to the auction house, and the greater the potential risk to the seller.

- *Low reserves result in low estimates and discourage fair bidding.* When a rare or important piece comes to auction with a low reserve, it will have an equally low estimate. This can discourage people who are not knowledgeable about gems or jewelry from bidding a fair price, because all too often they rely on the estimates as an indicator of the true value (see chapter 2). Thus, they feel foolish bidding much more than the estimate, and they are confused when a piece does succeed in selling for a much higher price. When this happens, they often conclude that someone just got caught up in auction fever and overpaid.

If the estimate is very low, this can also send a signal to the trade that the piece comes from a private estate where the seller doesn't know the value of the item. When this happens, it sometimes encourages dealers to bid together in order to buy it cheaply and then split the profits when they sell it later. This is known as *collusion,* and it is against the law in the United States. But it can be difficult to control and difficult to prove.

I vividly remember an experience where this is probably just what occurred. I had seen an exceptional ring that contained a rich green six-carat emerald with no visible inclusions (flaws) and, when I examined it with the microscope, showed no evidence of any clarity enhancement (see chapter 17). Such emeralds are extremely rare because surface-reaching cracks and fissures are routinely filled with various substances to make them less visible. At the time, I was searching for an exceptionally fine emerald for clients, and called them immediately about the emerald at the auction. My clients were looking for an emerald between three and four carats and were prepared to spend about $125,000, at wholesale, for the stone. We had seen stones in the three- to four-carat range that had not been oiled or clarity enhanced, but none could compare in color and clarity to the emerald in this ring. On the basis of my extensive search, we estimated that the current wholesale value of the emerald coming up at auction would have been over $300,000. The auction estimate on the emerald ring was $35,000 to $45,000. While I knew that this stone would bring much more than the estimate, we decided to attend the auction and see if we got lucky (after all, there was no laboratory documentation, and maybe it would not get attention). We were prepared to bid up to $110,000, plus the buyer's premium. As the bidding began, I noticed many emerald dealers in the room, but only one was bidding against us. We finally reached our limit of $110,000, and the dealer against whom we'd been bidding went one more bid and acquired the stone for $120,000. I knew from my experience with other rare gems that this ring should have brought at least $200,000 from an emerald dealer. So why didn't it? I think I know why. I had seen the dealer who had bid against us speaking to several emerald dealers before the sale, and the same group was huddled together in a restaurant immediately following the sale. There is no question in my mind that this was a case of their having agreed not to bid against one another in order to keep the price down, and to split a future profit. But I couldn't see a way to prove it. And I couldn't help wondering what they would have paid had we not been bidding against them—possibly much less.

- *Auction house evaluations and appraisals may be unreliable.* As we've already discussed, it is in the best interest of the auction house to convince the seller to consign gems and jewelry at the lowest possible price. This means that the "value" they place on a piece may be unreliable. Don't make the mistake of regarding the auction house as the expert to whom you should turn to learn what something is worth.

  In addition to unreliable valuations, sometimes auction houses lack the expertise to accurately identify an important gemstone or to recognize unusually rare or valuable quality. They may identify a synthetic as natural or an exceptionally fine natural stone as a synthetic.

  *Before* going to the auction house with something to sell, you should first locate an *independent gemologist-appraiser* with respected credentials (see appendix) to find out exactly what the auction house has and, most of all, what it is really worth. Only by learning the value of what you have *before* you go to an auction house to consign something can you protect yourself from consigning it at too low a price.

  A knowledgeable gemologist-appraiser can also help you determine what a fair reserve and estimate should be. In some cases, the gemologist may be willing to accompany you to the auction house to help you negotiate the reserve and estimate, or take the piece to the auction house for you as your agent.

- *The process may be lengthy with no guarantee your piece will sell.* Most auction houses are very careful about what they accept for auction, and will not accept pieces unless they think they will sell. Nonetheless, while most items will sell at a good sale, 20 to 25 percent will still go unsold. And if for some unforeseen reason auction attendance and bidding are weak, the percentage of unsold lots can be much higher. Once your piece is accepted and consigned to the auction house, there is normally a three-to-four-month period during which the auction house has possession of the piece (for photography, catalog production, exhibitions, and so on). If your piece sells and brings a good price, it will be worth the wait and anticipation. But if it fails to sell, then you will pay a nominal fee to the auction house and have nothing to show for it.

As you can see, buying and selling at auction are not without some degree of risk, but the more you know about where the risks exist, the less likely you will be to fall victim to them. We hope we haven't discouraged you but rather have opened your eyes to those areas in which you need to be most astute. Now, armed with this information, you are ready to take the next step toward buying and selling at auction.

You've seen in chapters 2 and 3 how the process works. But even more important than understanding the process, you must understand how to judge the gemstones and jewelry that interest you—what to look for, and what to look out for—if you are going to be successful at auction. Because of the intricacies and complexities of the gem and jewelry field, the emphasis in the remaining chapters will be on giving you what you need to know to be more confident about the gemstones themselves and the jewelry they adorn.

If you take the information provided here to heart, you'll find that the auction market can be a great source of some of the world's finest gems and jewelry, record-setting treasures, and great bargains, too.

## PART 2 ♦
# BECOMING FAMILIAR WITH GEMS

# 5 ♦ GETTING STARTED

GEMS SHOULD NEVER BE BOUGHT AS A GAMBLE—THE UNEDUCATED consumer will always lose. This is a basic rule of thumb. The best way to take the gamble out of buying a particular gem is to familiarize yourself with the gem. While the average consumer can't hope to make the same precise judgments as a qualified gemologist, whose scientific training and wealth of practical experience provide a far larger database from which to operate, the consumer can learn to judge a stone as a "total personality" and learn what the critical factors are—color, clarity (also referred to in the trade as *perfection*), cut, brilliance, and weight—and how to balance them in judging the gem's value. Learning about these factors and spending time in the marketplace looking, listening, and asking questions before making the purchase will prepare you to be a wise buyer more likely to get what you really want at a fair price.

Try to learn as much as you can about the gem you want to buy. Examine stones owned by your family and friends, and compare stones at several different jewelry stores, noting differences in shades of color, brilliance, and cut. Go to a good established jewelry store and ask to see fine stones. If the prices vary, ask why. Let the jeweler point out differences in color, cut, or brilliance; if he or she can't, go to another jeweler with greater expertise. Do the same at several fine auction houses. Begin to develop an eye for what constitutes a fine stone by looking, listening, and asking good questions.

## How to Use a Loupe

A loupe (pronounced *loop*) is a special type of magnifying glass. The loupe can be very helpful in many situations, even for the beginner. With a loupe you can check a stone for chips or scratches, or you can examine certain types of noticeable inclusions more closely. Remember, however, that even with a loupe you will not have the knowledge or skill to see or understand the many telltale indicators that an experienced jeweler or gemologist can spot. No book can provide you with that knowledge or skill. Do not allow yourself to be deluded or let a little knowledge give you false confidence. Nothing will more quickly alienate knowledgeable people or mark you faster as easy prey for the disreputable.

The loupe is a very practical tool to use once you master it, and with practice it will become more and more valuable. The correct type is a 10x, or ten-power, "triplet," which can be obtained from any optical supply house. The triplet type is recommended because it corrects two problems other types of magnifiers have: traces of color normally found at the outer edge of the lens, and visual distortion, also usually at the outer edge of the lens. In addition, the loupe must have a black housing around the lens, not chrome or gold, either of which may affect the color you see in the stone.

The loupe *must* be 10x because the United States Federal Trade Commission requires grading to be done under ten-power magnification. Any flaw that does not show up under 10x magnification is considered nonexistent for grading purposes.

With a few minutes' practice you can easily learn to use the loupe. Here's how:

1. Hold the loupe between the thumb and forefinger of either hand.
2. Hold the stone or jewelry similarly in the other hand.
3. Bring both hands together so that the fleshy parts just below the thumbs are pushed together and braced by the lower portions of both hands just above the wrists (the wrist portion is actually a pivot point).
4. Now move both hands up to your nose or cheek, with the loupe as close to your eye as possible. If you wear eyeglasses, you do not have to remove them.

A 10x Triplet Loupe

How to hold a loupe
when examining a stone

5. Get a steady hand. With gems it's very important to have steady hands for careful examination. With your hands still together and braced against your face, put your elbows on a table. (If a table isn't available, brace your arms against your chest or rib cage.) If you do this properly you will have a steady hand.

Practice with the loupe, keeping it approximately one inch (more or less) from your eye and about an inch from the object being examined. Learn to see through it clearly. A 10x loupe is difficult to focus initially, but with a little practice it will become easy. You can practice on any object that is difficult to see—the pores in your skin, a strand of hair, a pinhead, or your own jewelry.

Play with the item being examined. Rotate it slowly, tilt it back and forth while rotating it, and look at it from different angles and different directions. It won't take long before you are able to focus easily on anything you wish to examine. If you aren't sure about your technique, a knowledgeable jeweler will be happy to help you learn to use the loupe correctly.

## WHAT THE LOUPE CAN TELL YOU

With practice and experience (and further education if you're really serious), a loupe can tell even the amateur a great deal. For a gemologist it can help determine whether the stone is natural, synthetic, glass, or a doublet (a composite stone, to be discussed later), and it can reveal characteristic flaws, blemishes, or cracks. In other words, the loupe can provide the necessary information to help you know whether the stone is in fact what it is supposed to be.

For the beginner, the loupe is useful in seeing these features:

- *Hallmarks and trademarks.* Assay marks (revealing gold or platinum content), hallmarks, trademarks, engraved messages, and names provide important clues to provenance and value. Sometimes they are difficult to see because of where they are located, or because they are worn, but a loupe enables you to see marks that are often missed.

- *Chips, cracks, or scratches on the facet edges, planes, or table.* While zircon, for example, looks very much like diamond because of its pronounced brilliance and relative hardness, it chips easily. Therefore, careful examination of a zircon will often show chipping, especially on the top and around the edges. Glass, which is very soft, will often show scratches. Normal wear can cause it to chip or become scratched. Also, if you check around the prongs, the setter may even have scratched it while bending the prongs to hold the stone.

In such stones as emeralds and opals, the loupe can also help you determine whether or not any natural cracks are really serious, how close they are to the surface, how deep they run, or how many are readily visible.

For jewelry, you can also notice wear, see worn or broken prongs, and detect poor repairs or alterations when you see traces of solder.

- *The workmanship that went into the cutting of a gem or the creation of a piece of jewelry.* For example, is the symmetry of the stone balanced? Does it have the proper number of facets for its cut? Is the proportion good? Few cutters put the same time and care into cutting glass as they do into a gem. For jewelry, examine the front and back for intricate detailing.

- *The sharpness of the facet edges.* Harder stones will have a sharp edge, or sharper boundaries between adjoining planes or facets, whereas many imitations are softer, so that under the loupe the edges between the facets are less sharp and have a more rounded appearance.

- *Bubbles, inclusions, and flaws.* Many flaws and inclusions that cannot be seen with the naked eye are easily seen with the loupe. But remember, many are not easily seen unless you are very experienced. The presence of inclusions is not as serious in colored stones as in diamonds, and they don't usually significantly reduce the value of the stone. However, the *kind* of inclusions seen in colored stones can be important. They often provide the necessary key to positive identification, determine whether a stone is natural or synthetic, and possibly locate the origin of the stone, which may significantly affect the value. With minimal experience, the amateur can also learn to spot the characteristic bubbles and swirl lines associated with glass.

The loupe can tell you a great deal about the workmanship that went into cutting a gem or creating a jewel. It can help a professional decide whether a gem is natural, synthetic, a doublet, or glass. It can provide the clues about a gem's durability and its country of origin. It can provide clues to jewelry period authenticity, repairs, and alterations. But spotting these clues takes lots of practice and experience.

When you use a loupe, remember that you won't see what the experienced professional will see, but with a little practice, it can still be a valuable tool and may save you from a costly mistake.

## PARTS OF A STONE

One of the most important things to learn is how to look at a gem, even if you won't see all that a gemologist will. Let's begin by making sure you understand the terms you will be hearing and using to describe what you want—especially terms pertaining to the stone's cut and the names for the parts of a cut stone.

It's important to be familiar with a few general terms that are commonly used in reference to faceted stones. The parts of a stone can vary in proportion and thus affect its brilliance, beauty, and desirability. This will be discussed later in greater detail.

- **Girdle.** The girdle is the edge or border of the stone that forms its perimeter; it is the edge formed where the top portion of the stone meets the bottom portion—its "dividing line." This is the part usually grasped by the prongs of a setting.
- **Crown.** The crown is also called the *top* of the stone. This is simply the upper portion of the stone: the part above the girdle.
- **Pavilion.** The pavilion is the bottom portion of the stone, the part from the girdle to the culet.
- **Culet.** The culet is the lowest part, or point, of the stone. It may be missing in some stones, which can indicate damage, or—particularly with colored stones—it may not be part of the original cut.

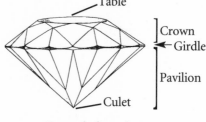

Parts of a faceted stone

- **Table.** The table is the stone's largest facet, often called the face, the flat area on the very top. The term *table spread* is used to describe the width of the table facet, often expressed as a percentage of the stone's total width.

## THE CUT OF THE STONE

The most important—and least understood—factor that must be evaluated when one considers any gem is the *cut*. When we talk about cut, we are not referring to the shape but to the care and precision used in creating a finished gem from the rough. There are many popular shapes for gemstones. Each shape affects the overall look of the stone, but if the stone is cut well, its brilliance and value endure no matter what shape it is. For the average consumer, choosing a shape is simply a matter of personal taste. Some of the most popular shapes are pictured here.

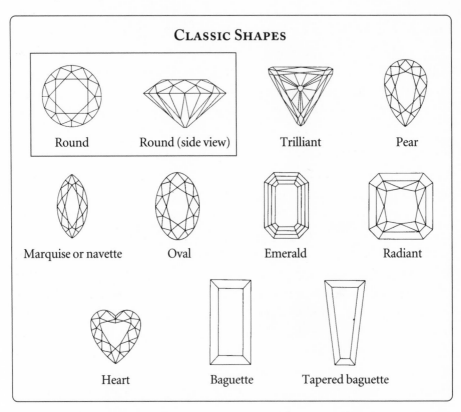

**CLASSIC SHAPES**

Round    Round (side view)    Trilliant    Pear

Marquise or navette    Oval    Emerald    Radiant

Heart    Baguette    Tapered baguette

## *Make* Makes a Big Difference

The shape of the stone may affect the personality it displays, but it is the overall cutting that releases its full beauty. A term used by professionals to describe the overall quality of the cutting is *make*. This term pertains to the overall precision of the cutting, especially the proportioning and finish (polish and symmetry). Having a "good make" is especially important in diamonds. A diamond with an "excellent make" will sell for much more than one with a "fair make." The difference in price between a well-cut diamond and one that is poorly cut can be as much as 50 percent or more. Even more important, careless cutting, or cutting to get the largest possible stone from the rough, can sometimes result in faults that may make a stone more fragile and vulnerable to breakage. Such stones should sell for much less, although the fault may not be visible without careful examination by an expert. Here we will discuss cutting in a general way; it will be discussed in greater detail later.

## How to Know Whether a Stone Is Well Cut

The precision of the cutting dramatically affects the beauty and value of any stone. This is especially true in *faceted* stones, those on which a series of tiny flat planes (facets or faces) have been cut and polished. (Nonfaceted stones are called *cabochons;* these are discussed in chapter 16.) You should also keep in mind that there are several cutting styles used for faceted stones: brilliant cut, as seen in round diamonds (using many triangular and kite-shaped facets); step cut, as seen in emerald-cut stones (using trapezoid or rectangular facets); and mixed cut, which combines both styles.

Whichever faceting style is used, by following some general guidelines for looking at faceted gemstones, you can better determine both the quality of the stone and the quality of the cut. The first thing to keep in mind is that if the basic material is of good quality, the way it is cut will make the difference between a dull, lifeless stone and a beautiful, brilliant one. In diamonds, the cutting and proportioning have the greatest influence on the stone's brilliance and fire. In colored gems, the perfection of the cut is not as important as with diamonds, but proportioning remains critical because it significantly affects the depth of color as well as the stone's brilliance and liveliness.

Look at the stone face-up, through the top (table). This is the most critical area to view, since it is the one most often noticed. If you are looking at a diamond, does it seem to sparkle and dance across the whole stone, or are there dead spots? In a colored gem, does the color look good from this direction? Is the table centered and symmetrical?

Table centered
but not symmetrical

Table off-center
and asymmetrical

Table centered and
symmetrical—the ideal

A quick way to check the symmetry of a round diamond is to look at the table edges. The lines should be straight, regular, and parallel to one another. The table edges should form a regular octagon, with the edges meeting in sharp points. If the lines of the table are wavy, the overall symmetry is not good, and the symmetry of the adjoining facets will also be affected.

Next, look at the stone from the side. Note the proportion of the stone both above and below the girdle.

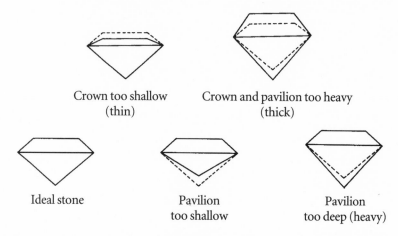

Crown too shallow
(thin)

Crown and pavilion too heavy
(thick)

Ideal stone

Pavilion
too shallow

Pavilion
too deep (heavy)

The stone's proportion—whether it is too thin or too thick—will have a marked effect on its overall beauty. With colored stones, the relative terms of thickness or thinness vary greatly because of the inherent optical properties of different gems. As a general guide when you are considering colored stones, keep in mind these three points:

1. If the stone appears lively and exhibits an appealing color when viewed through the table, the proportion is usually correct and acceptable for that particular stone, no matter how it appears (thick or thin).

2. The depth of color (tone) will become darker as the stone is cut thicker, particularly if the bottom portion (pavilion) is deep and broad.

3. A stone's depth of color will become lighter as the stone is cut thinner. This is especially important when you are considering a pastel-colored stone. A pastel stone should always have fairly deep proportioning.

The effects of cut and proportioning will be discussed in greater detail in parts three and four, as the factors affecting cut and proportioning are somewhat different for diamonds and colored gems. It is an important first step, however, to become aware of general views and to begin to have a feeling about what looks right.

## Understanding Weight—
## What Is a Carat and How Does It Affect Value?

Carat weight affects both the *size* of a gem and its *value*. In fact, weight can have a dramatic impact on both, but not in the way you may think. Carat weight is something most people think they understand but few really do. Most think of "carat" as a *size*, but it is really a measurement of *weight*. While it is related to the size, unless you understand the difference, you may be very disappointed.

All gems, except pearls and coral, are sold by the *carat* (ct), not to be confused with *karat* (kt), which in the United States refers to gold purity. Since 1913, most countries have agreed that a carat weighs 200 milligrams, or ⅕ of a gram. Carat weight is often stated in terms of *points*. This is particularly true of stones under 1 carat. There are 100 points to a carat, so if a stone weighs 75 points, it weighs ⁷⁵⁄₁₀₀ of a carat, or ¾ of a carat.

I wish to stress the point that a carat is a unit of weight, not size. Most people think that a 1-carat stone is a particular size—the size they have come to associate with the size of a 1-carat diamond. They think that a 1-carat diamond, a 1-carat ruby, and a 1-carat emerald will all appear the same size and have the same dimensions. This is not the case.

Some stones weigh more than others, because the density (specific gravity) of the basic material is heavier. Ruby is heavier than diamond or emerald, so a 1-carat ruby will be *smaller* in size than an identically shaped and proportioned diamond or emerald. Emerald weighs less than diamond, and much less than ruby, so a 1-carat emerald cut in the same shape and with the same proportioning as a diamond will look *larger* than the diamond and *much* larger than the ruby. A lighter substance requires more mass to attain the same weight; a heavier substance takes less mass to attain the same weight.

Certain sizes have become associated with diamonds (see the chart on the next page) because certain formulas have been established for diamond cutting, and diamonds are always cut to essentially the same set of parameters. This means that a 1-carat round diamond will always measure approximately 6.5 millimeters in diameter, a 2-carat round diamond will measure 8.2 mil-

# SIZES AND WEIGHTS OF VARIOUS DIAMOND CUTS

| Weight (ct) | Emerald | Marquise | Pear | Brilliant |
|:---:|:---:|:---:|:---:|:---:|
| 5 | | | | |
| 4 | | | | |
| 3 | | | | |
| 2½ | | | | |
| 2 | | | | |
| 1½ | | | | |
| 1¼ | | | | |
| 1 | | | | |
| ¾ | | | | |
| ½ | | | | |

limeters, and so on. Even fancy shapes such as oval and pear are always more or less a particular size at a particular weight, as you can see in the chart. It is these sizes that come to mind when people think of carat weight, and they are often mistakenly transferred to colored gemstones. When most people describe the size gemstone they want in terms of carat weight, they are really visualizing a size that is associated with diamonds. When people say they want a 1-carat sapphire, for example, what they really mean is that they want a sapphire that looks the size of a 1-carat diamond: about 6½ millimeters in diameter. But this is not what they will get. Since sapphire is much denser than diamond (it weighs about 25 percent more), a 1-carat round sapphire cut to the same proportions as a 1-carat diamond will look 25 percent smaller. In order to get the same size as a 1-carat diamond, they would have to ask for a 1¼-carat sapphire. And so on.

## Carat Weight Is Not a Reliable Guide to Colored Gemstone *Size*

Unlike diamonds, there are no set "proportions" for cutting colored gemstones to get maximum brilliance, because light performs differently in every gemstone group, so size will vary with each different gemstone. Some cutters also try to get the heaviest possible weight out of a stone and cut them overly deep, while other cutters may cut a shallow stone in order to lighten color if the color of the rough is too dark. If a cutter cuts a deep stone, but all the weight is in the bottom of the stone, it can look smaller than another stone that weighs half as much. Or, if it is cut shallow, it might look twice as large as another. In short, you can find two stones that have the same *weight*, but one will be *twice as large* as the other!

As we have explained, you cannot rely on the carat weight given in descriptions to provide any indication of size. If you rely on the carat weight alone, without knowing the actual dimensions (that is, the size of the piece—its measurements) you may end up buying something much smaller or larger than you wanted and end up very disappointed. Keep this in mind when reading descriptions of gems and jewelry given by online sellers. And when looking at photos in printed catalogs, find out whether or not they are "actual" size; if not, be sure to ask for the exact dimensions of pieces you are considering.

## How Does Carat Weight Affect Value?

The carat weight is a significant factor in determining the value of a gemstone. Stones with higher carat weights are rarer than those with lesser weight and, thus, costlier on a cost-*per-carat* basis. As a result, the cost of a 2-carat stone will be *more* than twice the cost of a comparable 1-carat stone; the cost of a comparable 3-carat stone will be *much more* than three times the cost of a 1-carat stone; and so on. In diamonds, for example, a good 1-carat stone might cost $7,500 *per carat*, for a total of $7,500 for the stone; the cost of a comparable 2-carat stone might be $10,000 per carat, for a total of $20,000; and the cost of a comparable 3-carat stone, $12,000 per carat, for a total of $36,000. In the rarest qualities, the differences in cost between a 1-carat, 2-carat, and 3-carat diamond will be even greater, because diamonds with rare color and clarity become even rarer as the weight increases.

In colored gemstones, carat weight also affects value—even more so than in diamonds. Generally speaking, the rarer the gemstone and the finer its quality, the more the carat weight will impact the cost per carat; the more common the gemstone, the less impact. There is very little difference in the cost per carat of aquamarines between 1 to 3 carats, for example. Among rubies, however, the difference in the cost per carat between an exceptional 1-carat stone and another weighing 3 carats could easily exceed 300 percent per carat!

Where diamonds are concerned, there are fairly reliable price guides that quickly show the impact of carat weight on the cost of a diamond in a particular shape and quality. Unfortunately this is not the case with colored gemstones because there are no universally accepted quality grading systems. It takes time and experience to develop an understanding of the extent to which the carat weight can affect the cost of a particular gem in a particular quality.

## BEFORE BEGINNING

As you look at any fine gem or jewelry, keep in mind the importance of looking at stones side by side and comparing them. Many of the factors discussed in the following chapters will become clearer when you have actual stones before you to examine, and you will gain a deeper understanding and appreciation for the gem you are considering. Gem and jewelry specialists at the auction house will also be happy to take time to help you understand differences in quality and cost.

## PART 3 ♦
# DIAMONDS

# 6 ♦ What Is a Diamond?

CHEMICALLY SPEAKING, A DIAMOND IS THE SIMPLEST OF ALL GEM-stones. It is plain, crystallized carbon—the same substance, chemically, as the soot left on the inside of a glass globe after the burning of a candle; it is the same substance used in "lead" pencils.

The diamond differs from these in its crystal form, which gives it the desirable properties that have made it so highly prized—its hardness, which gives it unsurpassed wearability; its brilliance; and its fire. (But note that while diamond is the hardest natural substance known, it *can* be chipped or broken if hit hard from certain angles, and if the *girdle*—the edge of the diamond that forms the perimeter—has been cut too thin, it can be chipped with even a modest blow.)

The transparent white (or, more correctly, *colorless*) diamond is the most popular variety, but diamond also occurs in colors. When the color is prominent it is called a *fancy-color* diamond. Diamond is frequently found in nice yellow and brown shades. Colors such as pink, light blue, light green, and lavender occur much more rarely. In diamonds, the colors seen are usually pastel. Deep colors in hues of red, green, and dark blue are extremely rare. Historically, most colored diamonds have sold for more than their colorless counterparts, except for light yellow or brown varieties. Yellow or brown in *very* pale shades may not be fancy-color diamonds but *off-color* stones, which are very common and sell for much less than colorless diamonds or those with a true "fancy" color.

India was one of the earliest-known sources of diamond, and the most important, until the eighteenth-century discovery of diamonds in Brazil. In the nineteenth century, a major diamond discovery was made in South Africa, and the twentieth century saw diamond discoveries in other African nations such as Botswana and Angola, and in Russia, Australia, and most recently Canada. Commercial diamond mining is also taking place in the United States.

Many diamonds mined today have no jewelry value because they are too tinted and heavily flawed, but they are used for many industrial purposes. Colorless and fancy-color diamonds remain rare, with red diamond being the rarest and most valuable of all gems.

## THE FOUR FACTORS THAT DETERMINE DIAMOND VALUE

Diamond quality and value are determined by four factors, which are called the *four Cs.* They are often listed as follows:

1. Color (body color or *absence* of color)
2. Clarity (degree of flawlessness)
3. Cutting and proportioning (often referred to as the *make*)
4. Carat weight (which affects the size)

In terms of determining beauty, however, we would rank them in a different order:

1. Cutting and proportioning
2. Color
3. Clarity
4. Carat weight

### Finding the Right Combination

Keep in mind, however, that the key to being happy with your diamond purchase is understanding how each of these four Cs affects beauty and durability, cost, and the stone *as a whole.* It may sound complicated at first, but when you begin looking at stones you'll see it really isn't. With a little experience, you'll decide which Cs are most important to you, and you'll know what to look for to get the right combination—one that meets your emotional *and* financial needs.

Because each factor is a lesson in itself, we have devoted a chapter to each, except for carat weight, which is covered in chapter 5. We will begin with a discussion of diamond cutting and proportioning because it is the least understood and because we think it's the most important factor in terms of the stone's beauty. Equally important, as we mentioned earlier, the cutting of a diamond has a significant effect on cost and can even affect the stone's durability.

# 7 ♦ JUDGING CUT AND ITS EFFECT ON BEAUTY

IT IS IMPORTANT TO DISTINGUISH EXACTLY WHAT *CUT* MEANS IN REF-erence to diamonds and other stones. *Cut* does not mean *shape*. Shape pertains to the outline of the diamond's perimeter. The selection of shape is a matter of individual preference. No matter which shape is selected, its cutting must be evaluated.

There are several different cutting styles: *brilliant* cut, *step* cut, and *mixed* cut. A brilliant cut uses many facets, usually triangular and kite-shaped, arranged in a particular way to create maximum brilliance. A step cut uses fewer facets, usually trapezoid or rectangular, arranged in a more linear pattern (as you see in the emerald cut). Although usually less brilliant than those cut in a brilliant style, step-cut diamonds can produce a lively, fiery stone with a very elegant and understated personality. You often see step-cut triangle, square, and trapezoid shapes in Art Deco period jewelry (1920–1935). A mixed-cut style incorporates elements from both the step-cut and brilliant-cut styles.

The term *cut*—also referred to as the stone's *make*—is especially important because of its effect on the beauty and personality of the diamond. When we evaluate the cut, we are really judging the stone's proportioning and finish: the two factors that are most directly related to producing the *fire* (the lovely rainbow colors that flash from within) and the *brilliance* (the liveliness, the sparkle) that sets diamonds apart from all other gems. Regardless of the shape or cutting style, a stone with an excellent make will be exciting, while a stone with a poor make will look lifeless; it will lack the sparkle and personality we identify with diamonds. In addition, diamonds are often cut to make them appear larger. But a stone that looks much larger than another of the same weight will not be as beautiful as a smaller stone that is properly cut.

Differences in cutting can also affect the *durability* of a diamond. Some cutting faults weaken the stone and make it more susceptible to breaking or chipping.

Fine cutting requires skill and experience, takes more time, and results in greater loss of the "rough" from which the stone is being cut, resulting in a stone that yields less weight when finished. For all these reasons, a well-cut diamond commands a premium and will cost much more than one that is cut poorly.

There are many popular shapes for diamonds. Each shape affects the overall look of the stone, but if the stone is cut well, beauty and value endure no matter which shape you choose. We'll begin the discussion of diamond cutting with the round brilliant cut, since this is the most popular shape.

A modern round brilliant-cut diamond has fifty-eight facets. There are thirty-three on the top and twenty-four on the bottom, plus the culet—the "point" at the bottom, which normally is another tiny facet (although many diamonds today are cut without a culet). Round brilliant-cut stones that are small are referred to as *full-cut* to distinguish them from *single-cut* stones, which have only seventeen facets, or *Swiss-cut* stones with only thirty-three facets. Older pieces of jewelry such as heirloom diamond bands, or inexpensive pieces containing numerous stones, often contain these cuts instead of full-cut stones. They have less brilliance and liveliness than full-cut stones, but with fewer facets they are easier and less expensive to cut. Rings containing single-cut or Swiss-cut stones should sell for less than rings with full-cut stones.

When a round brilliant-cut diamond is cut well, its shape displays the most liveliness because it enables the most light to be reflected back up through the top. This means that round brilliant-cut diamonds will have greater brilliance, overall, than other shapes, but other shapes can also be very lively. New shapes are also appearing, some of which compare very favorably with round stones for overall brilliance and liveliness.

As a rule of thumb, if the top portion of the stone (the crown) appears to be roughly one-third of the pavilion depth (distance from girdle to culet), the proportioning is probably acceptable.

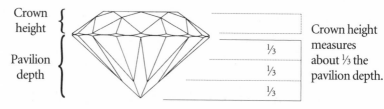

A well-proportioned stone

## How Cutting Affects Brilliance

**Light Reflection in an Ideally Proportioned Diamond**
Ideal proportions ensure the maximum brilliance. When
light enters a properly cut diamond, it is reflected from facet
to facet, and then back up through the top, exhibiting
maximum fire and sparkle.

**Light Reflection in a Diamond Cut Too Deep**
In a diamond that is cut too deep, much of the light is reflected to
opposite facets at the wrong angle and is lost through the sides.
The diamond appears dark in the center.

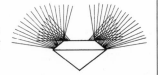

**Light Reflection in a Diamond Cut Too Shallow**
A diamond cut too shallow (to make it look larger) loses
brilliance. The eye sees a ring of dull reflection instead of
the great brilliance of a well-cut diamond.

## TYPES OF DIAMOND PROPORTIONING

The proportioning—especially the height of the crown in relation to the depth
of the pavilion, and the width of the table facet in relation to the width of
the stone—is what determines how much brilliance and fire the stone will
have. Several formulas for correct proportioning have been developed for
round diamonds. Stones that adhere to these very precise formulas are considered to have an "ideal" make and will cost more than other diamonds
because of the extra time and skill required to cut them, and because more
diamond "rough" is lost in the cutting.

## WHAT IS IDEAL?

Today great emphasis is placed on "ideal makes" to help people better understand the effect of precision cutting on the beauty and cost of a diamond, and
to provide guidelines to help them select a diamond that exhibits brilliance,
fire, and overall scintillation (the sparkle that results from the fire and brilliance working together). There are exceptions to all rules, however, and many
diamonds do not adhere to "ideal" parameters, yet are as brilliant and fiery as
those that do.

Diamond cutting is an art form that is still evolving, and technological
advances continue to shed new insights on how cutting affects the way light

travels through diamond to create a scintillating diamond. Today there are several slightly differing formulas for cutting an "ideal" stone, and there is no consensus as to what is best, but each results in an exceptionally beautiful stone. Generally speaking, diamonds that are cut with smaller tables exhibit more fire; those with larger tables exhibit more brilliance. Larger tables seem to be more in fashion today. But, as common sense may tell you here, both can't excel in the same stone. A larger table can create greater brilliance but may cause some reduction in fire; a smaller table area can increase fire but may reduce brilliance. The ideal would be a compromise that would allow the greatest brilliance and fire simultaneously. No one has come to agreement, however, on what the percentages should be, since some people prefer fire to brilliance, and vice versa. This is one reason why several different types of proportioning are found in diamonds, and "best" is usually a matter of personal preference.

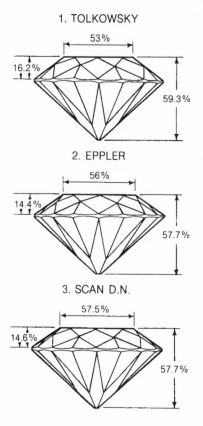

Three standards for "ideal" diamond proportioning

In 1919, Marcel Tolkowsky developed what he thought would be the best combination of angles to allow light to enter the stone and be reflected back in such a way as to create the most vivid fire combined with intense brilliance. The Tolkowsky cut provided the basis for the modern American ideal make, but today there are several variations of Tolkowsky's formula.

When you purchase a round diamond, ask how the make would be graded: ideal, excellent, very good, good, fair, or poor. A diamond with a fair or poor make should sell for less than a diamond with a good make. A diamond with a very good, excellent, or ideal make will sell for more. (See chapter 10 for more information on grading the make.)

Keep in mind that despite the effect of cutting on a diamond's beauty, durability, and cost, most laboratories do not yet grade the cut or indicate "ideal." The American Gem Society Laboratory (AGS), American Gemological Laboratories (AGL), and Professional Gem Sciences (PGS) do so. Diamond reports from the Gemological Institute of America (GIA) and other laboratories provide information about cutting that relates to the diamond's make, but you must understand how to interpret this information. (See chapter 10.)

## Other Popular Shapes

Unlike round diamonds, *fancy shapes*—all shapes other than round—have no set formulas, so evaluating the make of a fancy shape is more subjective. Table and depth percentage can vary widely among individual stones of the same shape, each producing a beautiful stone. Personal taste also varies with regard to what constitutes the "ideal" for shapes other than round. Nonetheless, there are certain visual indicators of good or poor proportioning—such as the bow tie effect—which even the amateur can learn to spot. There are recommended ratios for overall shape and symmetry, but a preferred shape is largely a personal matter.

## Cutting Faults in Popular Fancy Shapes

One of the most obvious indicators of poor proportioning in fancy shapes is the *bow tie* or *butterfly* effect: a darkened area across the center or widest part of the stone, depending on the cut. The bow tie is most commonly seen in the pear shape or marquise, but it may exist in any fancy shape. Virtually all fancy shapes cut today will exhibit some minimal bow tie effect. Nonetheless, the presence or absence of a bow tie is an indicator of proper proportioning. In poorly proportioned stones there is a pronounced bow tie; the more pronounced it is, the poorer the proportioning. The less pronounced the bow tie, the better the proportioning. The degree to which the bow tie is evident is the first indicator of a good or a poor make. A diamond with a pronounced bow tie should sell for much less than one without.

Marquise with a pronounced bow tie, or butterfly

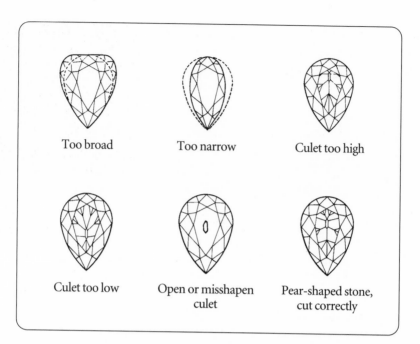

| Too broad | Too narrow | Culet too high |

| Culet too low | Open or misshapen culet | Pear-shaped stone, cut correctly |

As with the brilliant-cut diamond, fancy shapes can also be cut too *broad* or too *narrow,* and the pavilion can be too *deep* or too *shallow.*

Personal taste will always play a role in fancy shapes. Some prefer a narrow pear shape, for example, while others might prefer a fatter pear. Whatever the shape you are considering, you must ask yourself whether or not you find the stone exciting. Does it have a pleasing personality? Does it exhibit good brilliance and fire? Is the entire stone brilliant, or are there "dead" spots? Are there any cutting faults that might make it more susceptible to chipping? Then you must make the choice.

## Early Cuts Enjoy Renewed Popularity

As interest in antique and period jewelry is growing, the diamonds that adorn them are arousing renewed attention and gaining new respect. The way a diamond is cut is often one of the clues to the age of a piece. Older diamonds can be replaced or recut to modern proportions, but replacing or recutting stones mounted in antique or period pieces could adversely affect the value of the jewelry. To preserve the integrity of the piece, antique and period jewelry connoisseurs want original stones or, if stones have been replaced, at least stones cut in the manner typical of the period. The market is becoming increasingly strong for diamonds with older cuts, and prices are also strengthening.

Natural diamond crystal

As these early-cut diamonds receive more and more attention, a growing number of people are beginning to appreciate them for their distinctive beauty and personality and for the romance that accompanies them. The romantic element—combined with a cost that is more attractive than that of new diamonds—is also making them an increasingly popular choice for engagement rings.

Some of the earlier cuts are the *table cut,* the *rose cut,* the *old-mine cut,* and the *old-European cut.* (Before 1919, when America began to emerge as an important diamond cutting center, most diamonds were cut in Europe. Thus, most old-European cut diamonds were cut before the first quarter of the twentieth century.) Some of the earliest diamond jewelry contained *uncut* diamonds, those in the natural, octahedral crystal shape—which looks like two pyramids put together, base to base.

The *table cut* illustrates history's earliest cutting effort. By placing the point of a diamond crystal against a turning wheel that held another diamond, the point could be worn down, creating a squarish, flat surface that resembled a tabletop. Today we still call the flat facet on the very top of the stone the table facet.

**TABLE CUT**

A table-cut diamond. Note the tablelike flat surface on the top, where the crystal point was polished off. The remainder of the crystal is left unchanged.

The *rose cut* is a sixteenth-century cut, usually with a flat base and facets radiating from the center in multiples of six, creating the appearance of an opening rosebud. The rose cut appears in round, pear, and oval shapes.

**ROSE CUT**

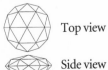

Top view

Side view

Double rose cut          Full rose cut

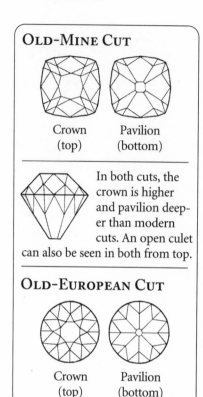

### OLD-MINE CUT

Crown (top)    Pavilion (bottom)

In both cuts, the crown is higher and pavilion deeper than modern cuts. An open culet can also be seen in both from top.

### OLD-EUROPEAN CUT

Crown (top)    Pavilion (bottom)

The *old-mine cut* is a precursor of the modern round cut. This cut has a squarish or "cushion" shape (a rounded square). The proportions follow the diamond crystal, so the crown is higher and the pavilion is deeper than in modern stones. The table is very small, and the culet is very large and is easily seen from the top (resembling a "hole" in the diamond). These lack the brilliance of modern stones but often exhibit tremendous fire. The old-mine cut is enjoying a resurgence in popularity today.

Appearing in the mid-1800s, the *old-European cut* is similar to the old-mine cut but is round rather than squarish, with fifty-eight facets. The crown is higher than in modern cuts but not as high as in the old-mine cut; it has a deep pavilion, but not as deep as in old-mine cuts. The culet is still "open" but is smaller than in old-mine cuts.

In addition to the early cuts described above, two other older cuts are enjoying renewed popularity: the *cushion cut,* with a small table, high crown, and large culet, which resembles the old-mine cut but is usually more elongated; and the *Asscher cut,* a more or less

Old Asscher in a modern setting    Old cushion cut

square emerald cut that, like old-European and old-mine cut diamonds, is characterized by a very high crown, deep pavilion, small table, large culet, and very canted corners (in some cases the angles formed at the corners are so pronounced that the stone resembles an octagon). Although exhibiting less brilliance than modern-cut diamonds, the cushion and Asscher cuts both exhibit very fiery personalities, and they offer a distinctive look with a classic character.

Older cutting styles once popular for use as side stones, or to create interesting design elements, are also enjoying renewed popularity. Among the most popular are two *step-cut* shapes—the trapezoid and the half-moon—and the briolette.

The *trapezoid* and *half-moon* cuts are often seen in Art Deco period jewelry (1920–1935) and make especially elegant choices to use with emerald-cut diamonds (which are also step cut) and colored gemstones. Here the understated character of

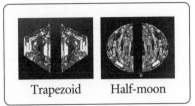

Trapezoid     Half-moon

the trapezoid and half-moon cuts is very complementary; while they are lively, their brilliance is not overpowering, as it often is with modern brilliant cuts.

The *briolette* is fashioned into a "drop," completely encircled with tiny triangular facets. A single briolette can be worn as a pendant, or multiple briolettes can be suspended from almost any piece of jewelry. We are again seeing briolettes used in earrings and brooches and suspended in multiples, like a fringe, from necklaces.

Briolette

## ARE DIAMONDS WITH OLD CUTS VALUABLE?

Old cuts can be very beautiful. The finest examples of these earlier cutting styles exhibit intense fire and have tremendous allure, especially among collectors and those who appreciate authentic jewelry from these earlier periods. By today's standards, however, they lack brilliance, and a very large culet may detract from the stone's beauty.

Until recently, old-mine cut and old-European cut diamonds have been evaluated by comparison with modern-cut stones. Value has been determined by estimating the color, the clarity, and the weight the stone would *retain* if it were recut to modern proportions. However, this practice is now changing because of the increasing demand for old cuts, as mentioned earlier.

We don't suggest recutting old diamonds if they are in their original mountings. The overall integrity and value of the piece would be adversely affected.

If the setting has no special merit, the decision must be an individual one, based on whether or not the stone appeals to you. As I have said, some older cuts are very lovely, while others may look heavy, dull, or lifeless. An unattractive older cut may benefit from recutting, and although it will lose weight, it may have equal or greater value because of the improved make. In addition, recutting can sometimes improve the clarity grade of an older stone. Finally, before deciding whether or not to recut, you should note that the increasing popularity of older cuts is driving prices higher, since they are difficult to find. In addition to their unique personalities, old cuts can have a distinctive character that sets them apart from more modern cuts.

# 8 ♦ Judging Color

COLOR IS ONE OF THE MOST IMPORTANT FACTORS TO CONSIDER WHEN selecting a diamond, because one of the first things most people notice is whether or not the diamond is white or, more accurately, *colorless* (there actually are *white* diamonds, but they are extremely rare and not very attractive). It is also one of the most significant factors affecting value.

Color refers to the natural body color of a diamond. The finest and most expensive "white" diamonds are absolutely colorless, as in pure springwater. Most diamonds show some trace of yellowish or brownish tint. Diamonds also occur in every color of the rainbow. Natural-colored diamonds are called *fancy-color* diamonds (see chapter 13). Fancy colors include red, pink, orange, violet, blue, green, yellow, brown, and every shade in between.

## How to Look at a Diamond to Evaluate Color

In colorless diamonds, color differences from one grade to the next can be very subtle, and a difference of several grades is difficult to see when a diamond is mounted. Keep in mind that it is impossible to accurately grade color in a mounted diamond. When looking at an unmounted stone, however, even an amateur can learn to see color differences if the stone is viewed properly.

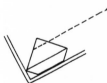

Examine the stone through the pavilion, with the table down.

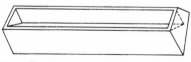

A grading trough, available in plastic or folding white cardboard stand-up packs.

Because of the diamond's high brilliance and dispersion (fire), the color grade cannot be accurately determined by looking at the stone from the top, or face-up, position. It is best to observe color by examining the stone through the pavilion, with the table down. Use a flat white surface such as a folded white business card, or a *grading trough*, which can be purchased from a jeweler's supply house. When a stone is mounted, simply position the piece of jewelry in a way that permits you to view the diamond in the same manner as shown here.

# What Is Body Color?

When we discuss body color in white (colorless) diamonds, we mean how much yellow or brown tint can be seen. We are not referring to the rare natural-color diamonds that occur in such shades as blue, green, yellow, and red, which are designated in the trade as fancy-color diamonds.

Today, most white diamonds in the United States and other countries are graded on an alphabetical scale beginning with the letter D. This letter designation is part of a color grading system introduced by the Gemological Institute of America (GIA) and is used extensively in the diamond trade worldwide. The GIA classification progresses from D, the rarest classification on this scale (colorless), through the alphabet to Z, getting progressively more tinted. The grades D, E, and F are exceptionally fine and are the rarest; they are the only grades that should be referred to as colorless.

## Diamond Color Grades

| | | |
|---|---|---|
| COLORLESS | D<br>E<br>F | Loose diamonds appear colorless. |
| NEAR COLORLESS | G<br>H<br>I<br>J | When mounted in a setting, these diamonds may appear colorless to the untrained eye. |
| FAINT YELLOWISH* TINT | K<br>L<br>M | Smaller diamonds look colorless when mounted. Diamonds of ½ carat or more show traces of color. |
| VERY LIGHT YELLOWISH* TINT | N<br>O<br>P<br>Q<br>R | These diamonds show increasingly yellow tints to even the untrained eye, and appear very "off-white." |
| TINTED LIGHT YELLOWISH* | S<br>T<br>U<br>V<br>W<br>X<br>Y<br>Z | |

* Usually yellow, but can be brown or gray

# COMMONLY USED DIAMOND COLOR GRADING SYSTEMS

The GIA and American Gem Society (AGS) grading systems are the most commonly used in the United States. The GIA system is the most widely used in the world. Scandinavian diamond nomenclature (Scan D.N.) is often used in Scandinavian countries, as well as a system developed by CIBJO (the International Confederation of Jewelry, Silverware, Diamonds, Pearls, and Stones). Participating member nations include most European nations, Japan, and the United States. Another system, HRD, is applied by the Belgian Diamond High Council.

| AGS | GIA | SCAN D.N. UNDER 0.50 CARAT | SCAN D.N. 0.50 CARAT AND OVER | CIBJO UNDER 0.47 CARAT | CIBJO 0.47 CARAT AND OVER | HRD |
|---|---|---|---|---|---|---|
| 0 | D | White | River | Exceptional white | Exceptional white (†) | Exceptional white (†) |
| 0 | E | White | River | Exceptional white | Exceptional white | Exceptional white |
| 1 | F | White | Top wesselton | Rare white | Rare white (†) | Rare white (†) |
| 2 | G | White | Top wesselton | Rare white | Rare white | Rare white |
| 3 | H | White | Wesselton | White | White | White |
| 4 | I | Slightly tinted white | Top crystal | Slightly tinted white | Slightly tinted white (I) | Slightly tinted white |
| 5 | J | Slightly tinted white | Crystal | Slightly tinted white | Slightly tinted white (J) | Slightly tinted white |
| 6 | K | | Top cape | Tinted white | Tinted white (K) | Tinted white |
| 6 | L | | Top cape | Tinted white | Tinted white (L) | Tinted white |
| 7 | M | | Cape | | | |
| 7 | N | | Cape | | | |
| 8 | O | | | | | |
| 8 | P | Tinted color | Cape / Light yellow | Tinted color | Tinted color | Tinted color |
| 8 | Q | | Light yellow | | | |
| 9-10* | R | | | | | |
| 9-10* | S-X -Z | | Yellow | | | |

*AGS grade 9 corresponds to GIA, R–U inclusive. AGS grade 10 corresponds to GIA, V–Z inclusive.

† The use of the term *blue-white* is discouraged today, since it is usually misleading.

Left side margin labels (top to bottom): Small mounted stones appear colorless — Mounted stones appear colorless — Mounted stones appear increasingly tinted — Mounted stones appear yellow

# Natural Color and HPHT Processed

Color differences can be subtle, but the difference in cost can be extreme (see the price comparison charts in chapter 14). It is important to know the precise color grade, but it is even more important to know whether the color is natural or the result of some type of treatment. In chapter 12 we discuss several fraudulent techniques that have been used on colorless diamonds for many years, as well as new techniques that are being applied routinely to certain types of diamonds. Where colorless diamonds are concerned, until recently the techniques to alter color produced results that were temporary, and any competent gemologist could detect the treatment. This is no longer true; the latest techniques are difficult to detect and require sophisticated testing.

A new process, developed in the 1990s, uses high-pressure/high-temperature annealing (often referred to as the HPHT process) to transform very tinted, off-white diamonds into colorless and near-colorless stones, ranging from D through H in color. These stones were originally referred to as GE-POL diamonds but are now called Bellataire™ diamonds. The results are permanent and irreversible. Unlike earlier treatments, detection requires sophisticated testing available only at major gem-testing laboratories (see appendix).

Not all tinted diamonds can be transformed into colorless or near-colorless diamonds. Only very rare diamond types respond to HPHT whitening techniques. Of all the diamonds mined, reports estimate that fewer than 2 percent produce the desired effect. Today the process is also being used to produce fancy-color yellow, pink, and blue diamonds (see chapter 13).

## Caution Auction Goers:
## HPHT "Colorless" Diamonds Sold as "Natural"

In addition to GE-POL and its Bellataire™ brand, other companies are producing colorless diamonds that have been whitened by this process. We do not know how many are now being sold, or when they actually began to enter the marketplace, but we do know that some are being sold without any disclosure. While we are unaware of any that have been purchased at auction up to now, you cannot ignore the possibility. Diamonds treated in every other manner have been sold at auction, and HPHT diamonds will be no exception. Equally important, before being aware of the use of this technology on diamonds, the major gem-testing laboratories were not checking for it, nor did they have the data to understand how to detect it. This is no longer the case, but caution must be exercised when you buy any fine, colorless diamond to ensure that you know whether or not the color results from this technology. Labs such as the GIA, the Swiss Foundation for the Research of Gemstones (SSEF), and the European Gemological Laboratory (EGL) will grade diamonds treated in this manner, indicating the use of this process on the report, usually under "Comments." GIA also requires that the words "HPHT Processed" be laser-inscribed on the stone's girdle before issuing the grading report. Be sure to reconfirm that the color is natural when you are considering any diamond with a laboratory report issued between 1997 and 2000.

## WHAT IS FLUORESCENCE?

If the diamond you are considering is accompanied by a diamond grading report issued by the GIA or another respected lab, it will indicate whether or not the diamond has some degree of *fluorescence.* Fluorescence refers to whether or not a stone produces a color reaction when exposed to ultraviolet radiation—a color seen *only* when the stone is exposed to ultraviolet radiation. Whether or not a diamond fluoresces, and the strength of its fluorescence (faint, weak, moderate, strong, very strong) are determined by viewing the diamond with a special lamp called an ultraviolet lamp, which emits only ultraviolet radiation. When we say that a white (colorless) diamond fluoresces blue, we mean that its color will appear to be blue when we view it under the pure ultraviolet light produced by the ultraviolet lamp. The stone is really a colorless diamond and will appear colorless in normal light. Some diamonds fluoresce; others do not. A diamond can fluoresce any color, but most diamonds fluoresce blue, white, or yellow.

It is important to note whether or not a diamond fluoresces, and what color it fluoresces, because there are varying wavelengths of ultraviolet radiation all around us. Ultraviolet radiation is present in daylight (that's what causes sunburn) and wherever there are fluorescent light fixtures (those long tube lights you see in the ceilings of many stores and office buildings). This means that, depending upon the strength of a diamond's fluorescence, and the intensity of the ultraviolet radiation in the light source, its color may not appear the same in all lights.

A diamond that fluoresces a strong blue, for example, might appear whiter in daylight, or in an office with fluorescent lights, because the ultraviolet radiation present will cause the diamond to emit some degree of blue, masking any faint yellow or brown tint that might be present. The same stone might appear less white when seen at home in incandescent light—any warm light, such as a household lightbulb—where you see the stone's true body color, without the benefit of any fluorescence stimulated by ultraviolet radiation. A white diamond that fluoresces "strong yellow" can look more yellow in some lights. But remember, whatever color is produced by fluorescence, it occurs *only* in daylight or fluorescent light.

To ensure that the true body color is being graded, a professional always tests a diamond for fluorescence with an ultraviolet lamp before color grading it. Blue fluorescence is more common than white or yellow. Some white diamonds that fluoresce blue may actually look blue-white in the right light. The results of a recent study conducted by the GIA showed that consumers found the presence of blue fluorescence to be a benefit; participants in the study actually preferred diamonds that fluoresced blue to other diamonds because they seemed "whiter," despite the fact that you will not really notice fluorescence with the naked eye.

## Does Fluorescence Affect Value?

Generally, the presence or absence of fluorescence has little if any effect on value. However, *if the stone has a strong yellow fluorescence it may sell for 10 to 15 percent less,* since this will make the stone appear more yellow in some lights than another stone with the same color grade.

Blue fluorescence may be considered an added benefit—a little bonus—because it may make the stone appear whiter in some lights, and yet there may be no difference in cost or the stone may sell at a modest *discount* (although this may change after the results of the GIA study). You must be careful, however, to look closely at stones with *very strong* blue or yellow fluorescence; some will have an oily or murky appearance. If the stone appears murky or oily in daylight or fluorescent light, it should sell for *much* less than comparable stones without the murky cast.

In fancy-color diamonds (see chapter 13), fluorescence can affect value if it alters the color to make it less pleasing or less intense. Note that fluorescence is *not* always indicated on laboratory reports. If not, be *sure* to check to see whether there is fluorescence and, if so, how strong. If there is fluorescence, be sure to check the color of the stone in different types of light; you may like it in daylight and hate it in lamplight, or vice versa.

# What Is a Chameleon Diamond?

A *chameleon* diamond is one that changes color when exposed to heat! Several diamonds that show this very unusual phenomenon have been sold recently at auction, and they make interesting conversation pieces. Whatever color they exhibit in natural or fluorescent light, or when heated, usually becomes more yellow when they are left in the dark for a time.

# Dirt Affects Perception of Color

A dirty diamond will not look white, nor will it sparkle. An accumulation of dirt, especially greasy dirt, will give a diamond a yellowish cast.

This principle applies especially when you are looking at old jewelry for possible purchase. When you are considering old diamond pieces, pay particular attention to whether or not it is impacted with dirt accumulated by years of use. If it is, there is a possibility that the diamond will have a better color grade than it may appear to have at first glance. This is because the dirt may contain varying amounts of fatty deposits (from dishwashing, cosmetics, etc.), which yellow with age. When this type of dirt builds up and is in contact with the diamond, it will also make the diamond appear more yellow.

# Settings Affect Perception of Color

The color of the metal in the setting can affect your perception of the color of the stone, sometimes adversely and sometimes beneficially. The yellow gold environment may mask the degree of yellow in a tinted diamond, or it may give a colorless diamond an undesirable yellow tint. The setting can also affect future color grading should you ever need an updated insurance appraisal.

This is important to remember when judging diamonds you are thinking of purchasing at auction. If there is no diamond grading report from a recognized lab, you can misjudge them. It is sometimes helpful to slip a white card or paper between the diamond and the mounting to try to more accurately determine color.

# 9 ◆ JUDGING CLARITY

FLAW CLASSIFICATION—ALSO CALLED *CLARITY* GRADE—IS ONE OF THE criteria used to determine the value of a diamond. As with all things in nature, however, there is really no such thing as "flawless." Even though some very rare diamonds are classified "flawless," the term is somewhat misleading, and you must be sure you understand what it really means.

When we talk about this classification, we are referring to the presence of tiny, usually microscopic, imperfections. The word *flaw* suggests something bad, but this is not really the case; rather, the flaw grade simply provides part of the complete description of the stone. It is important to understand that as diamonds form in nature, *every* diamond develops certain types of internal characteristics. They might be microscopic cracks shaped like feathers—some are quite lovely when viewed with the microscope—or microscopic diamond crystals, or even crystals of some other gemstone! *Every diamond contains distinctive internal characteristics.* In the jewelry trade, these internal characteristics are called *inclusions,* something included within the stone as it was forming in nature.

Each diamond's internal picture—its internal character—is unique. No two are alike, so the clarity picture can be an important factor in identifying a specific diamond.

## To What Extent Does Clarity Affect the Beauty of a Diamond?

It is very important to understand that clarity may have little or no effect on the beauty of a diamond if it falls within the first eight clarity grades discussed later in this chapter (FL through SI). Few people can discern any visible difference between stones until they reach the imperfect grades, and even then it is sometimes difficult to see anything in the stone without magnification.

Many people mistakenly believe that the clarity grade affects a diamond's brilliance and sparkle. This is not true; the clarity grade has little effect on a diamond's visible appearance except in the very lowest grades. Many people think that the better the clarity, the more brilliant and sparkling the diamond. Perhaps it is the term itself, *clarity,* that leads to the confusion (and the reason we don't like the term *clarity grade*). Whatever the case, as discussed in chapter 7, it is the precision of the *cutting* that determines how brilliant and sparkling a diamond will be.

To the buyer, the flaw grade, or clarity grade, is important because it indicates, on a relative basis, how "clean" the diamond is, and this ranking has a significant effect on cost. The cleaner the stone, the rarer; the rarer the stone, the costlier.

Diamonds don't have to be flawless to be beautiful and sparkling. As you will see when you shop and compare, you can find very beautiful, sparkling diamonds in a wide range of clarity grades. Juggling the clarity grade can give you tremendous flexibility in getting a whiter or larger diamond for your money. Just keep in mind that you won't see differences with the eye alone, so you must take care to know for sure what the specific clarity grade is.

## How Is the Clarity Grade Determined?

Diamonds used in jewelry are usually very clean, and little if anything can be seen without magnification. This is starting to change as an increasing number of diamonds with visible cracks or other inclusions enter the market—stones in the $I_1$ through $I_3$ range and below—but for the most part, differences in clarity cannot normally be seen simply by looking at the stone with the naked eye. The clarity grade is based on what can be seen *when the diamond is examined by 10X magnification* under a loupe (see chapter 5). The clarity grade is based on the number, size, color, and location of inclusions or blemishes in the stone. The flawless grade is given to a stone in which no imperfections can be seen internally (inclusions) or externally (blemishes) when examined with 10X magnification, although at higher powers inclusions will be visible even in a flawless diamond. For clarity grading purposes, if an inclusion can't be seen at 10X, it doesn't exist.

Clarity grading requires extensive training and practice, and proper grading can be done only by an experienced jeweler, dealer, or gemologist. If you want to examine a diamond with the loupe, remember that only in the lowest grades will an inexperienced person be able to see inclusions or blemishes easily, and even with the loupe it will be difficult to see what a professional will see easily. Few amateurs will see anything at all in the highest clarity grades.

## COMMONLY USED CLARITY GRADING SYSTEMS

There are several recognized clarity grading systems in use worldwide, but the system used most widely in the United States and an increasing number of other countries was developed by the Gemological Institute of America (GIA). The terms *clarity grade* and *flaw grade* may be used interchangeably, but today the term *clarity* is more commonly used.

The most widely recognized clarity grading scales were introduced by these organizations:

- CIBJO (International Confederation of Jewelry, Silverware, Diamonds, Pearls, and Stones); participating member nations that use this system include Austria, Belgium, Canada, Denmark, Finland, France, Great Britain, Italy, Japan, Netherlands, Norway, Spain, Sweden, Switzerland, United States, and Germany
- Scan D.N. (Scandinavian Diamond Nomenclature)
- GIA (Gemological Institute of America)
- AGS (American Gem Society)
- HRD (Hoge Raad voor Diamant, the Diamond High Council of Belgium)

The chart on the following page shows the relationship between the GIA system and others used internationally.

## HOW DOES THE CLARITY GRADE AFFECT DIAMOND VALUE?

We will use the GIA system to explain clarity and its effect on value because it is the most widely used in the United States. As you can see from the comparison chart, other systems now use similar classifications. Should you have a diamond with a report from one of these, you can use this chart to find the corresponding GIA grade.

On the GIA scale, FL is the grade given to a stone that has no visible flaws, internal or external, when examined under 10X magnification. Only a highly qualified person will be able to determine this grade. If you are using a loupe as you examine diamonds, remember that it is very difficult for the

# COMMONLY USED DIAMOND FLAW (CLARITY) GRADING SYSTEMS

| CIBJO UNDER 0.47 CARAT | CIBJO 0.47 CARAT AND OVER | HRD | SCAN D.N. | GIA | AGS |
|---|---|---|---|---|---|
| Loupe clean | Loupe clean | Loupe clean | FL | FL | 0 |
| | | | IF (Internally Flawless) | IF | 1 |
| VVS | $VVS_1$ | $VVS_1$ | $VVS_1$ | $VVS_1$ | |
| | $VVS_2$ | $VVS_2$ | $VVS_2$ | $VVS_2$ | 2 |
| VS | $VS_1$ | $VS_1$ | $VS_1$ | $VS_1$ | 3 |
| | $VS_2$ | $VS_2$ | $VS_2$ | $VS_2$ | 4 |
| SI | $SI_1$ | SI | $SI_1$ | $SI_1$ | 5 |
| | $SI_2$ | | $SI_2$ | $SI_2$ | 6 |
| Piqué I | Piqué I | $P_1$ | 1st Piqué | $I_1$ (Imperfect) | 7 |
| | | | | | 8 |
| Piqué II | Piqué II | $P_2$ | 2nd Piqué | I2 | 9 |
| Piqué III | Piqué III | $P_3$ | 3rd Piqué | I3 | 10 |

VV = Very, Very      S = Slight or Small
V = Very      I = Inclusion or Included or Imperfect (Imperfection)

For example, VVS may be translated to mean Very, Very Slightly (Included); or Very, Very Small (Inclusion); or Very, Very Slightly (Imperfect). Some jewelers prefer to classify the stone as "very, very small inclusion" rather than "very, very slightly imperfect" because the former description may sound more acceptable to the customer. There is, in fact, no difference.

inexperienced viewer to see flaws that may be readily observable to the experienced jeweler, dealer, or gemologist, and you will not have the experience to determine whether or not a diamond is flawless. Often the novice is unable to see any flaws, even in SI grades, even with use of the loupe. A flawless, colorless, correctly proportioned stone, particularly in a one-carat size or larger, is *extremely* rare and is priced proportionately much higher than any other grade. Some jewelers insist there is no such thing available today.

*IF* is the grade given to a stone with no internal flaws and with only minor external blemishes that could be removed with polishing, such as nicks, small pits not on the table, and/or girdle roughness. These stones, in colorless, well-proportioned makes, are also rare and are priced proportionately much higher than other grades.

$VVS_1$ and $VVS_2$ are grades given to stones with internal flaws that are very, very difficult for a qualified observer to see. These grades are also difficult to obtain and are priced at a premium.

$VS_1$ and $VS_2$ are grades given to stones with very small inclusions, difficult for a qualified observer to see. These stones are more readily available in good color and cut, and their flaws will not be visible except under magnification. These are excellent stones to purchase.

$SI_1$ and $SI_2$ grades are given to stones with flaws that a qualified observer will see fairly easily under 10**x** magnification. They are not as rare as the higher grades, so they are less costly; in these grades, flaws may sometimes be visible without magnification when the stones are examined from the back or laterally. These grades are still highly desirable, and since they cannot normally be seen with the naked eye when mounted, they may enable one to select a stone with a higher color, or in a larger size, when working with a limited budget.

The *imperfect* grades are given to stones in which flaws may be seen by a qualified observer without magnification; they are readily available and are much less expensive. They are graded $I_1$, $I_2$, and $I_3$. (These grades are called *first piqué* (pronounced pee-kay), *second piqué*, and *third piqué* in some classification systems.) $I_1$, $I_2$, and *some* $I_3$ grades may still be desirable if they are brilliant and lively, and if there are no inclusions that might make them more susceptible than normal to breaking. They should not be automatically eliminated by a prospective purchaser who desires lovely diamond jewelry. As a general rule, however, imperfect grades may be difficult to resell should you ever try to do so.

## CLARITY ENHANCEMENT

Today, technological advances have made it possible to improve diamond clarity. Several clarity enhancement techniques are available; some are more or less permanent, and others are definitely not permanent. Unfortunately, clarity enhancement frequently is not disclosed, either to jewelers themselves or by jewelers to their customers. It is important to buy diamonds from knowledgeable, reputable jewelers who check for such treatments. In addition, before buying any diamond, you must ask whether or not the stone has been clarity enhanced. If the stone has been enhanced, ask what method was used, and be sure this is stated on the bill of sale. In addition, be sure to ask about special care requirements that might be necessitated by the process.

The two most widely used methods of clarity enhancement are lasering and fracture filling.

## Lasering

Laser treatment is used today to make flaws less visible and thus improve the stone aesthetically. Laser technology makes it possible to "vaporize" black inclusions so they practically disappear. With the loupe, however, an experienced jeweler or gemologist can usually see the "path" cut into the diamond by the laser beam—this path may look like a fine, white thread starting at the surface of the stone and traveling into it—and other indicators of lasering. The effects of the laser treatment are permanent. If a lasered diamond is accompanied by a diamond grading report issued by a respected lab, the report will state that the stone is lasered.

A lasered stone should cost less than another with the "same" clarity, so it may be an attractive choice for a piece of jewelry—as long as you *know* it's lasered and therefore pay a fair price for it. You must be sure to ask whether or not the diamond is lasered. Some countries don't require disclosure, and for several years the Federal Trade Commission suspended the requirement to disclose lasering in the United States. This position was reversed—disclosure is now required—but it may take several years for compliance to be restored. If a lab report does not accompany the stone, you must be sure to ask explicitly, and verify it with an independent gemologist-appraiser.

## Fracture Filling

Fractures—cracks or breaks—that would normally be visible and detract from the beauty of a diamond can often be filled with a nearly colorless, glasslike substance. After filling, these breaks virtually disappear and will no longer be seen, except under magnification. Filling is *not* a permanent treatment, and special precautions are required when cleaning and repairing jewelry containing a filled diamond. With proper care, such stones may remain beautiful for many years. Careless handling, however, can cause the filler to leave the stone or change color, resulting in a much less attractive diamond. Some filling materials are much more stable than others, but at present it is usually not possible to know what filler has been used in a given stone. Should the filler be accidentally removed, your jeweler can have the treatment repeated to restore the stone's original appearance. The GIA will not issue a grading report on a filled diamond, but other labs will (indicating the grade it appears to be after filling).

Filled diamonds cost much less than other diamonds. They can be a very attractive and affordable alternative as long as you know what you are buying, understand the limitations, and pay the right price. Be sure to ask explicitly whether or not the stone has been fracture-filled, and if the stone does not have a report from a respected lab (see appendix), get a statement *on the bill of sale* as to whether or not it is fracture-filled.

# 10 ♦ DIAMOND GRADING REPORTS:
## HOW TO READ THEM

TODAY, FEW FINE DIAMONDS OVER ONE CARAT ARE SOLD WITHOUT A diamond grading report (or certificate, as they are also called) from a respected laboratory. Reports issued by the Gemological Institute of America (GIA) Gem Trade Laboratory are the most widely used in the United States and in many countries around the world, but reports from other laboratories (see appendix) are also highly respected.

A grading report does more than certify the stone's genuineness; it fully describes the stone and evaluates each of the critical factors affecting its quality, beauty, and value. Grading reports can be very useful for a variety of reasons. The information they contain can provide verification of the "facts" as represented by the seller and enable one to make a safer decision when purchasing a diamond. Another important function of reports is to verify the identity of a specific diamond at some future time—if, for example, it has been out of one's possession for any reason. For insurance purposes, the information provided on the report will help ensure replacement of a lost or stolen diamond with one that is truly of comparable quality.

Reports aren't necessary for every diamond, and many beautiful diamonds used in jewelry are sold without them. But when you are considering the purchase of a very fine diamond weighing one carat or more, we strongly recommend that the stone be accompanied by a report from one of the laboratories listed in the appendix, even if it means having a stone removed from its setting (no reputable lab will issue a full grading report on a mounted diamond) and then reset. If you are considering a stone that lacks a report, it is easy for a jeweler or appraiser to obtain one.

The availability and widespread use of these reports can, when properly understood, enable even those without professional skills to make valid comparisons between several stones and to reach more informed buying decisions. The key is in knowing how to read the reports properly.

## Don't Rely on the Report Alone

Reports can be an important tool to help you understand differences affecting rarity and price. But we must caution you not to let them interfere with what you *like* or really want. Remember, some diamonds are very beautiful even though they don't adhere to established standards. In the final analysis, use your own eyes and ask yourself how you *like* the stone. I had a customer who was trying to decide between several stones. Her husband wanted to buy her the stone with the "best" report, but she preferred another stone, which, according to what was on the reports, wasn't as "good." They decided against the "best" stone and bought the one that made her happiest. The important thing is that they knew exactly what they were buying and paid an appropriate price for that specific combination of quality factors. In other words, they made an *informed* choice. The reports gave them assurance as to the facts and greater confidence that they knew what they were really comparing.

## Improper Use of Reports
## Can Lead to Costly Mistakes

As important as diamond grading reports can be, they can also be misused and lead to erroneous conclusions and costly mistakes. The key to being able to rely on a diamond report—and having confidence in your decision—lies in knowing how to read it properly.

When trying to decide between two diamonds accompanied by diamond grading reports, buyers all too often make a decision by comparing just two factors evaluated on the reports—color and clarity—and think they have made a sound decision. This is rarely the case. No one can make a sound decision based on *color* and *clarity* alone. In fact, when significant price differences exist between two stones of the same color and clarity, you will find that often the cheaper stone is *not* the same quality and not the better value.

Color and clarity provide only part of the total picture, and differences in price usually indicate differences in quality that you may not see or understand. With *round* diamonds, *all* the information you need is on the report, but you need to understand what all the information means before you can make valid comparisons.

Properly used, diamond grading reports can give you a more complete picture and enable you to make sounder comparisons and to determine who is offering good value. Reading reports may seem complicated at first, but if you take time to learn, and seek the help of a knowledgeable jeweler, you'll be amazed at how much more interesting—and unique—you'll find each diamond will become!

Before you begin, however, we must offer one important word of caution: *Don't make a purchase relying solely on any report without making sure the report matches the stone, and that the stone is still in the same condition described.* Always seek a professional gemologist, gemologist-appraiser, or gem-testing laboratory to confirm that the stone accompanying the report is, in fact, the stone described there, and that the stone is still in the same condition indicated on the report. We know of instances where a report has been accidentally sent with the wrong stone. In some cases, deliberate fraud is involved.

## HOW TO READ A DIAMOND GRADING REPORT

**What date was the report issued?** It is very important to check the date on the report. It's always possible that the stone has been damaged since the report was issued. This sometimes occurs with diamonds sold at auction. Since diamonds can become chipped or cracked with wear, one must always check them. For example, you might see a diamond accompanied by a report describing it as flawless. If this stone were badly chipped *after the report was issued,* however, the clarity grade could easily drop to VVS, or in some cases even lower. Needless to say, in such a case, value would be dramatically reduced.

**Who issued the report?** Check the name of the laboratory issuing the report. Is the laboratory one that is known and well respected? If not, the information on the report may not be reliable. In the United States, respected laboratories that issue diamond reports include the Gemological Institute of America Gem Trade Laboratory (GIA/GTL), American Gemological Laboratories (AGL), American Gem Society (AGS), Professional Gem Sciences (PGS), and International Gemmological Institute (IGI). Respected European labs issuing diamond reports include the Belgian Diamond High Council (HRD), Laboratory Gübelin (Swiss), and Swiss Gemmological Institute (SSEF, Swiss). (See the appendix for additional information on these and other laboratories.)

Whichever report you are reading (see the end of this chapter for sample reports), all will provide similar information, including these specific features:

- *Identity of the stone.* This verifies that the stone is a diamond. Some diamond reports don't make a specific statement about identity because they are called *diamond* reports and are issued only for genuine diamonds. If the report is not called a "diamond grading report," then there must be a statement attesting that the stone described is a genuine diamond.

- *Weight.* The exact carat weight must be given.

- *Dimensions.* Any diamond, of any shape, should be measured and the dimensions recorded as a means of identification, especially for insurance/identification purposes. The dimensions given on a diamond report are very precise and provide information that is important for several reasons. First, the dimensions can help you determine that the diamond being examined is, in fact, the same diamond described in the report, since the likelihood that two diamonds will have exactly the same carat weight and millimeter dimensions is slim. Second, if the diamond has been damaged and recut since the report was issued, the millimeter dimensions may provide a clue that something has been altered, which may affect the carat weight as well. Any discrepancy between the dimensions on the report and those that you or your jeweler get by measuring the stone should be a red flag to check the stone very carefully. Finally, the dimensions on the report also tell you whether the stone is *round* or *out-of-round*. Out-of-round diamonds sell for less than those that are more perfectly round. Roundness is explained below in greater detail.

- *Proportioning, finish, girdle thickness, culet, color, and clarity.* These are covered individually on the following pages.

## Round, Brilliant-Cut Diamonds Are "Well-Rounded"

In round diamonds, the stone's *roundness* will affect value, so it is determined very carefully from measurements of the stone's diameter, gauged at several points around the circumference. For a round diamond, the report will usually give two diameters, measured in millimeters and noted to the hundredth: for example, 6.51 rather than 6.5, or 6.07 rather than 6.0, and so on. These indicate the highest and the lowest diameter. Diamonds are very rarely perfectly round, which is why most diamond reports will show two measurements. Recognizing the rarity of truly round diamonds, some deviation is permitted, and the stone will not be considered "out-of-round" unless it deviates by more than the established norm, which, in a one-carat stone, is approximately 0.10 millimeter. As the size of a diamond increases the tolerances also increase.

Depending on the degree of out-of-roundness, price can be affected by 10 to 15 percent, or much more if the stone is noticeably out-of-round. The greater the deviation, the lower the price should be.

## Dimensions for Fancy Shapes

While the dimensions for fancy shapes are not as important as they are for round diamonds, there are length-to-width ratios that are considered "normal," and deviations may result in price reductions of 15 percent or more.

## EVALUATING PROPORTIONING FROM THE REPORT

As discussed earlier, good proportioning is as critical to a diamond as it is to the man or woman who wears it! The proportioning—especially the depth percentage and table percentage—is what determines how much brilliance and fire the stone will have.

The information provided on diamond reports pertaining to proportions is critically important for *round, brilliant-cut diamonds.* Unfortunately, it is only of minimal use with fancy shapes. For fancies, you must learn to rely on your own eye to tell whether or not the proportioning is acceptable: Are there differences in brilliance across the stone? Or flatness? Or dark spots such as bow ties resulting from poor proportioning? (See chapter 7.)

Evaluating the proportioning of a diamond is as critical as evaluating the color and clarity grades. Diamonds that are cut close to ideal proportions (see chapter 7) and stones with excellent makes can easily cost 15 to 25 percent more than a diamond cut with average proportions; diamonds with poor makes sell for 10 to 20 percent less; very badly proportioned stones can be priced as much as 25 to 40 percent less than one with average proportions. As you can see, *the difference in cost between one diamond with ideal proportioning and another with poor proportioning—even where the color and clarity are the same—could be 40 percent or more.* The information on a diamond report can help you evaluate the proportioning and know whether or not you should be paying more or less for a particular stone.

## Depth Percentage and Table Percentage Affect Beauty

To determine whether or not a round stone's proportioning is good—which is so critical to its beauty—look at the section of the report that describes *depth percentage* and *table percentage*. The depth percentage represents the depth of the stone—the distance from the table to the culet—as a percentage of the width of the stone. The table percentage represents the width of the table as a percentage of the width of the entire stone. These numbers indicate how well a round stone has been cut in terms of its proportioning, and they must adhere to very precise standards. Your eye may be able to see differences in sparkle and brilliance, but you may not be able to discern the subtleties of proportioning. The percentages on the report should fall within a fairly specific range in order for the stone to be judged acceptable, excellent, or poor.

How one calculates these percentages will not be discussed here, but it is important for you to know what the ranges are, as outlined in the following guidelines. Some reports also provide information about the *crown angle,* which tells you the angle at which the crown portion has been cut. This angle will affect the depth and table percentage. Normally, if the crown angle is between 34 and 36 degrees, the table and depth will be excellent; between 32 and 34 degrees, good; between 30 and 32 degrees, fair; and less than 30 degrees, poor. If the exact crown angle is not given, it is probably considered acceptable. If not, there is normally a statement indicating that the crown angle exceeds 36 degrees or is less than 30 degrees. But once again, use your own eye to determine whether or not you like what you see. We've seen diamonds that are very beautiful despite having angles that are not within the norm.

*Depth percentage.* A round diamond cut with a depth percentage between 58 and 64 percent is normally a lovely, lively stone. You should note, however, that girdle thickness will affect depth percentage. A high depth percentage could result from a thick or very thick girdle, so when you are checking the depth percentage on the diamond report, check the girdle information as well.

Stones with a depth percentage over 64 percent or under 57 percent will normally be too deep or too shallow to exhibit maximum beauty and should sell for less. If the depth percentage is too high, the stone will also look smaller than its weight indicates. If the depth percentage is exceptionally high, brilliance can be significantly reduced, and a darkish center may also be produced.

## DEPTH PERCENTAGE GUIDELINES

| Depth Percentage | Effect on Price |
|---|---|
| *Ideal*—approximately 58 to 60% | 20 to 30% more* |
| *Excellent*—60 to 62% | 10 to 20% more* |
| *Good*—62 to 64% | ———— |
| *Fair*—64 to 66% | 15 to 25% less |
| *Poor*—over 66% or less than 57% | 20 to 40% less |

*For *round* diamonds, combined with the right table percentage and fine overall cutting

If the depth percentage is too *low,* brilliance will also be significantly affected. We've seen diamonds that were so shallow—stones with such low depth percentages—that they had no brilliance and liveliness at all. When dirty, such stones look no better than a piece of glass. We avoid stones with depth percentages over 64 percent or under 57 percent. If you are attracted to such stones, remember that they should sell for much less per carat.

*Table percentage.* Round stones cut with tables ranging from 53 to 64 percent usually result in beautiful, lively stones. Diamonds with smaller tables usually exhibit more *fire* than those with larger tables, but stones with larger tables may have more *brilliance.* As you will see, table width affects the stone's personality, but deciding which personality is more desirable is a matter of personal taste.

## TABLE PERCENTAGE GUIDELINES

| Table Percentage | Effect on Price |
|---|---|
| *Ideal*—from 53 to 58% | 20 to 30% more* |
| *Excellent*—up to 60% (up to 62% in stones under ½ carat) | 10 to 20% more* |
| *Good*—to 64% | ———— |
| *Fair*—over 64 to 70% | 15 to 30% less |
| *Poor*—over 70% | 30 to 40% less |

*For *round* diamonds, combined with the right depth percentage and fine overall cutting

# Finish

Under *finish* on the diamond report, you will find an evaluation of the stone's *polish* and *symmetry*. Polish serves as an indicator of the care taken by the cutter. The quality of the stone's polish cannot be ignored in evaluating the overall quality of a diamond, as well as its cost and value. As with a pair of fine leather shoes, the better the polish, the brighter the surface luster!

Polish can be described on the report as *excellent, very good, good, fair*, or *poor*. The price per carat should be less on stones with fair or poor polish. Cost per carat is usually more for stones that have very good or excellent polish.

Symmetry describes several factors: (1) how the facet edges align with one another, (2) whether or not the facets from one side of the diamond match corresponding facets on the opposite side, and (3) whether or not facets in the top portion of the diamond are properly aligned with corresponding facets in the bottom portion. When the symmetry is described as fair or worse, something is usually out of line.

In evaluating symmetry, the most important area to check is the alignment of the crown (top) to the pavilion (bottom). If it is not good, it will make a visual difference in the beauty of the stone, and correspondingly in its price. To check for proper alignment here, simply look at the stone from the side to see whether or not the facets just above the girdle align with the facets just beneath the girdle.

When the top and bottom facets don't line up, it indicates sloppy cutting and, more important, diminishes the overall beauty of the diamond. This will reduce price more than other symmetry faults.

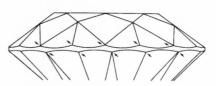

Misalignment of crown and pavilion

# How Does the Girdle Affect Value?

The girdle is another important item described on diamond grading reports. The report will indicate whether or not the girdle is polished, or faceted, and how thick it is. Girdle thickness is very important for two reasons: (1) it affects *value*, and (2) it affects the stone's *durability*.

Girdle thickness ranges from extremely thin to extremely thick. Diamonds with girdles that are excessively thin or thick normally sell for less than other diamonds. An extremely thin girdle increases the risk of chipping. Remember that despite their legendary hardness, diamonds are brittle, so a very thin edge poses a greater risk.

If a diamond has an extremely thick girdle, its cost should also be reduced somewhat because the stone will look smaller than another diamond of the same weight with a more normal girdle thickness. This is because extra weight is being consumed by the thickness of the girdle itself. (See chapter 7.)

In some cases a very thick girdle is acceptable. Shapes that have one or more points, such as the pear shape, heart, or marquise, can have thick to very thick girdles in the area of the points and still be in the acceptable range. Here the extra thickness in the girdle helps protect the points themselves from chipping.

Generally, a diamond with an extremely thin girdle should sell for less than one with an extremely thick girdle because of the stone's increased vulnerability to chipping. However, if the girdle is much too thick (as in some older diamonds), the price can also be significantly less because the stone can look significantly smaller than other stones of comparable weight.

## The Culet

The culet looks like a point at the bottom of the stone, but it is normally another facet—a tiny, flat, polished surface. This facet should be *small* or *very small.* A small or very small culet won't be noticeable from the top. Some diamonds today are actually pointed. This means that there really is no culet—that the stone has been cut straight down to a point instead. The larger the culet, the more visible it will be from the top. The more visible it is, the lower the cost of the stone. Stones described as having a large or "open" culet, as in old-European or old-mine cut diamonds (see chapter 7), are less desirable because the appearance of the culet causes a reduction in sparkle or brilliance at the very center of the stone. For the same reasons, a chipped or broken culet will seriously detract from the stone's beauty and significantly reduce the cost.

## COLOR AND CLARITY GRADES

The color and clarity grades found on a diamond report are the items with which most people are familiar, and they have already been discussed in detail in chapters 8 and 9. They are important factors in terms of determining the value of a diamond, but as the preceding discussion has shown, they do not tell the whole story.

The placement, number, type, and color of internal and external flaws will be indicated on a diamond report, and may include a plotting—a diagram showing all the details. Be sure you carefully note all the details in addition to the cumulative grade. Remember, the placement of imperfections can affect value (see chapter 9). You should pay special attention to the section that says "Key to Symbols." This is where lasering will be indicated if the diamond is lasered. This means that the clarity grade indicated is *after* lasering. Its cost should be 15 to 20 percent less than another diamond with the "same" clarity grade. With regard to *fracture filling,* a reliable diamond grading report cannot be issued on a fracture-filled diamond, so most laboratories will not grade diamonds that have been clarity enhanced by this method. Most will return the stone *ungraded,* with a notation that it is fracture-filled. Some labs will provide a "qualified" clarity grade, indicating that the stone is fracture-filled and that the grading cannot be precise.

## A Word About Fluorescence

Fluorescence, if present, will also be indicated on a diamond grading report and will be graded faint, weak, moderate, strong, or very strong. Some reports indicate the color of the fluorescence (blue, yellow, white, and so on). If the fluorescence is moderate to very strong and the color is not indicated, you should ask the jewelry specialist at the auction house to check for you and tell you what color the stone fluoresces. A stone with strong yellow fluorescence should sell for less, since it will appear more tinted when worn in daylight or under fluorescent lighting. The presence of blue fluorescence will not detract and in some cases may be considered a bonus, since it may make the stone appear whiter than it really is when seen in daylight or fluorescent lighting. However, if the report shows a very strong blue fluorescence, be sure to view the stone in daylight or fluorescent light to see whether or not there is an oily or murky appearance to the diamond. If so, it should sell for less; if not, its value should not be affected.

Reports on fancy-color diamonds may not include fluorescence. If not, be sure to have the auction house check. If they do not have the means, be sure to look at the diamond in different types of light. Find a way to see it in lamplight *and* daylight *and* fluorescent light to see whether or not its color changes and, if it does, whether or not you like it in *all* types of light. If the diamond is a very rare color, such as green, be sure it appears green in all lighting conditions. If not, you should pay much less.

## PAY ATTENTION TO "COMMENTS"

On the GIA diamond grading report, and on most other reports issued by major laboratories, there is a section under which additional comments are provided. What is worth noting here is important, and you should be sure you understand what the comment tells you. Here you will find comments on characteristics such as the presence of *graining*. Grain lines can be seen only when examining the diamond while slowly rotating it. They will appear in a group of two, three, or four pale brown lines, and they appear and disappear, usually instantaneously. If they cannot be seen from the crown side of the diamond and are small, they will not affect the grade adversely. Graining may not affect the appearance or value of a stone at all, but sometimes graining can reduce brilliance, so you should look more closely at the stone to make sure it doesn't affect its beauty.

Under "Comments," you will also find special notations regarding crown or pavilion angles, indicating that the angle at which the upper or lower portion of the stone has been cut may be less than or greater than the norm. Here again, you must look carefully at the stone to be sure its beauty has not been diminished by faulty cutting.

Last, but not least, this is where you will find any notation regarding certain treatments, such as clarity enhancement or the new high-pressure/high-temperature (HPHT) process used to enhance diamond color. If the laboratory issues a report on a diamond that has been treated in some manner, the presence of some type of enhancement will be noted under "Comments."

# GIA GEM TRADE LABORATORY

A Division of GIA Enterprises, Inc.
A Wholly Owned Subsidiary of the Nonprofit Gemological Institute of America, Inc.

10012345

580 Fifth Avenue
New York, New York 10036-4794
(212) 221-5858
FAX: (212) 575-3095

5355 Armada Drive
Carlsbad, California 92008-4699
(760) 603-4500
FAX: (760) 603-1814

FEB 02 1998

## DIAMOND GRADING REPORT

THE FOLLOWING WERE, AT THE TIME OF THE EXAMINATION, THE CHARAC-
TERISTICS OF THE DIAMOND DESCRIBED HEREIN BASED UPON 10×
MAGNIFICATION (FULLY CORRECTED TRIPLET LOUPE AND BINOCULAR
MICROSCOPE), DIAMONDLITE AND MASTER COLOR COMPARISON
DIAMONDS, ULTRAVIOLET LAMPS, MILLIMETER GAUGE, CARAT BALANCE,
PROPORTIONSCOPE, AND ANCILLARY INSTRUMENTS AS NECESSARY.

RED SYMBOLS DENOTE INTERNAL CHARACTERISTICS (INCLUSIONS).
GREEN SYMBOLS DENOTE EXTERNAL CHARACTERISTICS (BLEMISHES).
SYMBOLS INDICATE TYPE, POSITION AND APPROXIMATE SIZE OF
CHARACTERISTICS. DETAILS OF FINISH ARE NOT SHOWN. DIAGRAM MAY
BE APPROXIMATE.

**KEY TO SYMBOLS**
- ○ CRYSTAL
- ↖ FEATHER
- · PINPOINT
- ⌃ NATURAL

**SHAPE AND CUTTING STYLE** .. ROUND BRILLIANT
- Measurements .... 6.90 - 6.97 X 4.20 MM.
- Weight .......... 1.25 CARATS

**PROPORTIONS** ...
- Depth .......... 60.6 %
- Table .......... 61 %
- Girdle .......... MEDIUM TO SLIGHTLY THICK, FACETED
- Culet .......... VERY SMALL
- FINISH
  - Polish ........ VERY GOOD
  - Symmetry ...... VERY GOOD

**CLARITY GRADE** .. VS1

**COLOR GRADE** ... F

Fluorescence ..... NONE

**COMMENTS:**
 "GIA 10012345" has been inscribed on the girdle of this diamond.

ORIGINAL

**GIA GEM TRADE LABORATORY**

GIA Gem Trade Laboratory

**GIA CLARITY GRADING SCALE**

| | VVS₁ | VVS₂ | VS₁ | VS₂ | SI₁ | SI₂ | I₁ | I₂ | I₃ |
|---|---|---|---|---|---|---|---|---|---|
| Flawless | | | X | | | | | | |
| Internally Flawless | | | | | | | Included | | |

**GIA COLOR GRADING SCALE**

| D | E | F | G | H | I | J | K | L | M | N | O | P | Q | R | S | T | U | V | W | X | Y | Z | Fancy Grades |
|---|---|---|---|---|---|---|---|---|---|---|---|---|---|---|---|---|---|---|---|---|---|---|---|
| | X | | | | | | | | | | | | | | | | | | | | | | |
| Colorless | | | Near Colorless | | | Faint Yellow | | | Very Light Yellow | | | | | | | | | | Light Yellow | | | | Yellow | |

This report is not a guarantee, valuation or appraisal. The recipient of this report may wish to consult a credentialed
Jeweler or Gemologist about the importance and interrelationship of cut, color, clarity and carat weight.

Copyright © 1989 - 1997 GIA Gem Trade Laboratory

**NOTICE: IMPORTANT LIMITATIONS ON REVERSE**

GIA reports do not give a cut grade. Note laser inscription under "Comments" section.

# American Gemological Laboratories

Olympic Tower
645 Fifth Ave. Suite 1105
New York, N.Y. 10022
(212) 935-0060
(212) 935-0071

# Diamond Certificate

The information contained in this report represents the opinion of American Gemological Laboratories regarding the characteristics of the diamond(s) submitted for examination.

This analysis is based on measurements and also on observations made through a binocular darkfield microscope and in a controlled lighting environment utilizing master comparison stones. Mounted diamonds are graded only to the extent that mounting permits examination.

**CERTIFICATE NO.**   SAMPLE

**DATE:**   15 May 1989

| | |
|---|---|
| **SHAPE and CUT:** | Round Brilliant |
| **CARAT WEIGHT:** | 1.22 Cts. |
| **MEASUREMENTS:** | 6.95 - 7.06 x 4.04 mm. |
| **PROPORTIONS** | |
| Depth % | Good (4) |
| Table Diameter % | 59.5% |
| Girdle Thickness | 60% |
| | Medium; Faceted |
| **FINISH GRADE:** | Very Good - Good (3-4) |
| **CLARITY GRADE:** (10X Magnification) | VVS$_1$* |
| **COLOR GRADE:** | E* |
| UV Fluorescence | Moderate Blue |
| **COMMENTS:** | *Minor details of finish not plotted. |
| | *Transitional color grade. |

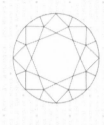

Diamond Proportions

Girdle Diameter = 100%
Table %
Depth %
Crown
Pavilion Depth
Girdle Thickness
Culet

**Clarity Scale (GIA)**

| Fl | IF | VVS$_1$ | VVS$_2$ | VS$_1$ | VS$_2$ | SI$_1$ | SI$_2$ | I$_1$ | I$_2$ | I$_3$ |
|---|---|---|---|---|---|---|---|---|---|---|

**Color Scale (GIA)**

| D | E | F | G | H | I | J | K | L | M | N | O | P | Q | R | S through Z | Z+ |
|---|---|---|---|---|---|---|---|---|---|---|---|---|---|---|---|---|
| Colorless | | | Near Colorless | | | | Faint Yellow | | | | Very Light Yellow | | | | Light Yellow | Fancy Yellow |

Internal characteristics shown with red symbols, external with green. Symbols indicate nature and position of identifying characteristics, not necessarily their size. Setting prongs on mounted stones are shown with black symbols. Minor details of finish not plotted.

This report prepared by **American Gemological Laboratories, Inc.**

Martin J. Anderson, G.G.

Original

SOURCE: AMERICAN GEMOLOGICAL LABORATORIES

AGL reports describe the cut and finish and provide a numerical grade.

## Cut Scale — AGS

| 0 | 1 | 2 | 3 | 4 | 5 | 6 | 7 | 8 | 9 | 10 |
|---|---|---|---|---|---|---|---|---|---|----|
| AGS Ideal | AGS Excellent | AGS Very Good | AGS Good | | | AGS Fair | | | AGS Poor | |

## Color Scale

| AGS | 0 | 0.5 | 1.0 | 1.5 | 2.0 | 2.5 | 3.0 | 3.5 | 4.0 | 4.5 | 5.0 | 5.5 | 6.0 | 6.5 | 7.0 | 7.5 | 8.0 | 8.5 | 9.0 | 9.5 | 10.0 | To | Fancy Yellow |
|-----|---|-----|-----|-----|-----|-----|-----|-----|-----|-----|-----|-----|-----|-----|-----|-----|-----|-----|-----|-----|------|----|--------------|
| GIA | D | E | F | G | H | I | J | K | L | M | N | O | P | Q | R | S | T | U | V | W | X | Y Z | Fancy Yellow |
| | COLORLESS | | | NEAR COLORLESS | | | FAINT YELLOW | | | VERY LIGHT YELLOW | | | | | LIGHT YELLOW | | | | | | | | |

## Clarity Scale

| AGS | 0 | 1 | 2 | 3 | 4 | 5 | 6 | 7 | 8 | 9 | 10 |
|-----|---|---|---|---|---|---|---|---|---|---|----|
| GIA | FLAWLESS / IF | VVS1 | VVS2 | VS1 | VS2 | SI1 | SI2 | I1 | I2 | I3 | |

## Key to Symbols

| | | | | | |
|---|---|---|---|---|---|
| Bruise | × | Crystal | ○ | Laser Drill Hole | ⊙ |
| Cavity | ⊘ | Extra Facet | ∧ | Natural | ∧ |
| Chip | ∧ | Feather | ⌇ | Needle | ╱ |
| Cleavage | ╱ | Indented Natural | ⩙ | Pinpoint | • |
| Cloud | ⋰ | Knot | ◎ | Twinning Wisp | ∿ |

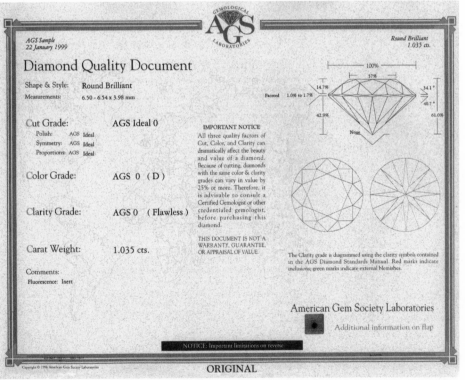

AGS reports provide a cut grade. Note the scale they use to indicate the quality of cutting.

certificate no.          000000000

The HRD Certificates Department is BELTEST accredited for the quality examination of polished diamonds under ref. N° 047.

This certificate is established in conformity with the "International Rules for Grading Polished Diamonds", approved by the World Federation of Diamond Bourses and the International Diamond Manufacturers Association at the May 1978 Congress (rev. ed. 1995), and may not be reproduced by any means whatsoever unless complete.

The stone in accordance with the above mentioned number has been identified as a natural gem diamond and has the following description :

| | |
|---|---|
| shape | brilliant |
| weight | 1.02 ct |
| clarity grade | loupe-clean |
| fluorescence | nil |
| colour grade | exceptional white (E) |
| measurements | 6.58-6.64mm x 3.89mm |
| proportions | very good |
| girdle | thin 2.5% |
| culet | pointed |
| table width | 65% |
| cr. height | 12.5% |
| pav. depth | 44% |
| finish grade | very good |
| comments | |

**clarity grade**
(magnification 10 ×)

| | |
|---|---|
| loupe-clean | X |
| vvs 1 | |
| vvs 2 | |
| vs 1 | |
| vs 2 | |
| si 1 | |
| si 2 | |
| p 1 | |
| p 2 | |
| p 3 | |

**colour grade**

| | |
|---|---|
| exceptional white + | |
| exceptional white | X |
| rare white + | |
| rare white | |
| white | |
| slightly tinted white | |
| tinted white | |
| tinted colour | |

**proportions**

| | |
|---|---|
| very good | X |
| good | |
| unusual | |

**finish grade**

| | |
|---|---|
| very good | X |
| good | |
| medium | |
| poor | |

antwerpen, 11/03/1996

gemmologists

identification marks :
negligible external characteristics

The characteristics of the above mentioned diamond have been established by scientific measurements and observations, carried out in the laboratory of the Diamond High Council.

Red symbols refer to internal and green symbols to external characteristics.
The symbols do not usually reflect the actual size of the characteristics.
The characteristics have been indicated in order to clarify the description and/or for further identification.

SOURCE: HOGE RAAD VOOR DIAMANT (THE DIAMOND HIGH COUNCIL OF BELGIUM)

HRD describes the quality of the cut and finish.

**LON** 0091285

## The Gem Testing Laboratory
## of Great Britain

## LONDON DIAMOND REPORT

| | |
|---|---|
| Carat weight: | 2.30 |
| Colour grade: | F RARE WHITE + |
| Clarity grade: | VVS 2 |
| Shape and cutting style: | ROUND BRILLIANT |
| Measurements: | 9.06 - 9.13 x 5.16 mm |
| Proportions: Height: | 56.7% |
| Table: | 68 % |
| Polish: | VERY GOOD |
| Symmetry: | GOOD |
| Girdle: | VERY THIN TO THIN |
| UV-fluorescence: | FAINT |
| Comments: | |

This Report does not make any statement with respect to the monetary value of the diamond.
Only the original report with signature and embossed stamp is a valid identification document.

The Gem Testing Laboratory of Great Britain is the official CIBJO recognised Laboratory for Great Britain.

### The Gem Testing Laboratory of Great Britain

GAGTL, 27 Greville Street,
London, EC1N 8SU, Great Britain

Telephone: +44 171 405 3351
Fax: +44 171 831 9479

Signed **SAMPLE**

Date 22nd May 2001

No cut grade is provided although essential
information pertaining to cutting is given.

# PROFESSIONAL GEM SCIENCES

An Independent Laboratory for the
Study and Grading of Diamonds and Gemstones

5 S. Wabash Avenue, Suite 1905
Chicago, IL 60603
Phone (312) 920-1541
Fax (312) 920-1547

·

550 S. Hill Street, Suite 1595
Los Angeles, CA 90013
Phone (213) 622-2387
Fax (213) 622-3138

·

Toll Free (800) 235-3287

www.progem.com

# CERTIFICATE OF QUALITY

## IDENTIFICATION

| | | | |
|---|---|---|---|
| Species | Natural Diamond | Report Number | XdSAMPLE |
| Variety | Diamond | Date | May 08, 2001 |
| Shape & Cut | Round Brilliant Cut | | |

| | | | |
|---|---|---|---|
| Carat Weight | 0.75 ct. | Precision Weight | 0.7565 ct. |
| Clarity Grade* | VS1 | Graining | Nil |
| Color Grade** | F | Fluorescence | Very Faint |

### Clarity Representation
Internal Characterisitcs are shown in red. External Characteristics are shown in green. Extra facets are shown in black. Symbols indicate the position of identifying characterstics, not necessarily their size. Hairline feathers in the girdle, minor bearding, and minor details of polish and finish are not shown.

### KEY TO SYMBOLS

| | |
|---|---|
| Feather | Crystal |
| Cloud | Natural |

## CUT INFORMATION

| | | | |
|---|---|---|---|
| Dimensions | 5.78 - 5.87 x 3.62 mm. | Total Depth | 62.1% |
| Table Width | 56% | | |
| Crown Angle | 35.5° | Crown Height | 16.0%* |
| Pavilion Angle | 40.5° | Pavilion Depth | 43.0%* |
| Girdle Thickness | Thin to Slightly Thick, Frosty, Smooth | Average | 3.1%* |
| | | *TOTAL | 62.1% |
| Culet Size | Small, Polished (1.0%) | | |

## FINISH

| | |
|---|---|
| Polish | Very Good to Excellent |
| Symmetry | Good to Very Good |

## COMMENTS
Ideal Cut. Additional pinpoints not shown.

* Clarity grade determined at 10x magnification with a corrected loupe.
** Color grade determined by comparison to approximately 1 carat size, master comparison diamonds.
*** Color Analysis determined by comparison to Munsell color order standards as presented in the book *The World of Color.*

**Note: Please read the important limitations to this report printed on the reverse side.**

Security Control Number
SAMPLE

QUALITY CONTROL By:

*Thomas E. Tashey Jr.*

Thomas E. Tashey, Jr., G.G., F.G.A.

©2001 PGS, INC

This report provides a cut grade in the "Comments" section.
Here the cut is graded "ideal."

# SSEF SCHWEIZERISCHES GEMMOLOGISCHES INSTITUT
# SSEF INSTITUT SUISSE DE GEMMOLOGIE
# SSEF SWISS GEMMOLOGICAL INSTITUTE

Offiziell anerkannt am 27/04/78 von der

## CIBJO

INTERNATIONALE VEREINIGUNG SCHMUCK, SILBERWAREN, DIAMANTEN, PERLEN UND STEINE

CONFEDERATION INTERNATIONALE DE LA BIJOUTERIE, JOAILLERIE, ORFEVRERIE, DES DIAMANTS, PERLES ET PIERRES

INTERNATIONAL CONFEDERATION OF JEWELLERY, SILVERWARE, DIAMONDS, PEARLS AND STONES

## Diamond Report
## Diamant Expertise Nr. CH 10392

| | |
|---|---|
| Carat weight/Gewicht/Poids: | 1.558 ct |
| Colour grade/Farbe/Couleur: | white (H) |
| Purity grade/Reinheit/Pureté: | VVS 2 |
| Shape and cut/Schliffform/Taille: | round brilliant |
| Measurements/Abmessungen/Mesures: | 7.42 - 7.48 x 4.56 mm |
| Proportions/Proportion: Height/Höhe/Haut. | 61 % Table/Tafel 63 % |
| Finish: Symmetry/Symmetrie/Symétrie: | very good |
| Polish/Politur/Polissage: | very good |
| Girdle/Rundiste/Rondiste: | medium, faceted |
| UV-fluorescence/Fluoreszenz: | medium |
| Comments/Bemerkungen/Commentaires: | internal growth characteristics |
| | This colourless diamond shows no evidence of HPHT treatment |

SSEF

8 November 1996 ni

SPECIMEN

Falknerstrasse 9, 4001 Basel, Tel. 061/262 06 40, Fax 061/262 06 41

Note the statement regarding the absence of
High-Pressure/High-Temperature Treatment

# 11 ◆ Is It a Diamond
## or a Diamond Imposter?

HOW CAN YOU TELL IF A STONE IS REALLY A DIAMOND? AS WE HAVE said many times, unless you are an expert—or consult one—you cannot be sure about the identification of a stone. Nevertheless, you can perform a few simple tests that will reveal most diamond imposters quite quickly. Here are a few things to look for.

*Is newsprint readable or observable through the stone?* If the stone is a round, modern-cut stone and is loose or mounted in such a way as to allow you to place it table-down over some small newsprint, check whether you can see or read any portion of the lettering. If so, it is not a diamond. Refraction of light within a genuine diamond is such that you will not be able to see any of the letters in the newsprint.

*Is the stone glued into the setting?* Diamonds are seldom glued in. Rhinestones often are.

*Is the back open or closed?* If the stone is a properly set diamond, the back of the setting will usually be open, allowing you to readily see a portion of the pavilion. Some antique pieces containing rose-cut or single-cut diamonds may have closed backs, and some of today's finest custom designers may use a closed-back technique. Otherwise, if a piece has a closed back it is probably rhinestone, the back being closed to conceal silver foil applied to the back of the stone to create greater brilliance.

Recently a young woman called and asked us to examine an antique diamond ring she'd inherited from her great-grandmother. She mentioned that as she was cleaning it, one of its two diamonds had fallen out of the setting, and inside the setting she saw what she described as pieces of "mirror." She added, "Isn't that strange?" Of course our suspicions were immediately aroused, and upon examination of the piece, they were completely confirmed.

When we saw the ring, we could immediately understand why she felt it was a valuable heirloom. It was beautiful, with a classic design. It held two "diamonds" appearing to be approximately one carat each. The ring mounting was finely worked platinum filigree. But the design of the mounting, which had been common in her great-grandmother's day, made viewing the stones from the side of the ring almost impossible. The top of the stone and the beautiful platinum work were visible, but little more could be seen. Furthermore, the back was not completely enclosed; a small round hole would easily have led to the assumption that the stones were the real thing, since the setting wasn't completely closed, as were most imitations at that time. The "set" diamond appeared to be a well-proportioned old-mine cut with very good color. The loose stone, however, with some of the "shiny stuff" still clinging to it, lacked brilliance and fire.

This was one of the finest examples of fraud we had seen in a long time. The "stones" were well cut and proportioned; the mounting was beautifully worked in a precious metal; the stones were held by very small prongs, which was typical of good design at that time. But inside the mounting, backing the stones, was silver foil. They were not genuine diamonds but foil-backed glass.

The use of silver foil is an effective method of "creating" a diamond. It acts as a mirror to reflect light and makes the stone appear so brilliant and lively that it can pass as a diamond. The foiling seen today consists of making the back facets into true mirrors and then giving the backs of these mirrors a protective coating of gilt paint. These are then set in jewelry so that their backs are hidden.

It's a sad story but not an altogether uncommon one. We don't know how many more rings as cleverly done exist today, but approximately 5 percent of the antique jewelry we see is set with fake gems. Fine glass imitations (often referred to as "paste") have been with us since the Venetians of the Renaissance period perfected the art of glassmaking. Fraud, unfortunately, has been with us since time immemorial. Don't allow yourself to be deluded into believing that something you possess is "genuine" simply because it is "antique" or has "been in the family" for a long time.

**How many facets are visible on the top?** In cheaper glass imitations, only nine top facets are usually visible, as opposed to thirty-three visible top facets in a diamond or "good" simulation. Single-cut or Swiss-cut diamonds (see chapter 7) will also show only nine facets on top, but they will be set in open-back mountings, whereas cheap glass imitations are usually set in closed-back mountings.

*Does the girdle of the stone appear to be "frosted"?* The girdles of most diamonds are unpolished, with a ground-glass–like appearance that suggests frostiness. Some diamond imitations also have a frosted appearance, but of all of these, a diamond has the whitest frostiness—like clean, dry, ground glass. On the other hand, some diamonds do have polished or faceted girdles, and thus no frostiness will be present. You can develop an eye for this by asking a reliable jeweler to point out the differences between a polished girdle, an unpolished girdle, and a faceted girdle.

*Is the cut symmetrical?* Since diamond is so valuable and symmetry so important to its overall appearance and desirability, the symmetry of the faceting on a diamond will be very carefully executed, whereas in diamond simulations the symmetry of the facets may be sloppy. For example, the eight kite-shaped facets (sometimes called bezel facets) will often be missing one or more points on the side, or on the top or bottom, showing a small straight edge rather than a point. This sloppy faceting can be an important indication that the stone in question is not a diamond, since it indicates that the cutter did not take proper care. It should be noted that some poorer-grade or old-cut diamonds may also show sloppiness.

*Are the crown and the pavilion of the stone properly aligned?* While occasionally a diamond may show partial misalignment, imitations are frequently and often badly misaligned.

*Are the facet edges or faces scratched, chipped, or worn?* Diamond imitations include some stones that are very soft and/or brittle, such as zircon, GGG (an artificial simulation), Fabulite (an artificial diamond simulation also known as Wellington Diamond), and glass. Because of their lack of hardness and, in the case of zircon, their possible brittleness, these imitations will show wear easily, and one can often detect scratches or chips on the facet edges or faces. The edges are somewhat more vulnerable, and scratches or chips may be more easily seen there, so check the edges first. Then check the flat faces for scratches. Check both the areas that would be most exposed and the areas around the prongs, where a setter might have accidentally scratched the stone while setting it.

Zircon, a stone found in nature that is often confused with cubic zirconia (CZ), an artificial imitation, is relatively hard but very brittle, so it will almost always show chipping at the edges of the facets if the stone has been worn in jewelry for a year or more. Glass and Fabulite will also show scratches after minimal exposure to handling and wear. Fabulite further differs from diamond in its fire; it will show even more fire than diamond, but with a strong bluish cast.

In addition, with a very good eye or the aid of a magnifier, you can examine the lines or edges where the facets come together in these imitation materials. In diamond, these facet edges are very sharp because of the stone's spectacular hardness. In most simulations, however, since the stone is so much softer, the final polishing technique rounds off those edges, and that sharpness is absent.

Some diamond look-alikes, however, are more durable and resistant to noticeable wear. These include colorless synthetic spinel, colorless synthetic sapphire, colorless quartz, YAG (yttrium aluminum garnet; artificial), and CZ. While these may scratch or chip over time with regular wear and daily abuse, scratches or chips are not as numerous and will be less noticeable.

## AN IMPORTANT WORD ABOUT CUBIC ZIRCONIA

Cubic zirconia is the best diamond simulation made to date, and even some jewelers have mistaken these stones for diamonds. Cubic zirconia is almost as brilliant as diamond, has even greater fire (which masks its lesser brilliance), and is relatively hard, giving it good durability and wearability. It is also being produced today in fancy colors—red, green, and yellow—and can provide a nice diamond alternative as a means to offset or dress up colored stones in jewelry if diamonds are unaffordable.

But make sure you *know* what you are buying. For example, if you are considering a lovely amethyst or sapphire ring dressed up with "diamonds," make sure to ask whether the colorless stones are diamonds.

## How Can You Tell If You Have a CZ?

Some of the tests already discussed may help you detect a CZ. The following, however, may eliminate any remaining doubt. But once again, you need access to the stone to observe these clues and perform these tests. You can either bring a trained gemologist to an auction house or create an escrow account with a third party to gain access to the diamond before making a purchase.

*If it is a loose stone, have it weighed.* If you are familiar with diamond sizes (see page 88), you can estimate the diamond carat weight. A loose stone can be weighed on a scale, which most jewelers and auction houses have handy, and you can determine how much it should weigh if it is truly a diamond. If the weight is much greater than the diamond weight should be, based on its size, then it is not a diamond. A CZ is approximately 75 percent heavier than a diamond of the same size. For example, a CZ that is the same size as a 1-carat diamond will weigh 1¾ carats.

*Look at the girdle.* If the girdle is frosted, a subdued whiteness resembling slightly wet or oiled frosted glass will indicate CZ. Unfortunately, looking at girdles to differentiate between the appearance of frosted CZ and frosted diamond girdles requires considerable experience.

*Test the stone with a carbide scriber.* CZ can be scratched with a fine-point carbide scriber, also available at most jewelry supply houses for under $15. If the scriber is forcibly pushed perpendicularly to any of the facets (the table being the easiest) and then drawn across this flat surface, you will scratch it. You cannot scratch a diamond except with another diamond. But be sensible and considerate. Don't heedlessly scratch merchandise that doesn't belong to you—particularly if the jeweler or seller doesn't represent the stone as a diamond.

*Use an electronic diamond tester.* There are pocket-size diamond testers for under $300 that will tell you whether or not you have a diamond. If you follow the instructions, they are easy to use and fairly reliable. Most won't tell you what you have if it's *not* diamond; they will only confirm whether or not it *is* diamond.

If after making these tests you have some questions, take the stone to a qualified gemologist with lab facilities for positive identification.

## Synthetic Moissanite—A Sparkling Newcomer

A new diamond imitation is being sold today under the name *moissanite,* although it should be called *synthetic moissanite,* since what is being sold is not natural but created in laboratories. It is silicon carbide, named after Dr. Moissan, the French scientist who discovered it. Advertisements describe it as one of nature's rarest gems, but it does not occur in nature as a gemstone, only as a microscopic inclusion.

It made news upon its introduction because it fooled most electronic diamond testers, indicating "diamond" when tested! Many concluded that it was therefore indistinguishable from diamond, but this is far from the case. It has several distinctive characteristics that immediately separate it from diamond. Nevertheless, synthetic moissanite is being misrepresented as diamond in new and antique jewelry, and there have been several cases in which jewelers have switched stones, substituting synthetic moissanite for the original diamond. Gemologists can quickly and easily separate diamond from synthetic moissanite with simple tests, in most cases using only a 10x loupe. There are also new electronic diamond testers that can instantly distinguish between the two.

## A Word about Synthetic Diamonds

Synthetic diamonds are diamonds that are made in the laboratory. Unlike CZ, moissanite, and other diamond imitations, all of which differ from diamond physically and chemically, synthetic diamond *duplicates* the natural. That is, it is scientifically produced in a laboratory and has virtually the same physical and chemical properties. In essence, it is diamond. But it is not identical. Since it is grown in laboratories, it shows distinctive growth features not seen in natural diamonds, so all synthetic diamonds now being produced can be distinguished from natural diamonds. In many cases, however, identification requires sophisticated scientific instrumentation found only in major gem-testing laboratories. For this reason, we once again stress the importance of having laboratory documentation for any fine diamond. *Note:* Electronic diamond testers have become very popular and are very effective in distinguishing diamond imitations, such as CZ, YAG, Fabulite, and others, from diamond. However, they cannot distinguish between synthetic and natural diamonds, and they *will* indicate "diamond" when testing synthetic diamond.

Synthetic gem-quality diamonds are now commercially available in a range of sizes, shapes, and colors. Yellow, red, blue, and pink stones are now being produced in sizes up to two carats and are creating a sensation in the marketplace because they provide very beautiful alternatives to their much rarer, and much costlier, natural counterparts. Where colorless and near-colorless synthetic diamonds are concerned, laboratories have succeeded in producing them, but the production costs are still too high for them to be commercially viable at this time.

## Comparison of Diamonds and Diamond Look-Alikes

| Name of Stone | Hardness (Mohs' Scale 1–10) 1 = Soft, 10 = Hardest | Read-through* | Degree of Dispersion (Fire, Flashes of Color Observed) | Wearability |
|---|---|---|---|---|
| Diamond | 10 (Hardest natural substance in existence) | None, if properly cut | High; lots of fire and liveliness | Excellent |
| Strontium titanate (also known as Fabulite or Wellington Diamond) | 5–6 (Soft) | None, if properly cut | Extremely high; too high (much more than diamond); shows lots of blue flashes | Poor—scratches and wears badly |
| Cubic zirconia (CZ) | 8.5 (Hard) | Slight | Very high; lots of life | Very good |
| Gadolinium gallium garnet (GGG; produced very briefly) | 6.5 (Somewhat soft) | Moderate | High; almost identical to diamond | Fair—scratches easily; wears badly; sunlight causes brownish discoloration |
| Yttrium aluminum garnet (YAG; used extensively) | 8.5 (Hard) | Strong | Very low; almost no visible display of fire | Good |
| Synthetic rutile (shows yellowish color) | 6.5 (Soft) | None | Extremely high; lots of life—but strong yellowish flashes | Poor; scratches easily and shows excessive wear |
| Zircon | 7.5 (Moderately hard) | Moderate | Good; lively | Fair—hard but brittle, so chips easily and shows wear equivalent to much softer stones |
| Synthetic sapphire | 9 (Very hard) | Very strong | Very low; little life or display of color flashes | Very good |
| Synthetic spinel | 8 (Hard) | Very strong | Low; little "life" | Very good |
| Glass | 5–6.5 (Soft) | Very strong | Variable—low to good depending on quality of glass and cut | Poor; susceptible to scratches, chipping, and excessive wear |
| Synthetic moissanite | 9.25 (Very hard) | None | Extremely high; much too high for diamond; higher than CZ | Excellent |

*This technique—the ability and ease with which one can read print while looking through the stone—is reliable only when looking at round, brilliant-cut stones (although it is *sometimes* useful for ovals and some fancy cuts).

# 12 ♦ How to Avoid Fraud and Misrepresentation When Buying Diamonds at Auction

AS YOU HAVE SEEN, THERE ARE MANY WAYS THAT ONE CAN BE MISLED, either unintentionally or deliberately, when buying a diamond at auction. It is especially important to be very cautious, since many factors affect a stone's quality and value that cannot be judged with the naked eye. Again, we can't stress enough that you should personally view the stone before making a purchase to ensure you really like the way it looks, whether or not it has a diamond grading report. You must also take extra precautions to ensure that any representations as to quality are accurate, and to verify that any diamond accompanied by a respected laboratory report actually *matches* the report. When you are considering purchases from online auction vendors on sites such as eBay, this can sometimes be done by special arrangement with the seller before payment. With traditional auction firms, be sure you understand what is "guaranteed" in the capitalized headings, and be sure to ask the house expert to personally examine any diamond you are considering and to personally confirm whatever quality representations have been made. They may not be willing or able to do this, or may "qualify" the representations, but this should influence your decision with regard to the amount you are willing to bid. If you are unable to take such steps, then you must decide whether making this purchase is really worth the risk involved.

We also recommend examining diamonds out of the setting whenever possible in order to precisely grade them, because mountings make it very difficult, if not impossible, to see subtle differences that can dramatically affect cost. At many of the leading auction houses you will now see that important diamonds have been removed from their settings for just this reason: to enable prospective buyers to more accurately examine them. But this is often not the case, and rarely is it done with smaller stones (except for extremely rare fancy-color diamonds), so bid accordingly by establishing a bid that represents the worst-case scenario, and hope for the best case.

For buyers, the key to having a wonderful experience—or making a costly mistake—is understanding as much as possible about diamonds, and how it all works at auction. Most of this information has been covered in the preceding chapters. Now, if you take the time to follow these additional steps and learn about some of the things to look *out* for, you'll be well armed to avoid the pitfalls, enjoy the fun and excitement of the auction, and make a sparkling acquisition!

## Key Steps to Avoiding Fraud or Misrepresentation

- The first step is to buy from a reputable firm with experienced gemologists on staff, or if buying from an online auction site without a physical location where viewing is possible, being able to arrange for viewing and verification of representations before payment. Large, well-established auction houses usually have experts with gemological skills available to answer any questions you have, and often the diamonds they offer are accompanied by diamond grading reports from an internationally respected laboratory. Some smaller firms also have experienced gemologists and offer diamonds accompanied by diamond grading reports.

  Keep in mind that documentation is not always what it appears to be, and many diamonds sold at auction lack documentation. Dealing with a firm that has on-staff gemologists will make it easier for you to get information regarding quality in the absence of documentation, and to confirm the reliability of any documentation accompanying a stone.

- If an auction house has no gemologist on staff, consider retaining an independent gemologist to determine the quality and value of the diamond you are considering or, if there is accompanying documentation, to confirm its reliability.

- Think twice before bidding on diamonds offered by firms or individuals without gemological expertise and without documentation that supports the representations made in the catalogs or by the seller. Keep in mind that when buying from an online auction, you run a higher risk of being a victim of fraud or misrepresentation because of the concealed identity of the seller.

- Before making a purchase, ask yourself whether or not you will be able to find the seller again if what you bought turns out to be other than what was represented. Also bear in mind that when you buy from an auction house or online seller in another country, you may have no recourse, or it may be cost-prohibitive to try to deal with matters related to misrepresentation or fraud.

- When bidding on-line, be sure the vendor is willing to ship the stone to you or to a mutually acceptable third party for the express purpose of having a respected gemologist-appraiser or consultant verify all representations regarding quality *before you make payment.* If the vendor is not willing to agree to this, or to an escrow arrangement, here is our advice: don't buy from this vendor. *Note:* Be sure to keep copies of e-mail correspondence pertaining to any terms and conditions agreed to by you and the seller, especially regarding payment terms and verification. Beware of any vendor who offers to "refund your money if it isn't what it was represented to be." If the vendor has your money, it may be impossible to get it back, and you may end up stuck with something you don't want.

- Ask the right questions. Don't be afraid to ask direct, even pointed questions. The key to getting complete information about what you are buying is to ask good questions so you can be sure you are aware of important factors affecting quality and value. If the seller cannot answer important questions for lack of expertise, or for any other reason, your risk will be much greater. Keep that in mind before you bid. (To help you ask the right questions, we provide a complete list in chapter 24.)

## DIAMONDS REPRESENTED TO BE BETTER THAN THEY ARE—BEWARE OF BARGAINS!

Beware of bargains. Most are not. When a price seems too good to be true, it usually is, unless the seller doesn't know the true value of a piece.

Even the most reputable auction houses have been known to misrepresent diamonds. I remember examining an antique diamond ring that was coming up for auction at a very well-established auction house with an excellent reputation. The overall piece was very beautiful, and at first glance the diamond appeared to be very fine. It was very well cut, for the late nineteenth century, and had fine color, but when I examined it with my loupe, I discovered that it was fracture-filled! This was a surprise, especially given the age of the piece—and there was no question it was an "old" diamond. When I called it to the attention of the department head, I was told that it was "impossible" because the piece had been consigned by an elegant elderly lady from the British aristocracy. Finally, they agreed to submit the diamond to the GIA lab in New York, and the fracture filling was confirmed. How did this happen? Who knows? Maybe the owner's original stone had been switched, or perhaps someone had told her that there was a way to make it "look better" and she didn't realize exactly what had been done to it. But in any event, it was a fracture-filled diamond and would have been sold without disclosure had someone not discovered it and insisted that it be sent to the lab.

During the sale, the auctioneer stated "this diamond may be treated." Note that the auctioneer was not fully forthright; he *knew* the stone was fracture-filled. Since no one bid on the ring, no harm was done.

In general, at auction you need to guard against fraud or misrepresentation in the following areas:

- Color alteration and misgrading
- Flaw concealment and misgrading
- Certification—altered and counterfeit certificates

## Enhancing Color Artificially: High-Tech Treatment with Permanent Results

As discussed earlier, diamond color can be altered in many ways. Auction houses may be unable to detect some of the latest treatments such as the HPHT treatment already discussed, because they don't have the sophisticated scientific equipment necessary to detect such treatments or the trained technicians needed to operate them. Auction houses often rely on descriptions provided by consignors and on the accompanying documentation.

As a seller you should also have your diamond examined for any treatments. You may be unaware that a diamond you either inherited or were given was, in fact, treated. It is best to determine this in advance to avoid trouble later. In addition to HPHT treatment, there are also radiation treatments that produce permanent results.

Exposing off-color diamonds such as yellowish or brownish tinted stones (and also badly flawed stones in which the flaws would be less noticeable against a colored background) to certain types of radiation can result in the production of fancy-color stones. This treatment produces rich yellows, greens, and blues, and it greatly enhances salability because these colors are very desirable. In and of itself, radiation is not fraud; in fact, it may make a "fancy" color diamond affordable to someone otherwise unable to afford one. But again, just be sure that the stone is properly represented, that you know what you are buying, and that you are getting it at the right price—which should be much lower than that of the natural fancy.

## TEMPORARY COLOR ENHANCEMENT

*Touching the culet with ink.* Touching the culet or side of a slightly yellow stone with a coating of purple ink, such as that found in an indelible pencil, neutralizes the yellow, producing a whiter-looking stone. This can be easily detected by washing the stone in alcohol or water.

*Improving the color by using a sputtering technique.* This technique (also called "painting" the diamond) involves sputtering a very thin coating of a special substance over the stone or part of the stone, usually the back, where it will be harder to detect when mounted. The girdle area can also be "painted" with the substance and create the same effect. The substance, like indelible pencil, also neutralizes the yellow and thereby improves the color by as much as seven color grades, but unlike indelible ink, the substance will not wash off. It can be removed in two ways: by rubbing the stone briskly and firmly with a cleanser, or by boiling the stone carefully in sulfuric acid. If the stone is already mounted and is coated on the back, using cleanser is not feasible. The sulfuric acid method is the only way. *But please note:* Using sulfuric acid can be extremely dangerous and must be done only by an experienced person. We cannot overstate the hazards of conducting this test.

This technique is not frequently used, but stones treated in this manner do appear often enough to make it worth mentioning.

*Coating the diamond with chemicals and baking it in a small lab-type oven.* This technique also tends to neutralize some of the yellow, thereby producing a better color grade. This coating will be removed eventually by repeated hot ultrasonic cleanings, which will gradually erode the coating. A more rapid removal can be accomplished by the more dangerous method of boiling in sulfuric acid.

Treated stones must be represented as treated stones and should be priced accordingly. Unfortunately, in their passage through many hands, the fact that they have been treated (radiated or "bombarded") is too often overlooked or forgotten—intentionally or accidentally. Whether the color is natural or treated can often be determined by spectroscopic examination, which can be provided by a gem-testing laboratory (see appendix). Not all gemologists, however, are competent with spectroscopic procedures, and some fancy-color diamonds require examination with very sophisticated equipment not available to most labs. If your gemologist lacks the skill or equipment, stones can be submitted to a laboratory such as the GIA's Gem Trade Laboratory for verification. Most natural fancy-color diamonds sold by jewelers in the United States are accompanied by a GIA report.

## ERRONEOUS COLOR GRADING

Mistakes in grading of color may be unintentional (resulting from insufficient training or experience, or simply from carelessness), or they may be deliberate. You're safer to consider the purchase of a stone that has had such important data as color described in a diamond grading report issued by one of several different laboratories offering this service. Diamonds accompanied by reports usually sell for slightly more per carat, but they provide an element of security for the average consumer as well as credible documentation if you wish to sell this stone at some future time. If the stone you purchase is accompanied by such a report, be sure to verify the information with a qualified gemologist-appraiser or consultant. It may be too late, but you'll know what you really got, what it's really worth, and how much insurance you should buy to protect it.

## CLARITY ENHANCEMENT

Be especially alert to the possibility that clarity may be enhanced. The two most frequently used techniques are lasering inclusions and filling fractures. In both cases, dark inclusions or cracks that might normally be visible—in some cases, very visible—are concealed or become much less noticeable (these techniques are discussed in chapter 9). Be sure to ask whether or not the stone has been lasered or filled. As long as you know, and pay the right price, a clarity-enhanced diamond may be an attractive choice, but you should pay much less: fracture-filled diamonds purchased at auction should cost 50 to 65 percent less than another stone of "comparable" quality; lasered diamonds should cost 15 to 25 percent less.

## CERTIFICATION OF DIAMONDS

If you are considering the purchase of a very fine diamond weighing one carat or more and it is not accompanied by such a report, you are taking a risk because you cannot be sure of the quality. If you want to bid on a diamond without a report, and the auction house has a gemologist to assist you, the gemologist may be able to determine the quality for you, but remember that it is very difficult, often impossible, to grade a diamond properly when it is mounted, so the quality may be higher or lower than the gemologist estimates.

If you are considering bidding on a diamond from a firm or seller with no gemological expertise available, you increase your risk significantly. Bid accordingly.

## Altered and Fraudulent Documentation

Unfortunately, the confidence of the public in stones accompanied by diamond grading reports has given rise to the practice of altering and counterfeiting them.

Online sellers are increasingly using appraisals and gem-testing laboratory reports to instill confidence in buyers. Some bogus appraisals and lab reports have duped unsuspecting buyers into purchasing items that have been misrepresented. We have also seen diamonds accompanied by reports from highly respected labs where the quality of the stone does not match the description on the report. In other words, sometimes a different stone accompanies the report. Here again, on-staff gemologists can help you confirm the document and stone match. If there is no gemologist available, retain an independent consultant…or bid low.

The risk when buying on-line is obvious, even when there is documentation. If you can't confirm the facts before you pay, think twice before bidding.

*Altering certificates.* Sometimes information is changed on an otherwise valid certificate; for example, the flaw or color grade may be altered. If you have any question regarding the information on the certificate, make a phone call to the lab, giving the certificate number and date, to verify the information.

*Counterfeit certification.* Certificates from nonexistent labs are an increasingly common problem. Stones accompanied by fancy "certificates" from impressive-sounding labs that don't exist are appearing more and more frequently. If the certificate is not from one of the recognized labs we list in the appendix, it should be carefully checked. Have reputable jewelers in the area heard of this lab? Has the Better Business Bureau had any complaints? If the lab seems legitimate, call to verify the information on the certificate; if all seems in order, you can probably rest comfortably. Otherwise, you may need to have the facts verified by another gemologist or recognized lab.

*Switching the stone described on a report.* In some cases the report is bona fide but the stone has been switched. To protect both the consumer and the lab, some labs are taking advantage of ingenious techniques to ensure against switching. For example, a service called Gemprint utilizes laser technology to display a diamond's unique pattern of reflection and then records it photographically. The result is an electronic "fingerprint" of the diamond, which can be used for identification purposes. In addition, the GIA and other labs can now actually inscribe the stone's report number directly onto the diamond, along the girdle. It is visible only under magnification, but by using a loupe and examining the girdle, you might find an inscription of the report number. If so, you can be assured that it is the original report.

In the absence of such a mark, a competent gemologist can determine whether the stone and the report match, but there are also clues that you might be able to look for, or ask the on-staff gemologist to check for you. One clue to a switched stone might be provided by comparing the carat weight and dimensions given on the report. If the measurements and weight match exactly, the probability is slim that the stone has been switched, provided the report hasn't been altered. But it's always a good idea to contact the lab to confirm the details of the report, and then double-check all the information. If the measurements don't match, it's possible the diamond was damaged and recut. In this case, the type and placement of inclusions or blemishes may enable you to determine whether the stone in question is the one described on the report. Here again, the house gemologist can help determine this for you.

Unfortunately, if the stone has been mounted, it may be difficult to get precise measurements to compare. In this case, if there is any cause for suspicion, you may be taking a risk to buy the stone unless the seller allows you to have the stone removed from the setting and to have both the report and the stone verified by a qualified gemologist-appraiser or by the laboratory that issued the report.

# 13 ♦ Fancy-Color Diamonds

OF ALL THE GEMS ON EARTH, NOTHING SURPASSES THE PALETTE OF natural-color diamonds for beauty, distinctiveness, desirability, and rarity. Known as *fancy-color diamonds,* they occur in virtually every color and shade of color. Ruby red, baby pink, grass green, and sapphire blue diamonds rank among the rarest and most precious of all gems.

## What Causes the Color Seen in Fancy Diamonds?

When we talk about fancy-color diamonds, we must remember that the color seen can be *natural* or the result of some *treatment* used to transform an off-color diamond into a lovely fancy color.

Natural color in diamonds usually results from the presence of trace elements, although in some cases it can result from natural exposure to radiation (as the diamond was forming in the earth) or from damage to the crystal lattice structure. Natural-color yellow diamonds get their color from the presence of nitrogen, for example, and blue diamonds, from boron or hydrogen. In diamonds whose color is due to particular trace elements, the presence or absence of those trace elements can be ascertained through sophisticated testing procedures, providing an important key to determining whether color is natural or artificial.

With natural-color green diamonds, the color does not result from the presence of trace elements; green diamonds owe their color to exposure to radiation as they were forming in the earth, eons ago. This creates an unusual dilemma for gem-testing laboratories because there are also treated green diamonds that have been created by humans using modern radiation techniques. Since radiation is the cause of color in both cases, it poses some identification challenges for laboratories. In some cases a natural-color green diamond will contain certain unique identifying characteristics that distinguish it from the treated stone, and in some cases a treated green diamond will exhibit characteristics that identify it as treated, but many green diamonds lack conclusive evidence for positive identification. In such cases, a laboratory report will indicate that a positive determination cannot be made with gemological data currently available. This leaves the door open to the possibility that a positive determination might be made at some future time as new data come to light from continued research and technological advances, but there are no guarantees. In any event, if you are considering a natural green diamond, you must understand that it may be more difficult to find one with laboratory documentation confirming that the color is natural.

Fortunately, gem-testing laboratories are usually able to positively confirm origin of color in fancy-color diamonds, and cases where they cannot are the exception rather than the rule. For this reason, and since origin of color has such a significant impact on rarity and cost, we never recommend the purchase of a natural-color diamond without laboratory verification (see appendix), nor would we ever purchase one personally without such documentation.

## JUDGING FANCY-COLOR DIAMONDS

Fancy-color diamonds have always attracted connoisseurs and collectors, but today they are capturing the attention of a much wider audience. Demand—and pricing—are setting new records. If a fancy-color diamond is what you seek, take time to learn as much as you can about the specific colors you like and what is available; some colors occur in a wider range of sizes than others, and some are much rarer.

It is also important to take time to understand the four Cs as they relate to fancy-color diamonds—especially the subtle nuances of color and their impact on value—and to develop an eye for the important differences that affect not only the beauty and desirability of a particular stone but its cost.

Let's begin with the most important factor you must judge: color.

### Color: The Most Important Factor

While the four Cs apply to fancy-color diamonds as well as to colorless diamonds, the emphasis is clearly on color. In general, the rarer the color, the less impact clarity and cutting have on its value; the less rare the color, the more important clarity and cutting become. Many reports on fancy-color diamonds do not even include a clarity grade or information regarding cutting and proportioning except for the stone's shape.

In judging a fancy-color diamond, color is so paramount that it is important to understand how color is graded. You must carefully evaluate each of the following:

- Purity of color
- Depth of color (tone and saturation)
- Color distribution throughout the stone

Whether or not the color is *natural*—the origin of color—is also critically important, as I've already discussed, in the overall evaluation of color and its impact on price.

To properly evaluate the color of a fancy-color diamond, you must view the stone from the face-up position—looking at it with the table up, as you would see it when it is mounted in a piece of jewelry—which is very different from evaluating colorless diamonds (see chapter 8). From the *face-up* position, you must now evaluate each of the following characteristics:

**Purity of color.** This refers to the hue and the purity of the hue. Let's take yellow as an example. The color of a fancy yellow diamond might be described as yellow, orangish yellow, brownish yellow, brown-yellow, and so on. Understanding the differences in the wording is very important. The final word in the color description is the *hue;* the word or words preceding it are the *modifiers* of the hue. If there is no modifier, the color is a pure hue, which, depending upon the color, can be very rare. Some color combinations are rarer and costlier than others. For example, let's consider two diamonds: one orangy yellow and the other brownish yellow. In both cases, the hue is yellow, but since orange is rarer than brown, the orangy yellow stone would be more valuable than the brownish yellow stone.

Now let's look again at the description of the brownish yellow stone. Here the primary color is yellow, with a lesser degree of brown modifying the color. However, if the words were *reversed*—that is, yellowish *brown* rather than brownish *yellow*—the words would tell us the diamond is *brown* with some lesser amount of yellow modifying the color. Again, since brown is a much less rare color, a yellowish brown diamond would have less value than a brownish yellow.

When considering a fancy-color diamond, it is important to take time to understand the terminology used to describe the particular hue that interests you, what shades are available, and how they compare in terms of rarity and value.

***Depth of color.*** This refers to the *saturation* of color combined with the *tone*. *Saturation* refers to the denseness of the color. A pure yellow or pink diamond, for example, has minimal color saturation, while a brown or blue diamond has heavy color saturation. Most fancy-color diamonds occur in less saturated colors such as yellow. With the exception of brown diamonds, heavily saturated colors can be very rare and costly; ruby red and sapphire blue are among the rarest and costliest of all gems.

*Tone* has to do with how much *white* or *black* is present; that is, how "light" or "dark" the color is. If there is too much white, the stone will be too pale or even colorless; if there is too much black, it will be overly dark. Fancy "black" diamonds are popular today. These are typically opaque (that is, not transparent) and heavily included, and they usually sell for much less than other fancy colors. It is important to note that today black diamonds are being used increasingly in designer lines, but most of the stones used are treated to obtain the black color. There are also "white" diamonds that should not be confused with "colorless" stones. Fancy white diamonds are very rare, but they are usually milky or cloudy, which reduces their popularity and value.

Most diamond reports for fancy-color diamonds classify the depth of color using terminology similar to the following:

- Faint
- Very Light
- Light

(these first three categories are not truly "fancy colors")

- Fancy Light
- Fancy (Yellow, Orange, Brown, Blue, or whatever the color)
- Fancy Dark
- Fancy Deep
- Fancy Intense
- Fancy Vivid

The classification pertaining to the depth of color is extremely important. One tonal difference can dramatically affect value. But it is important to understand that *the number of classifications* is *not the same for every color.* Generally speaking, less saturated colors (such as pure yellow or pure pink) have fewer classifications, and more heavily saturated colors (such as blue) will have more classifications. If you are interested in a yellow diamond, for example, and decide you want a color that is richer than Fancy Yellow, the next classification following Fancy Yellow is usually Intense rather than Dark or Deep, although in some rare cases you will find a Deep classification. On the other hand, if you are looking at a diamond described as Fancy *Brownish* Yellow—which has a higher color saturation—you will find more tonal classifications, and it is not unusual to find a Fancy Deep classification that would have more color depth than Fancy but less than Intense. It would also be more expensive than Fancy Brownish Yellow but less expensive than Fancy Intense. In blue diamonds, you can also find a Dark and a Deep classification. And so on. What this really means is that *to accurately evaluate rarity and value, and to be sure you have found the depth of color that best suits your needs, you must be sure to find out what the specific tonal classifications are for the particular color you are considering.*

*Evenness of color.* A laboratory report will indicate under "Distribution" whether or not the color is evenly dispersed. Ideally, the distribution of the color should be even, but this is not always the case. Sometimes color occurs in zones, alternating with colorless zones, and the report will indicate uneven color distribution. Such stones may *appear* to have even color distribution when viewed from the top, and may be lovely and desirable, but they should cost less than one that has even distribution.

*Is the color natural?* In addition to the rainbow of colors in which diamond occurs naturally, diamonds can also be transformed into beautiful, desirable colors by several techniques, as mentioned earlier. Radiation techniques have been used for many years to change tinted, off-white diamonds into various shades of yellow, green, and blue-green. In most cases (green diamonds are often an exception), these can be easily distinguished from the natural by any competent gemologist. But new techniques are creating new challenges, and determining whether or not color is natural may require very sophisticated, high-tech procedures available only at a major gem-testing laboratory.

*HPHT process creates "fancy-color" diamonds.* Earlier we mentioned a new technique known as high-pressure/high-temperature annealing (HPHT) that can be used to transform very off-white and brownish diamonds into colorless and near-colorless diamonds (see chapter 8). HPHT techniques can also transform tinted off-white and brownish diamonds into a variety of "fancy" colors, from yellowish green and greenish yellow to exquisite shades of pink and blue. While the yellowish green and greenish yellow stones often have a distinctive look that sets them apart from most natural diamonds of comparable color, this is not the case with the pink and blue stones, which exhibit a color and other characteristics that make it very difficult to distinguish them from the natural.

Since natural fancy-color diamonds can be costlier than many colorless diamonds—and fancy-color blue and pink diamonds *much* costlier because of their rarity—I recommend that you obtain a laboratory report for any fancy-color diamond represented to have natural color. Most major labs will grade diamonds treated in this manner, indicating the treatment in a special comment on the report (see the sample fancy diamond reports at the end of this chapter).

An extra word of caution regarding pink and blue diamonds: Anyone considering the purchase of a diamond represented to be *natural blue* or *natural pink* must be sure it is accompanied by a *current* report: *a report issued by a major laboratory after December 2000.* If the report was issued between 1995 and 2001, request that the stone be resubmitted to a major lab for verification, or make the sale contingent upon getting this documentation (see appendix). Most laboratories were unaware of the use of HPHT techniques to create blue and pink colors until the year 2000, and diagnostic data with which to detect the treatment were not available until later that year. Since previous testing techniques would not have revealed the treatment, earlier reports may not be accurate.

## Clarity

Many fancy-color diamond reports do not include a clarity grade, especially if the color is exceptional or very rare. When a clarity grade is provided, the grading is based on the same criteria used for colorless diamonds (see chapter 9). It is important to understand that in fancy-color diamonds, flawlessness is even rarer than in colorless diamonds. Fancy-color diamonds are often graded "slightly imperfect" (SI), and "imperfect" (I) grades are also common. In fancy-color stones, SI and I grades do not carry the stigma associated with these grades in colorless diamonds, especially if the stone has a rare or unusually deep color. This is not to say that there are no "flawless" fancy-color diamonds, or stones in the rarer clarity grades, but if the color is rare, and the stone also has a rarer clarity grade, the cost will be disproportionately *much* higher.

As with colorless diamonds, enhancement techniques are being used to improve the appearance by filling fractures and lasering black inclusions so they will no longer be visible. Be sure to take the precautions recommended in chapter 9.

## Cutting and Proportioning

As already mentioned, most reports on fancy-color diamonds lack information pertaining to cutting and proportioning. As with clarity, the deeper and/or rarer the color, the less important the cutting. However, we should mention here that certain shapes are more common among fancy-color diamonds because, in addition to its proportioning, the shape itself and the cutting style (that is, step cut versus brilliant cut) can affect the intensity or evenness of the color.

## Shape Can Affect Intensity and Evenness of Color

If you are interested in a fancy-color diamond, you must allow some flexibility where shape is concerned. Certain shapes are rare and difficult, if not impossible, to find in fancy colors, while other shapes are much more readily available in almost any color. The emerald cut is especially difficult to find, and even round stones may be difficult to find in a particular color. The radiant cut, however, is frequently found.

Today's modern radiant and princess cuts have become especially popular for fancy-color diamonds, because the shape, proportioning, and facet arrangement result in *intensifying the color*. On the other hand, it is extremely rare to find a fancy-color diamond in an emerald cut, because the color won't look as intense. In fact, when emerald-cut diamonds with fancy colors are found in old jewelry, many diamond cutters immediately recut them into one of the new cuts, such as the radiant or princess, to intensify the color so they can obtain a report with a rarer color grade. I searched for an emerald-cut diamond with an Intense Yellow color for a client and it took many months to find just three stones, because Intense Yellow emerald-cut diamonds, recut and resubmitted to a laboratory, often receive a *Vivid* grade, the rarest and costliest of yellow diamonds.

The result is that emerald-cut diamonds in fancy colors are becoming ever more difficult to find. One of the most beautiful diamonds I ever saw was a square emerald-cut diamond, with a report that graded the color Vivid Yellow. Imagine an emerald cut with a Vivid grade, and the intensity of color! The stone's personality was truly regal, and I would certainly never want to see this stone recut because I appreciate its rarity—not just because its color is Vivid but because it is a Vivid emerald cut.

Some shapes are not desirable in a fancy-color diamond because they may cause the color to appear uneven. This is often the case when a fancy-color diamond is cut into a pear shape or a marquise shape, because these shapes usually exhibit a bow tie effect across the center of the stone—an effect created by light leakage—which usually causes the color to appear lighter across the area of the bow tie. Sometimes the difference is slight; sometimes it is pronounced. Such stones should sell for less; the more visible the color difference, the more impact on cost.

To help you become more familiar with fancy-color diamond reports and the types of documentation that you might encounter, the next few pages provide sample reports from some of the world's most respected laboratories. Price guides for fancy-color diamonds sold at auction are in chapter 14.

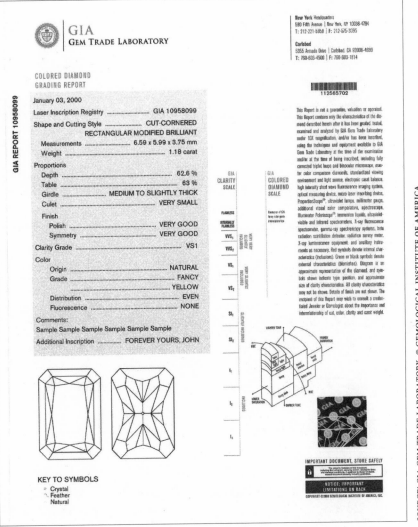

Here you will find information indicating origin of color ("natural"), depth of color ("fancy"), and distribution ("even"), along with other essential information describing the overall quality. Pay attention to what is included under "Comments"; this is where you would find reference to HPHT treatment, for example. Here you see that a laser inscription has been noted. GIA will also issue reports pertaining to color only.

SCHWEIZERISCHES GEMMOLOGISCHES INSTITUT
INSTITUT SUISSE DE GEMMOLOGIE
SWISS GEMMOLOGICAL INSTITUTE

**SSEF**

Gemstone Report
Expertise de pierre précieuse    No. 35888
Edelstein-Expertise

| | |
|---|---|
| Weight / Poids / Gewicht | 2.046 ct |
| Cut / Taille / Schliff | octagonal, step cut |
| Measurements / Dimensions / Masse | 7.71 x 7.54 x 4.91 mm |
| Colour / Couleur / Farbe | purplish red (fancy intense colour) |
| **IDENTIFICATION / IDENTIFIKATION** | D I A M O N D of natural coloration |
| Comments / Commentaires / Bemerkungen | The analysed properties confirm the authenticity of its coloration. |

Important note

The conclusions on this Gemstone Report reflect our findings at the time it is issued. A gemstone could be modified and / or enhanced at any time. Therefore, the SSEF may reconfirm at any time that a stone is in line with the Gemstone Report.

See other comments on reverse side.

Note importante

Les conclusions de cette expertise reflètent nos résultats au moment de son émission. A tout moment, une pierre précieuse, peut être modifiée et / ou son aspect amélioré. Par conséquent, le SSEF peut à tout moment contrôler la conformité entre la pierre et le certificat.

Voir autres commentaires au dos.

Wichtige Anmerkung

Die Befunde in dieser Edelstein - Expertise beschreiben den Zustand zum Zeitpunkt ihrer Erstellung. Ein Edelstein kann jederzeit verändert und / oder behandelt werden. Deshalb kann die SSEF die Übereinstimmung des Steins mit dem Zertifikat jederzeit nachprüfen.

Beachten Sie die Bemerkungen auf der Rückseite.

SCHWEIZERISCHES GEMMOLOGISCHES INSTITUT    SSEF
INSTITUT SUISSE DE GEMMOLOGIE
SWISS GEMMOLOGICAL INSTITUTE

Basel, 17 July 2000 ss

Dr. L. Kiefert, FGA            Prof. Dr. H.A. Hänni, FGA

magnification 2.0x

Falknerstrasse 9   CH-4001 Basel   Tel. + 41 (0)61 262 06 40    Fax + 41 (0)61 262 06 41

© Copyright by SSEF Swiss Gemmological Institute

This report provides essential information related to the color—depth ("Fancy Intense") and origin ("natural")—but there is no information about fluorescence. There is also no information about clarity or cut. The lab provides more detailed reports, but the owner of this stone requested information pertaining to its color only.

### The Gem Testing Laboratory
### of Great Britain

1242555

SAMPLE

## GEM TESTING REPORT

Examined a loose, yellow, oval, faceted stone, measuring approximately 16.30 x 12.15 x 7.85 mm. and weighing 10.20 ct.

Found to be a **NATURAL DIAMOND** of **NATURAL COLOUR.**

**COLOUR GRADE : FANCY INTENSE YELLOW**

The Gem Testing Laboratory of Great Britain is the official CIBJO recognised Laboratory for Great Britain

Only the original report with signatures and embossed stamp is a valid identification document.
This report is issued subject to the conditions printed overleaf.

### The Gem Testing Laboratory of Great Britain

GAGTL, 27 Greville Street,
London, ECIN 8SU, Great Britain

Telephone: +44 171 405 3351
Fax: +44 171 831 9479

SAMPLE

Signed_____      Signed_____

Sarah Mahoney FGA DGA                Stephen J. Kennedy FGA DGA

Date_____21st May 2001_____

This report provides information about color only, but note that information pertaining to the absence or presence of fluorescence (also called *luminescence*) is not provided. Reports including clarity and cutting are also available upon request.

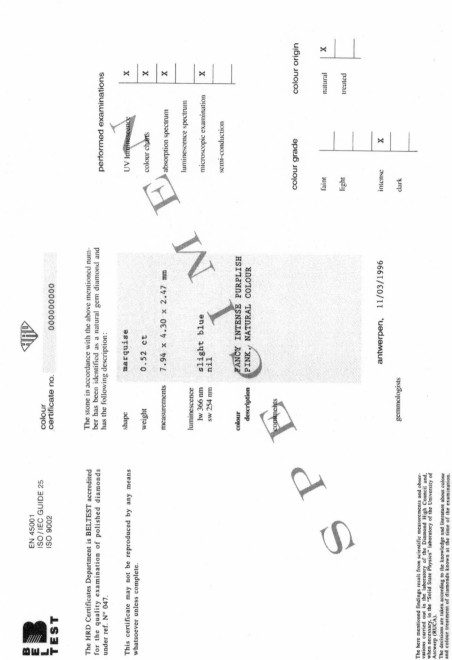

BELTEST

EN 45001
ISO / IEC GUIDE 25
ISO 9002

The HRD Certificates Department is BELTEST accredited for the quality examination of polished diamonds under ref. N° 047.

This certificate may not be reproduced by any means whatsoever unless complete.

colour
certificate no.     000000000

The stone in accordance with the above mentioned number has been identified as a natural gem diamond and has the following description:

shape               marquise

weight              0.52 ct

measurements        7.94 x 4.30 x 2.47 mm

luminescence
lw 366 nm           slight blue
sw 254 nm           nil

colour
description         FANCY INTENSE PURPLISH
                    PINK, NATURAL COLOUR

comments

                    antwerpen,  11/03/1996

gemmologists

performed examinations

UV luminescency            X
colour charts              X
absorption spectrum        X
luminescence spectrum
microscopic examination    X
semi-conduction

colour grade        colour origin

faint                   natural    X
light                   treated

intense    X
dark

The here mentioned findings result from scientific measurements and observations carried out in the laboratory of the Diamond High Council and, when necessary, in the "Solid State Physics" laboratory of the University of Antwerp (RUCA).
The decisions are taken according to the knowledge and literature about colour and colour treatment of diamonds known at the time of the examination.

This report was issued to confirm color only—purity, depth, and origin—without information on clarity or cutting. However, information on fluorescence (luminescence) *is* provided. Overall quality reports are also available.

# FANCY-COLOR DIAMONDS OFFER
## A RAINBOW OF CHOICES

Diamonds occur naturally in every color. Light brown and cognac shades are very affordable, while green, blue, and red diamonds are among the rarest gems on earth. The fancy-color diamond "peacock" and floral brooch attest to the palette of colors in which diamonds occur.

*Right:* Two natural **blue** diamond drops (0.95 and 1.05 carats) in diamond necklace, sold for $135,000 (Joseph DuMouchelle, Grosse Pointe, MI)

Fancy **deep blue** briolette-cut diamond (10.48 carats), sold for $2,700,000 (Phillips, Geneva)

Fancy **red** radiant-cut diamond (1.92 carats), sold for $1,500,000 (Phillips, New York)

Vivid yellow diamond ring (6.31 carats) by J.E. Caldwell & Company, circa 1940, sold for $232,250 (Weschler's, Washington, D.C.)

Fancy **intense yellow** emerald-cut diamond ring (30.14 carats), sold for $260,000 (Butterfields, San Francisco)

Vivid yellow emerald-cut diamond (11.52 carats). Estimate: $1,000,000 to $1,500,000 (Sotheby's, Geneva)

# Popular Diamond Shapes…Classic

Heart

Marquise

Round Brilliant

Pear

Oval

Emerald Cut

# ...And a Wide Variety of Jewelry, Old & New

Gold, pink tourmaline, and tsavorite ring, sold for $700 (sothebys.com)

Diamond and gold heart pendant, sold for $50 (ice.com)

Gold, green chalcedony, and coral pendant/brooch by Van Cleef & Arpels, sold for $2,600 (sothebys.com)

Modern peridot, diamond, and enamel brooch and earrings, sold for $5,060 (Weschler's, Washington, D.C.)

French enamel and gold locket and necklace, circa 1880, sold for $8,500 (Butterfields, San Francisco)

Platinum, aquamarine, and diamond brooch by Cartier, circa 1950, sold for $3,400 (sothebys.com)

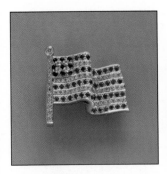

18K white gold, diamond, and colored stone flag brooch, sold for $715 (Sotheby's Arcade, New York)

Tomasino Saulini carved cameo, yellow gold, and enamel bracelet, circa 1850, sold for $8,050 (Joseph DuMouchelle, Grosse Pointe, MI)

Antique 14K gold-framed shell cameo depicting a dragon slaying, with an opening bid* of $500 (dickeranddicker.com)

# A WARM PALETTE OF RED AND PINK GEMSTONES

Red gems occur in a wide range of hues and tones to please every taste and budget.

Rubellite
(Red Tourmaline)

Morganite

Kunzite

Tourmaline

Rhodolite
Garnet

Topaz

Topaz

Ruby

Sapphire

Morganite

Red Beryl
(Red "Emerald")

Spinel

Rare red beryl, also referred to as red "emerald"—

*Right:* The crystal as it occurs in nature

*Far right:* A brilliantly cut and polished gem waiting to be set

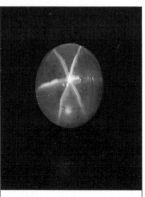

A six-rayed star ruby

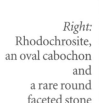

*Right:*
Rhodochrosite,
an oval cabochon
and
a rare round
faceted stone

# GREEN GEMS THAT EVERYONE WILL ENVY

Tsavorite Garnet

If green is your color, choices abound from pastel yellow-green to rich grass green.

Peridot

Tourmaline

Tourmaline

Emerald

Sapphire

Chrome Tourmaline

Tanzanite

Demantoid Garnet

Zircon

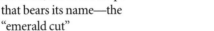

Emerald, cut in the shape that bears its name—the "emerald cut"

Paraiba Tourmaline

Fine Art Deco period brooch
with very fine green jadeite centerpiece

Laboratory-grown synthetics offer convincing and affordable alternatives to fine, rare natural gems. *Above*, laboratory-grown ruby, emerald, and sapphire

# CLASSIC SHAPES & CUTTING STYLES FOR COLORED GEMS

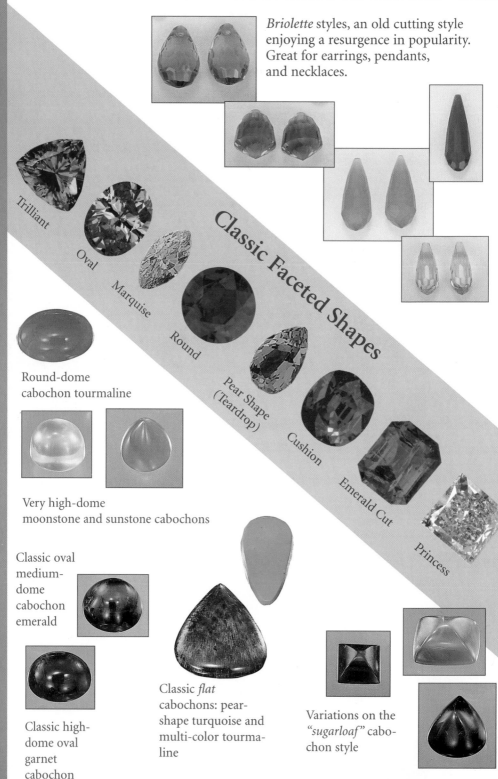

*Briolette* styles, an old cutting style enjoying a resurgence in popularity. Great for earrings, pendants, and necklaces.

Classic Faceted Shapes

Trilliant

Oval

Marquise

Round

Pear Shape (Teardrop)

Cushion

Emerald Cut

Princess

Round-dome cabochon tourmaline

Very high-dome moonstone and sunstone cabochons

Classic oval medium-dome cabochon emerald

Classic high-dome oval garnet cabochon

Classic *flat* cabochons: pear-shape turquoise and multi-color tourmaline

Variations on the *"sugarloaf"* cabochon style

# 14 ◆ Understanding Diamond Prices and What to Bid

ALL TOO OFTEN, PEOPLE LOOK FOR EASY ANSWERS TO COMPLEX PROB-
lems. Many would like to have a simple list of diamond grades and corresponding prices, by size, that one would expect to pay at auction. Unfortunately, this
is not possible because of the many variables that affect the auction market:
the economy, who is bidding, documentation accompanying the stone, attrac-
tiveness of the mounting, and so on. Also, as you have seen in the preceding
chapters, significant differences in price often result from subtle differences in
diamond quality that are not readily discernible to any but the professional.
Therefore, it is not possible to provide a simple answer to this complex question.

But this doesn't mean we can't provide some general guidelines that can
help you understand the *relative* effects of each of the four primary factors
used to determine the quality and corresponding value of a diamond, and
what you might expect to pay for a particular size and quality at auction. Some
of the charts at the end of this chapter provide a guide to diamond prices at
*retail*, and other charts provide a sampling of prices brought at auction. Once
you have calculated the retail value of a diamond in a particular size and quality, you can work backwards to determine what you might want to bid at auction, factoring in the potential risk along with the value of possibly retaining
a consultant to work with you to reduce the risks. Needless to say, when buying a diamond at auction, you want to pay less than what you would expect
to pay at a retail jewelry store. Generally speaking, once you've calculated the
retail value, divide that amount by 50 percent. This will serve as a good benchmark for deciding what the top end of your bid should be. If you succeed in
acquiring the stone at that price, or even a little more, you will have acquired
the diamond at a very good price. If you succeed in getting it for less, you
will have gotten an excellent buy (assuming, of course, that the quality assess-
ment is accurate)!

The rarity of a diamond in a particular quality or size may influence you to pay somewhat more than 50 percent of the retail value indicated in the following charts. Or, perhaps the beauty and workmanship in a distinctive antique setting make the piece especially desirable and worth more. Diamonds in less rare qualities and sizes, and stones readily available in the wholesale diamond market, may sell for as little as 25 percent of the retail value, but there are no hard and fast rules. We have also seen people bidding prices at auction that are much higher than the full retail value! Don't be lulled into thinking that whatever price you pay at auction is a good deal. This is not always the case.

When you buy diamonds that are set in a beautiful period setting or display exceptional old-world craftsmanship, the price often reflects more than just the intrinsic value of the diamonds, and the prices can often be staggering to someone who isn't knowledgeable about how much "jewelry" or "antique" value is added by a particular period or master jeweler. Also, if the stone is accompanied by a respected lab report, it is likely to encourage individuals or couples who are not diamond experts to feel more comfortable bidding and thus drive up the price to some degree. Conversely, a fine-quality diamond *without* a lab report may offer an especially good deal, but such stones also present a much higher risk unless you are working with a knowledgeable consultant.

The retail price guides are not hard price lists of what you should be paying in a jewelry store. Instead, they should be used as a guideline—a foundation on which you can place more current information that reflects the variations in a constantly fluctuating market. Keep in mind that the retail prices are for unmounted stones. Fine settings, one-of-a-kind pieces, and rare period settings can add substantially to the price.

Note that the prices given in the first three charts are for round brilliant-cut diamonds with good proportioning; stones with excellent or ideal proportioning will sell for more, while stones with poor proportioning can sell for *much* less. Diamonds having fancy shapes—shapes other than round—normally sell for 5 to 15 percent less. However, if a particular shape is in great demand, the price can be higher than for round stones. Antique and period cuts, such as the Asscher cut or cushion cut, are especially popular and enthusiastically sought in the auction arena; when well cut for their period, old cuts may sell for more than new cuts because of their distinctive personalities and their rarity in today's market.

Finally, before relying too heavily on the prices listed in this chapter, be sure you understand how to read and interpret *all* the information on any diamond grading report that accompanies a diamond you are considering, and make sure it is issued by a respected laboratory (see appendix). Such reports tell you what the quality of a diamond is, but they can also mislead you unless you know how to read and interpret the data. Be sure to ask the auction house expert to explain anything you don't understand and to advise you as to whether or not it has a positive or negative effect on the value of the diamond you are considering.

Keep in mind that laboratory reports accompanying diamonds sold at auction may be old; if so, they may not be reliable. Remember that diamonds can be damaged. A hard blow, for example, can cause a nick or crack that might result in a lower clarity grade. Repair of a damaged diamond may result in a stone that has been recut and weighs less than indicated on the original report. So it is especially important to ask whether or not the auction house or seller has double-checked to confirm that the report matches the diamond. If the auction house does not have an expert on staff, or if they are unable to confirm the facts on the report, be wary. Be especially wary when buying from an online auction service. Just having a lab report is not a guarantee! If you can't confirm the reliability of an accompanying report, the risk is very high that the diamond may not be the quality indicated.

If you succeed in acquiring a diamond at auction, be sure to have the facts verified by a qualified gemologist-appraiser. Should the diamond not be as represented, and if you have followed the advice above, many established auction houses, despite their limited responsibility, are willing to cancel the transaction and refund your money. You should also factor this possibility into your choice of an auction firm. It is also a good reason to select a gemologist-appraiser with recognized credentials (see appendix).

# Retail Price Guide for Round Brilliant-Cut Diamonds*

Notice both the tremendous price fluctuation among stones of the same size due to differences in the flaw grades and color grades, and the disproportionate jumps in cost *per carat*, depending upon size.

lightface indicates $\dfrac{\text{PRICE PER CARAT}}{\text{PRICE PER STONE}}$ in U.S. dollars
boldface indicates

## 1 Carat

COLOR GRADE

FLAW (CLARITY) GRADE

| | | D | E | F | G | H | I | J | K |
|---|---|---|---|---|---|---|---|---|---|
| | IF | 28,000 | 19,200 | 17,200 | 13,800 | 12,200 | 10,600 | 9,200 | 8,200 |
| | | **28,000** | **19,200** | **17,200** | **13,800** | **12,200** | **10,600** | **9,200** | **8,200** |
| | VVS₁ | 19,200 | 17,200 | 14,800 | 13,000 | 11,600 | 10,000 | 9,000 | 7,800 |
| | | **19,200** | **17,200** | **14,800** | **13,000** | **11,600** | **10,000** | **9,000** | **7,800** |
| | VVS₂ | 17,000 | 14,200 | 13,000 | 12,200 | 11,200 | 9,600 | 8,800 | 7,600 |
| | | **17,000** | **14,200** | **13,000** | **12,200** | **11,200** | **9,600** | **8,800** | **7,600** |
| | VS₁ | 14,200 | 13,600 | 12,800 | 11,800 | 11,000 | 9,200 | 8,400 | 7,400 |
| | | **14,200** | **13,600** | **12,800** | **11,800** | **11,000** | **9,200** | **8,400** | **7,400** |
| | VS₂ | 12,800 | 12,200 | 12,000 | 11,200 | 10,400 | 8,800 | 7,800 | 7,000 |
| | | **12,800** | **12,200** | **12,000** | **11,200** | **10,400** | **8,800** | **7,800** | **7,000** |
| | SI₁ | 11,400 | 10,800 | 10,600 | 10,000 | 9,400 | 8,200 | 7,400 | 6,400 |
| | | **11,400** | **10,800** | **10,600** | **10,000** | **9,400** | **8,200** | **7,400** | **6,400** |
| | SI₂ | 10,200 | 9,800 | 9,400 | 8,800 | 8,200 | 7,200 | 6,600 | 6,200 |
| | | **10,200** | **9,800** | **9,400** | **8,800** | **8,200** | **7,200** | **6,600** | **6,200** |
| | I₁ | 6,800 | 6,400 | 6,200 | 6,000 | 5,800 | 5,400 | 5,175 | 4,725 |
| | | **6,800** | **6,400** | **6,200** | **6,000** | **5,800** | **5,400** | **5,175** | **4,725** |

## 2 Carat

COLOR GRADE

FLAW (CLARITY) GRADE

| | | D | E | F | G | H | I | J | K |
|---|---|---|---|---|---|---|---|---|---|
| | IF | 44,400 | 33,400 | 29,200 | 23,200 | 20,200 | 15,400 | 13,000 | 11,000 |
| | | **88,800** | **66,800** | **58,400** | **46,400** | **40,400** | **30,800** | **26,000** | **22,000** |
| | VVS₁ | 32,800 | 29,200 | 23,600 | 21,200 | 17,600 | 14,800 | 12,600 | 10,400 |
| | | **65,600** | **58,400** | **47,200** | **42,400** | **35,200** | **29,600** | **25,200** | **20,800** |
| | VVS₂ | 29,200 | 24,000 | 21,600 | 19,200 | 16,400 | 14,200 | 12,200 | 10,000 |
| | | **58,400** | **48,000** | **43,200** | **38,400** | **32,800** | **28,400** | **24,400** | **20,000** |
| | VS₁ | 24,600 | 22,000 | 19,400 | 18,400 | 15,800 | 14,000 | 11,400 | 9,400 |
| | | **49,200** | **44,000** | **38,800** | **36,800** | **31,600** | **28,000** | **22,800** | **18,800** |
| | VS₂ | 19,200 | 19,000 | 18,000 | 17,400 | 14,600 | 13,000 | 10,400 | 8,800 |
| | | **38,400** | **38,000** | **36,000** | **34,800** | **29,200** | **26,000** | **20,800** | **17,600** |
| | SI₁ | 16,600 | 16,200 | 15,400 | 14,800 | 13,400 | 11,800 | 9,600 | 8,200 |
| | | **33,200** | **32,400** | **30,800** | **29,600** | **26,800** | **23,600** | **19,200** | **16,400** |
| | SI₂ | 13,200 | 13,000 | 12,800 | 12,000 | 11,000 | 9,400 | 8,600 | 7,400 |
| | | **26,400** | **26,000** | **25,600** | **24,000** | **22,000** | **18,800** | **17,200** | **14,800** |
| | I₁ | 7,800 | 7,400 | 7,200 | 7,000 | 6,800 | 6,600 | 6,200 | 6,000 |
| | | **15,600** | **14,800** | **14,400** | **14,000** | **13,600** | **13,200** | **12,400** | **12,000** |

* Prices compiled from *The Guide*, Gemworld International, Inc., and adjusted to retail.

## 3 Carat — COLOR GRADE

| FLAW (CLARITY) GRADE | | D | E | F | G | H | I | J | K |
|---|---|---|---|---|---|---|---|---|---|
| | IF | 67,600 | 47,800 | 40,800 | 31,400 | 25,000 | 19,800 | 15,400 | 14,000 |
| | | 202,800 | 143,400 | 122,400 | 94,200 | 75,000 | 59,400 | 46,200 | 42,000 |
| | VVS$_1$ | 48,000 | 41,000 | 31,800 | 25,800 | 22,400 | 17,800 | 14,600 | 13,400 |
| | | 144,000 | 123,000 | 95,400 | 77,400 | 67,200 | 53,400 | 43,800 | 40,200 |
| | VVS$_2$ | 41,400 | 31,800 | 26,600 | 23,200 | 20,600 | 17,000 | 14,000 | 12,400 |
| | | 124,200 | 95,400 | 79,800 | 69,600 | 61,800 | 51,000 | 42,000 | 37,200 |
| | VS$_1$ | 32,200 | 26,800 | 23,600 | 22,200 | 19,000 | 15,600 | 12,800 | 11,600 |
| | | 96,600 | 80,400 | 70,800 | 66,600 | 57,000 | 46,800 | 38,400 | 34,800 |
| | VS$_2$ | 26,400 | 23,800 | 22,400 | 19,800 | 17,000 | 13,800 | 11,600 | 10,400 |
| | | 79,200 | 71,400 | 67,200 | 59,400 | 51,000 | 41,400 | 34,800 | 31,200 |
| | SI$_1$ | 21,200 | 20,200 | 18,800 | 17,000 | 14,200 | 12,400 | 10,800 | 9,600 |
| | | 63,600 | 60,600 | 56,400 | 51,000 | 42,600 | 37,200 | 32,400 | 28,800 |
| | SI$_2$ | 16,200 | 15,200 | 14,200 | 13,400 | 12,600 | 11,200 | 9,800 | 8,400 |
| | | 48,600 | 45,600 | 42,600 | 40,200 | 37,800 | 33,600 | 29,400 | 25,200 |
| | I$_1$ | 11,800 | 11,000 | 10,200 | 9,600 | 9,000 | 8,000 | 7,600 | 6,800 |
| | | 35,400 | 33,000 | 30,600 | 28,800 | 27,000 | 24,000 | 22,800 | 20,400 |

\* Prices compiled from *The Guide*, Gemworld International, Inc., and adjusted to retail.

## RETAIL PRICE GUIDE FOR OLD-EUROPEAN CUT DIAMONDS*

Prices are per carat in U.S. dollars

| Color | ½ Carat | 1 Carat | 2–3 Carat |
|---|---|---|---|
| Color D–F | | | |
| VVS–VS | 6,500–7,500 | 9,200–13,000 | 14,600–26,000 |
| SI | 4,875 | 7,000–9,600 | 12,400–13,200 |
| I$_1$ | 3,250 | 5,000 | 5,600–7,000 |
| Color G–H | | | |
| VVS–VS | 5,500–6,450 | 7,200–10,000 | 11,200–14,000 |
| SI | 4,625 | 6,400–8,800 | 10,000–11,000 |
| I$_1$ | 2,875 | 5,500–6,000 | 6,300–7,500 |
| Color I | | | |
| VVS–VS | 4,375 | 6,800 | 9,000–11,000 |
| SI | 3,690 | 6,000 | 8,000–8,800 |
| I$_1$ | 2,375 | 5,000 | 7,000–7,250 |
| Color J–K | | | |
| VVS–VS | 3,975 | 6,200–7,250 | 8,000–9,600 |
| SI | 3,250 | 6,250 | 6,400–7,200 |
| I$_1$ | 2,125 | 4,625 | 6,000–7,000 |
| Color L–M | | | |
| VVS–VS | 3,250 | 6,250 | 6,400–7,200 |
| SI | 2,500 | 5,500 | 6,250–7,000 |
| I$_1$ | 1,875 | 4,000 | 4,500–5,500 |

*Retail prices are based on information provided by Michael Goldstein Ltd.

## Retail Price Guide for Rose-Cut Diamonds*
Prices are per carat in U.S. dollars

| Size | Carat | Color | Per Carat |
|------|-------|-------|-----------|
| 3–4 mm | 0.15–0.20 | H–J,VS–SI | 1,375–1,625 |
| | | K–M,VS–SI | 1,200–1,500 |
| 5 mm | 0.45 | H–J,VS–SI | 2,000–2,500 |
| | | K–M,VS–SI | 1,750–2,250 |
| 6 mm | 0.75 | H–J,VS–SI | 2,500–3,375 |
| | | K–M,VS–SI | 1,750–2,000 |

*Retail prices are based on information provided by Michael Goldstein Ltd.

## Retail Price Guide for Briolette-Cut Diamonds*
Prices are for bright goods, VS to SI clarity, and are per carat in U.S. dollars

| Weight | Brown | Cognac | K–M | H–I |
|--------|-------|--------|-----|-----|
| ½ carat | 375–600 | 750–1,050 | 1,375–1,750 | 2,440–2,750 |
| ¾ carat | 600–750 | 1,050–1,350 | 1,875–2,250 | 3,000–3,500 |
| 1 carat | 1,050 | 1,250–1,500 | 2,440–3,000 | 3,750–4,500 |

*Retail prices are based on information provided by Michael Goldstein Ltd.

## A Sampling of Diamonds Sold at Auction

| Size | Color | Clarity | Shape | House | $/Carat | Total $ |
|------|-------|---------|-------|-------|---------|---------|
| 2.04 | H | VS$_1$ | Round | Christie's | 5,645 | 11,516 |
| 2.99 | F | VS$_2$ | Round | Christie's | 7,467 | 22,326 |
| 3.02 | D | IF | Oval | Christie's | 19,065 | 57,576 |
| 3.09 | D | SI$_2$ | Oval | Christie's | 8,746 | 27,025 |
| 3.13 | G | SI$_1$ | Heart | Christie's | 6,356 | 19,894 |
| 4.02 | H | SI$_1$ | Round | Christie's | 5,553 | 22,323 |
| 4.60 | D | SI$_1$ | Round | Sotheby's | 13,288 | 61,125 |
| 7.67 | F | VS$_2$ | Pear | Christie's | 18,709 | 143,498 |
| 9.01 | H | SI$_1$ | Pear | Christie's | 11,043 | 99,497 |
| 10.03 | H | VS$_2$ | Oval | Sotheby's | 10,394 | 104,252 |
| 14.23 | I | VS$_2$ | Emerald | Sotheby's | 6,922 | 98,500 |
| 21.21 | D | IF | Oval | Christie's | 44,366 | 941,003 |
| 30.56 | I | SI$_1$ | Emerald | Sotheby's | 8,647 | 264,252 |
| 74.79 | D | IF | Pear | Christie's | 57,441 | 4,296,012 |

# Retail Price Guide for Fancy-Color Diamonds*

Prices are per carat in U.S. dollars

### C5–C7 FANCY LIGHT BROWN TO FANCY BROWN

| Wt. | FL–VVS | VS | SI | I₂ |
|---|---|---|---|---|
| Melee | NA | 600–1,200 | 525–900 | 450–750 |
| ¼ ct | NA | 750–1,650 | 675–1,500 | 600–975 |
| ½ ct | NA | 900–3,000 | 750–2,500 | 600–1,750 |
| ¾ ct | NA | 1,250–3,750 | 900–3,000 | 750–2,000 |
| 1 ct | NA | 1,500–4,500 | 1,250–4,250 | 900–2,500 |
| 2 ct | NA | 2,000–6,250 | 1,750–5,000 | 1,250–3,000 |
| 3 ct | NA | 3,000–7,000 | 2,500–6,250 | 1,750–4,750 |
| 4 ct | NA | 3,750–7,500 | 3,250–7,000 | 3,000–5,500 |
| 5 ct | NA | 7,500–9,000 | 6,250–8,000 | 3,750–7,500 |

### FANCY YELLOW

| Wt. | FL–VVS | VS | SI | I₂ |
|---|---|---|---|---|
| Melee | 1,050–2,250 | 900–2,000 | 750–1,875 | 600–1,625 |
| ¼ ct | 2,000–4,500 | 1,750–4,000 | 1,500–3,750 | 1,350–3,000 |
| ½ ct | 5,250–6,500 | 5,000–6,000 | 4,250–5,000 | 3,750–4,250 |
| ¾ ct | 6,000–7,000 | 5,750–6,500 | 5,000–6,250 | 4,250–5,000 |
| 1 ct | 7,200–7,600 | 6,800–7,200 | 6,400–7,000 | 5,600–6,000 |
| 2 ct | 12,000–12,600 | 10,400–12,000 | 10,000–11,600 | 8,000–9,000 |
| 3 ct | 13,000–14,000 | 12,000–13,000 | 10,000–12,000 | 9,200–9,800 |
| 4 ct | 14,000–16,000 | 13,000–15,000 | 12,000–13,000 | 10,000–11,000 |
| 5 ct | 16,000–18,000 | 15,000–17,000 | 13,000–15,000 | 11,000–13,000 |

### FANCY INTENSE YELLOW

| Wt. | FL–VVS | VS | SI | I₂ |
|---|---|---|---|---|
| Melee | NA | NA | NA | NA |
| ¼ ct | NA | NA | NA | NA |
| ½ ct | 6,800–7,400 | 6,400–7,000 | 6,000–6,800 | 3,500–5,500 |
| ¾ ct | 9,000–11,000 | 8,000–10,000 | 6,600–8,000 | 6,000–7,000 |
| 1 ct | 11,400–15,400 | 11,000–15,000 | 10,000–13,600 | 8,000–10,000 |
| 2 ct | 16,000–17,800 | 15,600–17,600 | 13,600–15,200 | 10,000–12,400 |
| 3 ct | 18,000–19,000 | 17,000–18,000 | 16,000–17,000 | 11,000–13,000 |
| 4 ct | 19,000–23,000 | 18,000–22,000 | 17,000–20,000 | 12,000–14,000 |
| 5 ct | 23,000–26,000 | 22,000–26,000 | 20,000–24,000 | 13,000–15,000 |

* Retail prices are based on *The Guide*, Gemworld International, Inc.

## FANCY LIGHT PINK

| Wt. | FL–VVS | VS | SI | I$_2$ |
|---|---|---|---|---|
| Melee | 2,250–3,250 | 2,000–3,000 | 1,750–2,500 | 1,625–2,375 |
| ¼ ct | 7,500–8,000 | 7,000–7,200 | 6,250–6,600 | 5,500–6,000 |
| ½ ct | 13,000–17,000 | 11,000–16,000 | 10,000–12,000 | 5,000–8,000 |
| ¾ ct | 30,000–34,000 | 24,000–30,000 | 18,000–24,000 | 12,000–16,000 |
| 1 ct | 36,000–42,000 | 32,000–40,000 | 30,000–36,000 | 22,000–26,000 |
| 2 ct | 72,000–90,000 | 70,000–86,000 | 60,000–80,000 | 40,000–50,000 |
| 3 ct | 110,000–150,000 | 100,000–140,000 | 90,000–130,000 | 60,000–70,000 |
| 4 ct | 160,000–220,000 | 150,000–200,000 | 120,000–140,000 | 100,000–110,000 |
| 5 ct | 240,000–260,000 | 200,000–220,000 | 160,000–200,000 | 120,000–160,000 |

## FANCY PINK

| Wt. | FL–VVS | VS | SI | I$_2$ |
|---|---|---|---|---|
| Melee | NA | NA | NA | NA |
| ¼ ct | 30,000–60,000 | 24,000–50,000 | 22,000–44,000 | 10,000–20,000 |
| ½ ct | 70,000–100,000 | 60,000–90,000 | 40,000–90,000 | 20,000–30,000 |
| ¾ ct | 80,000–110,000 | 70,000–120,000 | 50,000–80,000 | 30,000–40,000 |
| 1 ct | 120,000–160,000 | 100,000–140,000 | 80,000–140,000 | 50,000–70,000 |
| 2 ct | 200,000–270,000 | 150,000–200,000 | 120,000–180,000 | 60,000–80,000 |
| 3 ct | 300,000–500,000 | 250,000–400,000 | 180,000–260,000 | 150,000–200,000 |
| 4 ct | 350,000–500,000 | 350,000–450,000 | 250,000–300,000 | 170,000–220,000 |
| 5 ct | 500,000–700,000 | 400,000–600,000 | 300,000–600,000 | 300,000–450,000 |

## FANCY BLUE

| Wt. | FL–VVS | VS | SI | I$_2$ |
|---|---|---|---|---|
| Melee | NA | NA | NA | NA |
| ¼ ct | NA | NA | NA | NA |
| ½ ct | 120,000–130,000 | 80,000–120,000 | 60,000–80,000 | 40,000–50,000 |
| ¾ ct | 140,000–160,000 | 100,000–150,000 | 80,000–100,000 | 60,000–70,000 |
| 1 ct | 240,000–280,000 | 200,000–240,000 | 170,000–200,000 | 140,000–180,000 |
| 2 ct | 350,000–450,000 | 300,000–400,000 | 250,000–350,000 | 100,000–150,000 |
| 3 ct | 500,000–750,000 | 450,000–700,000 | 400,000–550,000 | 250,000–350,000 |
| 4 ct | 600,000–800,000 | 550,000–750,000 | 450,000–600,000 | 300,000–400,000 |
| 5 ct | 800,000–1,100,000 | 750,000–1,050,000 | 600,000–800,000 | 400,000–500,000 |

*Retail prices are based on *The Guide,* Gemworld International, Inc.

# A Sampling of Fancy-Color Diamonds Sold at Auction

| Color | Size | Clarity | Shape | House | $/Carat | Total $ |
|---|---|---|---|---|---|---|
| Yellow | 2.45 | VS$_1$ | Square | Sotheby's | 5,051 | 12,375 |
| Yellow | 2.48 | VS$_1$ | Square | Sotheby's | 5,051 | 12,526 |
| Yellow | 10.06 | VS$_2$ | Round | Christie's | 5,256 | 52,875 |
| Yellow | 3.54 | VS$_2$ | Marquise | Christie's | 6,306 | 22,323 |
| Intense yellow | 1.93 | SI$_1$ | Rectangular | Christie's | 7,915 | 15,276 |
| Intense yellow | 4.63 | SI$_2$ | Oval | Christie's | 9,644 | 44,652 |
| Intense yellow | 16.43 | VVS$_2$ | Square | Christie's | 10,408 | 171,003 |
| Intense yellow | 7.22 | VS$_1$ | Rectangular | Sotheby's | 10,457 | 75,500 |
| Deep grayish greenish yellow | 3.88 |  | Emerald | Sotheby's | 10,567 | 41,000 |
| Vivid orangy yellow | 5.47 |  | Cushion | Sotheby's | 18,439 | 100,861 |
| Vivid orangy yellow | 5.58 |  | Cushion | Sotheby's | 18,439 | 102,890 |
| Light green | 6.20 | VS$_1$ | Old-mine | Christie's | 18,710 | 116,002 |
| Brownish orangy pink | 9.51 | VVS$_2$ | Oval | Christie's | 23,764 | 225,996 |
| Vivid yellow-orange | 3.56 | SI$_1$ | Rectangular | Christie's | 32,584 | 115,999 |
| Vivid yellow | 4.18 | IF | Rectangular | Christie's | 64,593 | 269,999 |
| Intense green-blue | 0.93 |  | Pear | Christie's | 101,075 | 94,000 |
| Deep blue | 5.02 | IF | Marquise | Christie's | 176,494 | 886,000 |
| Purplish red | 0.41 |  | Round | Christie's | 229,268 | 94,000 |
| Fancy red | 1.92 | VS$_2$ | Rectangular | Phillips | 781,250 | 1,500,000 |

# PART 4 ◆

# COLORED GEMSTONES AND PEARLS

---

# 15 ♦ The Allure of Colored Gemstones

TODAY YOU CAN FIND MANY STONES IN A PARTICULAR COLOR AND gemstones in every color of the rainbow. If red is your color, in addition to ruby you can choose from red spinel, red tourmaline, red garnet, and even red "emerald" (technically, emerald is the *green* member of the beryl mineral family, but red beryl is even rarer than the green variety and is mined in only one place in the world: Utah). If green is your color, in addition to emerald you can find emerald green garnet, known as *tsavorite,* and fiery yellowish green garnet, known as *demantoid,* along with green sapphires, peridot, and green tourmaline in every shade of green imaginable. If you prefer blue, in addition to sapphire you have blue spinel, iolite, blue topaz, tanzanite, and blue tourmalines in a range of shades. There are also many more gemstones in distinctive and unusual colors, such as lilac-colored kunzite, fiery orange Mandarin garnet, purple sapphires and spinels, golden beryl, and tourmaline in dusty rose or peach or the remarkable rare *Paraiba* variety, whose beautiful "neon" shades of blue and green are considered by many to be the most exciting gemological discovery of the century in terms of color.

The color revolution that has taken place in retail jewelry stores has also hit the auction house. Today we find rare gems in every color, along with gems that change color depending on the light in which they are viewed—such as the rare alexandrite, which appears green in outdoor or fluorescent light and raspberry red indoors, in incandescent light—and "phenomenal" stones (those that exhibit an unusual optical effect) such as star sapphire and cat's-eye chrysoberyl. One of my favorite auction acquisitions was a pair of earrings, each of which contained a large cabochon cat's-eye aquamarine. It is difficult to find beautiful, bright aquamarine cabochons at all, but a pair with a strong "eye" effect, perfectly centered in each stone, was a real delight.

## AUCTIONS: A PRIMARY SOURCE FOR BUYING AND SELLING RARE AND UNUSUAL GEMSTONES

Colored gemstones have always captivated people, and this is no less true today. They are in high demand among collectors, connoisseurs, and jewelry lovers, especially rare and untreated varieties. But many of nature's most spectacular gemstones have all but disappeared from the traditional jewelry marketplace. The legendary Kashmir sapphire, for example, has become very rare because the mines that produced it have been closed for almost three-quarters of a century. In the case of Burmese ruby, ruby is still mined in Burma, but *fine-quality* material is scarce, and very little has been mined for many years. Finally, unstable political situations have made it difficult to mine and distribute certain gemstones.

The scarcity of exceptionally beautiful, top-quality gemstones in the commercial marketplace has brought dealers to the auction arena for many years, seeking a rare beauty among the old jewels they find there. And as more and more consumers are becoming aware that there are really *two* colored gemstone categories—natural and treated—we are finding more and more connoisseurs at auctions, seeking these rare gems and bidding more aggressively for them. So whether one is buying or selling, the auction venue has moved to center stage as the primary source.

Those seeking sapphires now turn to major auction firms in search of the rare, mysterious Burmese and velvety blue Kashmir varieties, with certificates confirming that they have not been treated in any way (see chapter 16). Among ruby lovers, major auction firms have become an important source of natural rubies from Burma and elsewhere. When it comes to emeralds, today there is intense competition for stones free of any clarity or color enhancement, and several extremely rare "red emeralds" have come to the auction block in recent years.

For those looking for rare gems in large sizes, few retailers can offer what you can find at major auction houses. The finest-quality natural sapphires in sizes over fifteen carats, along with top-quality natural rubies and emeralds in sizes over five carats, can still be found at major auction houses fairly frequently. We've seen fifteen-carat alexandrites of the finest quality at major auctions, when it is rare to find one over three carats in the wholesale marketplace. And for people who love unusual colors, auctions often offer gemstones in exotic colors not typically found in the neighborhood jewelry store.

Today, consumers turn to the auction arena to buy gems and jewelry because it has become increasingly difficult to find what they want at the traditional jewelry store. People who are interested in selling important gemstones or jewelry are turning to the auction arena in order to reach a wider audience of collectors and connoisseurs—a worldwide audience—in the hope of getting the highest possible price. And the auction houses have recognized how much interest there is in colored gemstones and have expanded their focus to include a wider range of rare and unusual gemstones than ever before. So it is a wonderful time to explore the auction arena in your search for colored gemstones.

Before you purchase any colored gemstone, however, it is important to understand as much as possible about the alternatives available today. The following chapters will help you understand everything you need to know about colored gemstones so you can make a wise choice and avoid costly mistakes.

# 16 ◆ JUDGING QUALITY IN COLORED GEMSTONES

WHAT IS THE DEFINITION OF A GEM? NO ONE HAS COME UP WITH A universally accepted definition, but most agree that a gemstone is a mineral (or in some cases, an organic material) that possesses unusual *beauty, durability*, and *rarity*. We would add one more factor: it must have cachet. That is, it must possess mystery, mystique, glamour—those things that bring it into the world of our dreams and make us yearn to possess it.

While somewhat subjective, and not without some exceptions, the first three criteria are always at the heart of how we classify stones and determine whether or not they are gems. The first, and perhaps the most important, is beauty. If it isn't beautiful, why would anyone want to possess it? But beauty alone is not enough. A gem must also be sufficiently durable to withstand the normal wear and tear of use, to stand the test of time. This is at the heart of why gemstones figure so prominently as heirlooms; they are durable. Their durability is the key to a gem's ability to retain its beauty and allure, to be passed on from generation to generation. Finally, we must consider the rarity factor, the most important in terms of valuation. Generally speaking, the rarer the gem, the more costly, and vice versa.

Here is an example that might put these factors into a more relevant scenario. Several years ago I came across several "gemstones"—emeralds, rubies, and sapphires—that had been consigned to an auction house for sale to the highest bidder. Each stone was encased in a small folder, accompanied by a "laboratory certificate" that basically identified the stone as genuine. I watched in disbelief as each stone was sold for anywhere from $50 to $300; not one of them was worth more than $5 (including the cost of the packaging)!

I couldn't believe anyone would be interested in bidding anything at all for these stones because they were, above all, terribly unattractive. The bidders, however, assumed that since they were "precious gems," they were valuable. One man said that he bought them for resale because, as he explained,

"How could I go wrong buying a three-carat emerald for $100?" He expected to sell it for several thousand dollars. He, and others like him, quickly found out how wrong they were. What they bought were not "gems" but common, low-quality stones worth nothing, and for which no one would pay a lot of money. I suggested they might want to use them to add color to the gravel in their driveway.

Let's look at why these emeralds, rubies, and sapphires were not "gems." While all of the stones were genuine, they were not "*gem*stones" because they failed to meet any of the three criteria above. First, they were not beautiful: they did not possess lovely colors, had no sparkle or liveliness, and lacked any allure whatsoever (in fact, they were plain ugly). In terms of durability, these stones had so many flaws and cracks they probably would have broken if anyone tried to set them into a piece of jewelry (and if they had survived being set, they would not have survived the first week of wear). And finally, in terms of rarity, stones of such poor quality are not rare at all but are carried away from mine sites in garbage trucks. Such low-quality emeralds, rubies, and sapphires are common; they can be found all over the world in inexhaustible quantities. There is no demand for such material, and it has no value.

Beauty, durability, and rarity are directly related to differences in *quality*. Had the quality been much finer, the stones would have been more beautiful and more durable. In addition, as quality improves, rarity increases. Rarer stones are more valuable, so the cost would have been greater. This is usually the case, especially with gemstones that have immediate recognition. But today, with newly discovered gemstones, we cannot understand the value-added factor as it relates to rarity without understanding the "fourth" factor: *cachet*.

Let's look at one of the recently discovered gemstones, tsavorite. Tsavorite is a member of the garnet family, and the finest-quality tsavorites possess a rich, deep emerald green color. It was discovered in Tsavo National Park in Kenya and introduced to the jewelry trade in the 1970s. Let's compare it with another green gem, emerald. In terms of beauty, tsavorite is more brilliant and equally beautiful (some think it even surpasses the beauty of emerald). It is also more durable, and fine-quality stones over two carats are even rarer than emerald. In terms of value, however, it costs about one tenth what emerald costs. If beauty, durability, and rarity are the only factors to consider, why isn't tsavorite more valuable than emerald? The answer is found in the fourth factor: it lacks cachet. In other words, people don't dream about owning one—at least, not yet. It is a gem's cachet that will ultimately affect demand, and this, combined with its rarity, is what will ultimately determine its value.

Tsavorite has a very brief history to date: less than thirty years. Other newcomers, such as red beryl (also known as red "emerald") and fiery orange Mandarin garnet, have even briefer histories. Many people have not yet even heard of them, and fewer still have seen them. All of this affects supply and demand. Currently, the supply of these gems is able to meet current demand. But as we move into the twenty-first century, and universal awareness and appreciation for these wonderful rare beauties increases, so will demand. And who knows—as people become more knowledgeable about the wide range of gemstone choices available, supply and demand ratios may go topsy-turvy, along with the prevailing hierarchy. Tsavorite may well become the "emerald" of the twenty-first century, red spinel the "ruby" of the twenty-first century, and Paraiba tourmaline may exceed prices paid for fine sapphires. In fact, *now* may be an ideal time to search for these gemstones, and if you can get them at auction prices and hold on to them for a few years, you may reap lucrative rewards.

But whatever choices you make, the key to selecting a true *gemstone,* one that will give you lasting beauty and value, lies in an understanding of, and appreciation for, quality differences.

## THE FOUR CS OF COLORED GEMS

We've already discussed the four Cs to consider in choosing a diamond (see chapter 6), but colored gems have four Cs of their own: color, color, color, and color! This statement may sound like an exaggeration, but not so much as you might think. Generally speaking, the finer and rarer the color, the less impact cutting, clarity, and carat weight have on the value of the gem. On the other hand, the more common the color, the more impact these other factors have.

When we discuss color, we are not talking simply about hue. Color science and the evaluation of color constitute a very complex area. But if you understand the various elements that must be factored into the evaluation of color, you can begin to look at colored gems in a totally different light.

Color is affected by many variables that make it difficult to evaluate precisely. Perhaps the most significant factor is light; the type of light and its intensity can affect color dramatically. In addition, color can be very subjective in terms of what is considered pleasing and desirable. Nonetheless, there has been extensive research and development in the field of color science, and experts are working to develop a viable color grading system. For the time being, however, a great degree of subjectivity reigns where colored gems are concerned, and no system has yet replaced the age-old eye-and-brain combination, coupled with years of experience with colored stones.

## THE KEY ELEMENTS IN DESCRIBING COLOR

The color we see in gems is always some combination of the pure spectral colors—which range from pure red to pure violet—coupled with varying degrees of brown, white, black, and gray. It is these latter colors, in combination with the spectral colors, that affect the tone of the color seen and that make the classification of color so difficult. For example, if white is present with red, you will have a lighter tone or shade of red; if black is present, a darker tone or shade. Depending on the degree of gray, white, black, or brown, an almost infinite number of color combinations can result.

As a general rule, the closer a stone's color is to the pure spectral hue, the better the color is considered to be; the closer it comes to a pure hue, the rarer and more valuable it is. For example, if we are considering a green stone, the purer the green, the better the color. In other words, the closer it comes to being a pure spectral green, having no undertone (tint) of any other color such as blue or yellow, the better the color. There is no such thing as a perfectly pure color in nature, however; color is always modified by an undertone of another hue. But these undertones can create very beautiful, unusual, distinctive colors that are often very desirable.

In describing color we will often refer to these factors:

- *Hue*—the precise spectral color (red, orange, yellow, green, blue, violet, indigo)
- *Intensity* (or saturation)—the brightness or vividness (or dullness or drabness) of the color
- *Tone*—how much black, white, gray, or brown is present (how light or dark the stone is)
- *Distribution*—the even (or uneven) distribution of the color

## VIEW COLORED GEMSTONES IN DIFFERENT TYPES OF LIGHT

The color of a stone can be drastically affected by the kind of light and the environment in which the examination is being conducted; that is, variables as disparate as the color of the wallpaper or the tint of a shirt can alter a stone's appearance. If examined under a fluorescent light, a ruby may not show its fullest red because most fluorescent lights are weak in red rays; this causes the red in the ruby to be diminished and to appear more as a purple-red. The same ruby examined in sunlight or incandescent light (an ordinary electric lightbulb), neither of which is weak in red rays, will appear a truer, fuller red. Because the color of a ruby is dependent on the "color temperature," or type of light used, it will always look best in warm light. A ruby looks even redder if examined against a piece of orange-yellow paper. For this reason, loose rubies are often shown in little envelopes, called parcel papers, that have a yellow-orange inner paper liner to show the red color to the fullest.

Blue sapphire, another intensely colored gem, comes in numerous tones of blue, from light to very dark—some so dark that they look black in incandescent (warm) light. Most sapphires, however, look bluest in fluorescent light, or daylight. Many contain some degree of green. The more green, the lower the price. Some even exhibit a color change; we've seen blue sapphires that were a magnificent blue in daylight turn to an amethyst purple in incandescent light. Some, like the stones from the Umba Valley in Tanzania, turn slightly lavender over time. The lighter blues are generally referred to as Ceylon-colored sapphire; the finest and most expensive blue sapphires generally come from Burma (now called Myanmar) and Kashmir and exhibit a rich, true blue in all kinds of light. Those from Kashmir exhibit a more subdued, soft, velvety look by comparison with Burmese or Ceylon-type sapphires.

An environment that is beneficial to your stone can also be created by the setting in which the stone is mounted. For example, an emerald-cut emerald mounted in a normal four-prong setting will not appear to have as deep a color as it will if mounted in a special box-type setting that completely encloses the stone so that light is prevented from entering its sides.

Be sure to view any colored gem you are considering in several different types of light.

## A WORD ABOUT COLOR DISTRIBUTION, OR ZONING

Even though zoning doesn't really describe color and is sometimes evaluated as part of the clarity grade, we think it should be discussed as part of color evaluation.

In some stones, the color isn't always evenly distributed but exists in zones, and sometimes the pattern created by alternating zones of color and colorlessness resembles stripes. Zoning is frequently observed in amethyst, ruby, and sapphire. *These zones are most easily seen if you look through the side of the stone and move it slowly while tilting and rotating it.*

Sometimes a stone in the rough is colorless, or nearly so, but has a spot or layer of color. If the cutter cuts the stone so that the culet is in the color spot, the whole stone will appear that color. If there is a layer and the cutter cuts the stone so that the layer lies in a plane nearly parallel to the table, the whole stone will look completely colored. Evenness of color and complete saturation of color are very important in determining the value of colored gems.

Even though you may not notice the zones themselves when looking at the stone from the top, a heavily zoned stone will lack the color vibrancy of another stone without such zoning. Normally, if the zoning isn't noticeable from the top, value is not dramatically reduced, but a stone with even color will appear more vivid from the

Zones of color
in a stone

top—the face-up position, as seen when mounted—and will cost more. And, depending upon the hue and tone, possibly much more.

## A WORD ABOUT COLOR-CHANGE STONES

Some stones exhibit a very strange phenomenon when viewed in different types of light: they change color completely. These stones are called color-change gems. There are color-change spinels, color-change sapphires, color-change garnets, and so on. In these gem families, however, the color-change phenomenon is rare. The gem alexandrite, on the other hand, always exhibits a color change, and its value is based largely on the degree of change. There are even color-change synthetics, such as the inexpensive synthetic color-change sapphire that is often misrepresented and sold as genuine alexandrite. Alexandrite is a bluish green gem in daylight or under daylight-type fluorescent light, and a deep red or purple-red under incandescent light.

Fine alexandrites over two carats are very difficult to find in most jewelry stores, but fine alexandrites in large sizes—even ten carats and above—are frequently seen at important gem and jewelry auctions, at very attractive prices. But one must take precautions against inadvertently buying a synthetic. Be sure to read more about alexandrite in chapter 19.

## FLUORESCENCE—HOW DOES IT AFFECT COLORED GEMSTONES?

As we discussed in chapter 8, fluorescence is a property that some gemstones have that causes the stone to show a distinct color when exposed to ultraviolet rays produced by an ultraviolet lamp. The color seen when viewed under ultraviolet light can be a more intense shade of the stone's normal body color, or an altogether different color. If you have ever visited a museum and seen common, drab-colored rocks suddenly light up in psychedelic colors when the room is darkened and the "black light" (a type of ultraviolet light) is turned on, then you have seen this phenomenon known as fluorescence. These minerals appear to be a certain color when seen in normal light, but they reveal altogether different colors under pure ultraviolet wavelengths (produced by an ultraviolet lamp). A gemstone's reaction to ultraviolet radiation can be an important key to identifying gemstones and detecting treated stones.

### Fluorescence Can Affect the Color Seen in Different Lighting Environments

Perhaps most important, fluorescence can affect the color we see—and a stone's color *trueness*—in all types of lighting. This is the case with Burmese ruby, for example. One characteristic that makes ruby of Burmese origin so desirable is its fluorescence. Thai rubies and Burma rubies will both show a nice red color in incandescent light (a warm light in which any red stone looks great), but a Thai ruby will look much *less* red than the Burma ruby when seen in daylight. This is because the Burma ruby *fluoresces* red under all ultraviolet wavelengths, and thus, when exposed to the ultraviolet radiation present in daylight, the fluorescent reaction will be stimulated, triggering a strong red body color.

With colored gemstones, it is essential to check the color the stone appears in different types of lighting.

# CLARITY

As with diamonds, clarity refers to the absence of internal flaws (inclusions) or external blemishes. Flawlessness in colored stones is perhaps even rarer than in diamonds. However, while clarity is important, and the cleaner the stone the better, flawlessness in colored stones does not usually carry the premium that it does with diamonds. Light, pastel-colored stones will require better clarity because the flaws are more readily visible in these stones; in darker-toned stones, the flaws may not be as important a variable because they are masked by the depth of color.

The type and placement of flaws is a more important consideration in colored stones than the presence of flaws in and of themselves. For example, a large crack (feather) that is very close to the surface of a stone—especially on the top—might be dangerous because it weakens the stone's durability. It may also break the light continuity, and it may show an iridescent effect as well. Iridescence usually means that a fracture or feather breaks through the surface somewhere on the stone. Such a flaw would detract from the stone's beauty and certainly reduce its value. But if the fracture is small and is positioned in an unobtrusive part of the stone, it will have a minimal effect on durability, beauty, and value. Some flaws actually help a gemologist or jeweler identify a stone, since certain types of flaws are characteristic of specific gems and specific localities. In some cases, a particular flaw may provide positive identification of the exact variety or origin and actually cause an increase in the per-carat value. (For more information on the types of inclusions found in colored gems, we recommend *Gem Identification Made Easy*.) However, a very fine colored gem that really is flawless will probably bring a disproportionately much higher price per carat because it is so rare. Flawless rubies, sapphires, emeralds, and so on should always be viewed with suspicion because they are so rare and their genuineness should be verified by a gem-testing lab. The newer synthetic gems are often flawless and are easy to confuse with genuine natural gems.

If the flaws weaken the stone's durability, affect color, are easily noticeable, or are too numerous, they will significantly reduce price. Otherwise, they may not adversely affect price. In some cases, if they provide positive identification and proof of origin, they may actually increase the cost rather than reduce it, as with Burmese rubies and Colombian emeralds.

Again, it is important to shop around, become familiar with the stone you wish to purchase, and train your eye to discern what is "normal" so you can decide what is acceptable or objectionable.

## CUT

Colored gems can be either *faceted* or cut in a nonfaceted syle called *cabochon*. Generally speaking, the preference in the United States until recently was for faceted gems, so the finest material was usually faceted. However, this was not always the case in other eras and other countries. In Roman times, for example, it was considered vulgar to wear a faceted stone. Preference also varies with different cultures and religions, and the world's finest gems are cut in both styles. Don't draw any conclusions about quality based solely on style of cut.

**Cabochon** is a facetless style of cutting that produces smooth rather than faceted surfaces. These cuts can be almost any shape. Some are round with high domes; others look like squarish domes (the popular sugarloaf cabochon); others are buff-topped, showing a somewhat flattened top.

Many people around the world prefer the quieter, often more mysterious personality of the cabochon. Some connoisseurs believe that cabochons produce a richer color. Whatever the case, today we are seeing much more interest in and appreciation for cabochons, and more beautiful cabochons than have been seen in the market in many years.

Sugarloaf cabochon (left) and traditional faceted gem (right)

**Faceted** is a style of cutting that consists of giving to the stone many small faces at varying angles to one another, as in various diamond cuts. The placement, angle, and shape of the faces, or facets, are carefully planned and executed to show the stone's inherent beauty—fire, color, brilliance—to fullest advantage. Today there are many new faceted styles, including "fantasy" cuts, which combine rounded surfaces with sculpted backs.

## The Importance of Cut

As stated earlier, cutting and proportioning in colored stones are important for two main reasons:

1. They affect the depth of color seen in the stone.
2. They affect the liveliness projected by the stone.

Color and cutting are the most important criteria in determining the beauty of a colored stone. After that, carat weight must be factored in; the higher carat weight will usually increase the price per carat, generally in a non-linear proportion (for more on weight, see chapter 5). If a colored stone was of a good-quality material to begin with, a good cut will enhance its natural beauty to the fullest and allow it to exhibit its finest color and liveliness. If the same material is cut poorly, its natural beauty will be lessened, causing it to look dark, too light, or even "dead."

Therefore, when you examine a colored stone that looks lively to your eye and has good color—not too dark and not too pale—you can assume the cut is reasonably good. If the stone's color is poor, or if it lacks liveliness, you must examine it for proper cut. If it has been cut properly, you can assume the basic material was poor. If the cut is poor, however, the material may be very good and can perhaps be recut into a beautiful gem. In this case you may want to confer with a knowledgeable cutter to see whether it is worthwhile to recut, considering cutting costs and loss in weight. If you don't know any cutters, the auction house, a gemologist-appraiser, or a local lapidary club may be able to recommend one.

## Evaluating the Cut of a Colored Gem

When you are examining the stone for proper cut, a few considerations should guide you:

*Is the shade pleasing, and does the stone have life and brilliance?* If the answer is yes to both questions, then the basic material is probably good, and you must make a decision based on your own personal preferences and budget.

*Is the color too light or too dark?* If so, and if the cut looks good, the basic uncut material was probably too light or too dark to begin with. Consider purchase only if you find the stone pleasing, and only if the price is right, i.e., significantly lower than stones of better color.

*Is the stone's brilliance even, or are there dead spots or flat areas?* Often the brilliance in a colored gemstone is not uniform. If the color is exceptional, subdued brilliance may not have a dramatic effect on its allure, desirability, or value. However, the less fine the color, the more important brilliance becomes.

## COLORED GEMSTONE CERTIFICATES

Systems for grading colored gemstones have not yet been established world-wide. As a result, certificates or grading reports for colored gemstones vary widely in the information provided. Reports for colored stones have a more limited value in some respects than diamond reports, which are widely relied on to describe and confirm diamond quality using precise, universally accepted standards, but they are still *very important.*

Today's synthetics, newly discovered gemstone materials, and increased use of treatments have created a need for laboratory reports that verify identity (the type of gem), genuineness (whether or not it is synthetic), and, if the stone has been treated, the method and *degree* of treatment. The most widely recognized reports for colored gemstones include those issued in the United States by the American Gemological Laboratories (AGL), Gemological Institute of America (GIA) Gem Trade Laboratory, and the American Gem Trade Association (AGTA) Gemological Testing Center; in Switzerland, leading firms are Laboratory Gübelin and Swiss Gemmological Institute (SSEF); in the United Kingdom, the Gemmological Association and Gem Testing Laboratory of Great Britain.

For any expensive colored gemstone today, especially if the gem is of unusual size or exceptional quality and rarity, laboratory reports should be obtained. Major auction houses are encouraging consignors to obtain them, and today they frequently accompany important gems and jewelry sold at auction. This is not always the case, for a variety of reasons, but the absence of such a report should raise a red flag and signal the need for extra precaution. And keep in mind that unless the gem has been described as natural by the auction house, in the capitalized headings in its catalog, you should assume it is treated, even if it is not. If you acquire a gemstone without documentation, you should get a laboratory report to confirm what you have; if the stone was treated, it is important to know how it was treated, whether the treatment is permanent or needs any special care, and the extent of the treatment (minimal, moderate, extensive, and so on). And you may discover that the gem was *not* treated—that you got lucky and obtained a natural gem that slipped through the cracks!

If you are planning to *sell* a fine colored gemstone, getting a laboratory report from a respected laboratory is essential if you want to obtain the highest possible price.

At the least, colored gemstone reports should identify the gemstone, verify whether it is natural or synthetic, and indicate whether the stone's color and clarity are natural or enhanced. If enhanced, the method and degree—that is, faint, moderate, heavy, and so on—should also be indicated. You can also request a *grading* report, which will provide, in addition to identity, a full description of the stone and a rating of the color, clarity, brilliance, and other important characteristics. This information is essential to understanding the stone's quality and is also invaluable for insurance.

Also, depending on the information the gemologist can obtain from the gemstone during examination, some laboratories will indicate country of origin, if requested. The AGL, the AGTA Lab, SSEF, and Laboratory Gübelin will indicate origin where possible; GIA will not indicate country of origin.

Fees for colored gemstone reports vary depending on the type of gem; the type of report requested; and the time, skill, and gemological equipment necessary to perform conclusive tests. An estimate can usually be provided by a telephone call to the laboratory.

When you are considering a colored gemstone that is accompanied by a report, keep in mind the different types of reports available. Also keep in mind that the information provided on the report is only as reliable as the gemologist performing the evaluation, so be sure the report is issued by a respected laboratory; if in doubt, check with one of the labs listed in the appendix to see if it is familiar with the laboratory in question. Next, ask yourself what the report really tells you—does it confirm identity and genuineness only? If so, remember that quality differences determine value—a genuine one-carat ruby, sapphire, or emerald can sell for $10 or $10,000 or more, depending on the quality of the particular stone. Being genuine doesn't mean a stone is valuable.

Treatment disclosure is essential. Whether or not a gem has been treated and, if so, the degree of treatment affect value and durability as well as appearance. Remember, auction firms are not obligated to reveal whether a stone has been treated or enhanced in the fine print description. It is up to the buyer to verify this. Furthermore, it is important to know whether or not the treatment is permanent and whether it necessitates special care. Take time to look at many stones, ask questions, and make comparisons. In this way you can develop a good eye and an understanding of the differences that affect quality rating, beauty, and value.

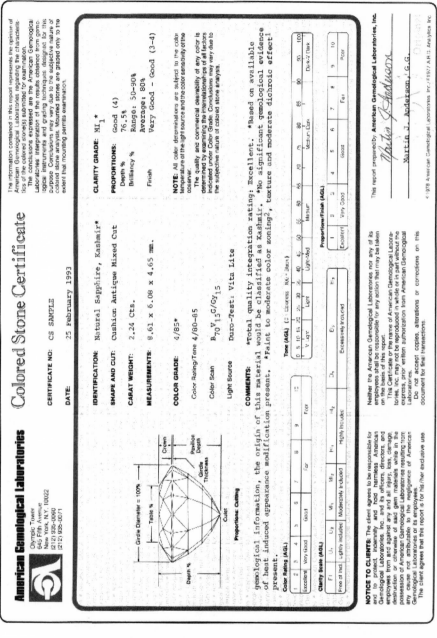

# American Gemological Laboratories

Olympic Tower
645 Fifth Avenue
New York, N.Y. 10022
(212) 935-0060
(212) 935-0671

## Colored Stone Certificate

**CERTIFICATE NO:** CS SAMPLE

**DATE:** 25 February 1993

**IDENTIFICATION:** Natural Sapphire, Kashmir*

**SHAPE AND CUT:** Cushion Antique Mixed Cut

**CARAT WEIGHT:** 2.24 Cts.

**MEASUREMENTS:** 9.61 x 6.08 x 4.65 mm.

**COLOR GRADE:** 4/85*

Color Rating/Tone 4/80-85

Color Scan $B_{70} V_{15} G/Gy_{15}$

Light Source Duro-Test: Vita Lite

**COMMENTS:** *Total quality integration rating: Excellent. *Based on available gemological information, the origin of this material would be classified as Kashmir. *No significant gemological evidence of heat induced appearance modification present. *Faint to moderate color zoning[2], texture and moderate dichroic effect[1] present.

The information contained in this report represents the opinion of American Gemological Laboratories regarding the characteristics of the colored stone(s) submitted for examination.
The conclusions expressed are the American Gemological Laboratories interpretation of the results obtained from gemological instruments and grading techniques designed for this purpose. Conclusions may vary due to the subjective nature of colored stone analysis. Mounted stones are graded only to the extent that mounting permits examination.

**CLARITY GRADE:** $MI_1$ *

**PROPORTIONS:**
Depth % Good (4)
Brilliancy % 76.5%
Range: 50-90%
Average: 80%
Finish Very Good - Good (3-4)

**NOTE:** All color determinations are subject to the color temperature of the light source and the color sensitivity of the observer.
The quality and commercial desirability of any color is determined by examining the interrelationships of all factors indicated under Color Grade. Conclusions may vary due to the subjective nature of colored stone analysis.

### Color Rating (AGL)

| 1 | 2 | 3 | 4 | 5 | 6 | 7 | 8 | 9 | 10 |
|---|---|---|---|---|---|---|---|---|---|
| Excellent | Very Good | Good | | Fair | | | | Poor | |

### Clarity Scale (AGL)

| FI | I1 | I2 | I3 | SI1 | SI2 | I1 | I2 | I3 | |
|---|---|---|---|---|---|---|---|---|---|
| Free of Incl. | Lightly Included | Moderately Included | | | | Heavily Included | | Poor | |

**Tone (AGL)** (G = Colorless  No = Black)

| 0 | 5 | 10 | 15 | 20 | 25 | 30 | 35 | 40 | 45 | 50 | 55 | 60 | 65 | 70 | 75 | 80 | 85 | 90 | 95 | 100 |
|---|---|---|---|---|---|---|---|---|---|---|---|---|---|---|---|---|---|---|---|---|
| | $C_1$ | | $V_{lgt}$ | | Light | | | Light-Med | | Medium | | | Medium-Dark | | | | | | Dark-Very Dark | |

| $C_1$ | | $D_1$ | $E_1$ | | $F_1$ | | $H_1$ | $P_1$ | | $I_1$ |
|---|---|---|---|---|---|---|---|---|---|---|
| Poor | | Fair | Good | | Very Good | | Good | Fair | | Poor |
| | | | Excessively Included | | | | Highly Included | | | |

### Proportions/Finish (AGL)

| 1 | 2 | 3 | 4 | 5 | 6 | 7 | 8 | 9 | 10 |
|---|---|---|---|---|---|---|---|---|---|
| Excellent | Very Good | | | Good | | Fair | | | Poor |

Neither the American Gemological Laboratories nor any of its employees shall be responsible for any action that may be taken on the basis of this report.
This Certificate or the name of American Gemological Laboratories, Inc. may not be reproduced in whole or in part without the express, prior written authorization from American Gemological Laboratories.
Do not accept copies, alterations or corrections on this document for final transactions.

This report prepared by: **American Gemological Laboratories, Inc.**

Martin L. Anderson

Martin J. Anderson, G.G.

© 1979 American Gemological Laboratories Inc. #19/7 A.H.I. Analytics Inc.

**NOTICE TO CLIENTS:** The client agrees to be responsible for and to protect, indemnify, and hold harmless American Gemological Laboratories, Inc. and its officers, directors, and employees from and against any and all injury, loss, damage, destruction or otherwise of said gem materials while in the possession of American Gemological Laboratories resulting from any cause not attributable to the negligence of American Gemological Laboratories or its employees.
The client agrees that this report is for his/her exclusive use.

SOURCE: AMERICAN GEMOLOGICAL LABORATORIES

A sample AGL colored gemstone report providing identification and a full quality evaluation, country of origin, and information pertaining to the absence of any significant treatment.

SCHWEIZERISCHES GEMMOLOGISCHES INSTITUT
INSTITUT SUISSE DE GEMMOLOGIE
SWISS GEMMOLOGICAL INSTITUTE

**SSEF**

Falknerstrasse 9
CH-4001 **Basel** / Switzerland

Telephone   061 / 262 0640
Telefax      061 / 262 0641
Postcheck   80-15013-2

TEST REPORT   No. 00000

on the authenticity of the following gemstone,
mounted in a brooch with diamonds

| | |
|---|---|
| Shape & cut: | antique cushion, modified brilliant / step cut |
| Total weight: | approximately  27.5 grams<br>(including mounting and diamonds) |
| Measurements: | approximately  24.10  x  14.05  x  12.40 mm |
| Calculated weight : | approximately  41 ct |
| Colour: | blue of medium saturation |
| Identification: | S A P P H I R E   (variety of corundum) |
| Comments: | The analysed properties confirm the authenticity<br>of this transparent sapphire.<br><br>No indications of thermal enhancement. |
| Origin: | Kashmir |

Important note: The conclusions on this Test Report reflect our findings at the time it is issued. A gemstone can be modified and / or
enhanced at any time. Therefore, the SSEF can reconfirm at any time that the stone is in accordance with the Test Report.

Please see comments on reverse side.

SSEF - SWISS GEMMOLOGICAL INSTITUTE
Gemstone Testing Division

Basel, 6 August 2001  ss

## SPECIMEN

Dr. L. Kiefert, FGA                    Prof. Dr. H.A. Hänni, FGA

A sample SSEF colored gemstone report providing identification,
treatment information, and country of origin.

## GÜBELIN
### GEM LAB

**EDELSTEIN-BERICHT · RAPPORT DE PIERRE PRECIEUSE
GEMSTONE REPORT**

No.                                          **SPECIMEN**
Datum · Date                                 16 May 2001

Gegenstand · Objet · Item                    One faceted gemstone

**Gewicht · Poids · Weight**                 **3.07 ct**

Schliff · Taille · Cut
   Form · Forme · Shape        oval
   Stil · Style · Style        modified brilliant cut
   Abmessungen · Dimensions · Measurements   11.16 x 7.98 x 5.53 mm

Transparenz · Transparence · Transparency    transparent

Farbe · Couleur · Colour                     **green**


                                             **IDENTIFIKATION · IDENTIFICATION**

                                             Spezies · Espèce · Species
                                             **NATURAL TOURMALINE**

                                             Varietät · Variété · Variety

Bemerkungen · Commentaires · Comments

**GEMMOLOGISCHES LABOR · LABORATOIRE GEMMOLOGIQUE · GEMMOLOGICAL LABORATORY**
Maihofstrasse 102 · CH-6000 Lucerne 9 · Switzerland · Tel. (41) 41 - 429 17 17 · Fax (41) 41 - 429 17 34
www.gubelinlab.com · e-mail: gubelinlab@compuserve.com

Christopher P. Smith, G.G.                   C. Dunaigre, A.G., DUG

Wichtige Anmerkungen und Einschränkungen auf der Rückseite · Remarques au verso · Important notes and limitations on the reverse.
Copyright © 1999 Gübelin Gem Lab Ltd.

A Gübelin report providing identification only. Note that "natural" tourmaline does *not* mean the stone is untreated; natural here means it is not a synthetic or imitation. This report does not provide treatment information, or quality information, but more complete reports are available upon request.

# 17 ◆ Colored Gemstones at Auction: Natural, Treated, Synthetic, and Imitation

THE ALLURE OF NATURAL COLORED GEMSTONES IS AS OLD AS TIME—and so is humankind's fascination with finding ways to improve, imitate, or duplicate them! This is equally true today, and new technology has enabled scientists to create new "gems" never seen before. Those who are enchanted by the world of colored gemstones today must understand what that world contains.

Among gemstones created by nature, we must now recognize that there are really two categories: gemstones that are *natural* and gemstones that have been *treated* to enhance their appearance. Among those created in the laboratories, there are also two categories: *synthetics* and *imitations*. They are not the same, and the first step to understanding and appreciating colored gemstones—and ensuring you get what you really want—is to make sure you understand all these differences.

## Natural or Treated

Let's begin with the two categories of gemstones created by nature: *natural* and *treated*. A natural gemstone is one that has been cut and polished but not artificially enhanced to improve its appearance in any way. A treated gemstone has been subjected to some type of treatment, or treatments, to improve the appearance. As long as the appearance is permanent and won't change over time, many people prefer treated gemstones because they are more affordable than their natural counterparts. Connoisseurs of the rarest and most prized gems, however, seek out the truly natural.

Before buying any colored gemstone, at auction or elsewhere, you must understand as much as possible about treatments. Gemstones are often treated to improve their color, brightness, and overall appearance, and retailers and auction firms alike have sold them. However, they are often sold without the facts about treatment having been disclosed. Traditional jewelry retailers are now governed by Federal Trade Commission guidelines that were recently revised and require disclosure of treatments. Auction houses, however, are not subject to the same requirements. Depending on the express disclaimers in their catalogs or elsewhere, you may have no recourse should you discover that what you purchased is extensively treated and not worth what you paid.

Sotheby's, like its competitors, clearly outlines its position on treatments. Here is what is stated in Sotheby's catalogs under "Treatment of Gemstones":

> Prospective purchasers are reminded that, unless the catalog description specifically states that a stone is natural, we have assumed that some form of treatment may have been used and that such treatment may not be permanent. Our presale estimates reflect this assumption.
>
> To the extent that Sotheby's has laboratory reports containing specific information on the treatment of a stone, these reports are made available for review by potential purchasers. Available reports from internationally recognized gemological laboratories will be noted in the description of the item. New forms of treatments and new scientific methods to discern them are constantly being developed. Consequently, there may be a lack of consensus among laboratories as to whether gemstones have been treated, the extent of the treatment, or the permanence of the treatment.

Sotheby's makes it clear: it is not their responsibility to divulge whether a stone is treated, nor is the presence of a laboratory report a guarantee. *It's buyer beware.*

The first step to protecting yourself from overpaying for a treated gem is to be aware of treatments and to understand that most rubies, sapphires, emeralds, and many other popular gemstones are routinely enhanced. While we have provided an overview of the treatments used on gemstones in this chapter (for detailed information see *Colored Gemstones: The Antoinette Matlins Buying Guide*), it is important to seek as much information as possible regarding treatments from auction house experts or other professionals. Keep in mind that when you buy colored gemstones at auction, there is always a higher degree of risk than when you buy from the traditional retailer, and, because of the complexity of colored gemstones, the risk is even greater than when you are buying diamonds. *Unless the gem you are considering is accompanied by a laboratory report, from a respected laboratory, indicating whether or not the color or clarity has been enhanced in any way, assume it is treated.*

It is also important to understand that some treatments produce permanent results, but others do not. Some treatments also make the gemstone more fragile. Be sure to ask whether or not the appearance can change or whether special care is required.

## GEMSTONE TREATMENT IS ROUTINE IN TODAY'S JEWELRY SCENE

The use of various treatments to improve the appearance of gemstones is not new. We find evidence of treatment in antique jewels, and ancient writings from Roman times attest to a long-standing knowledge of ways to improve the appearance of many gemstones. What is new, however, is the *routine* use of treatments, which began in the 1960s, necessitated by an ever-declining supply of natural, fine-quality gemstones. Natural emeralds, rubies, and sapphires—that is, gems not subjected to any type of artificial treatment or enhancement—have never been rarer than they are today. It is fair to say that if it were not for the use of various treatments, the supply of beautiful gemstones would be virtually depleted by now, and only the wealthiest and most powerful would be enjoying them.

Most treatments simply continue the process that Mother Nature started; all gems are exposed to heat, and many to radiation, as they are forming in nature. Today, most rubies, sapphires, and many other gemstones are routinely treated with *heat* or exposed to some type of *radiation* to change or enhance their color and improve clarity, and pricing is based on the assumption that enhancement has occurred. On the other hand, if the color of a gem is very fine, and if it can be documented by a respected gem-testing laboratory that the color is natural and that there is no clarity enhancement, the stone will command a much higher price because such stones are so rare and desirable.

## AUCTIONS MAY OFFER RARE NATURAL GEMSTONES IN A WORLD WHERE TREATMENTS ARE THE NORM

Since certain varieties of natural gemstones are so scarce today in fine quality because of depletion of the mines, it is very difficult to find them in jewelry stores. Even the finest salons may not have what you are seeking, and since these stones are equally scarce in the wholesale arena, it might take many weeks or months to locate the right one for you. For this reason, people seeking natural gems pay special attention to jewelry reentering the marketplace from private estates—jewelry that may contain old stones mined in days gone by, when fine material was still available and did not need to be subjected to any treatment to improve its appearance.

When private estates are liquidated, or when someone decides to sell old jewelry, it is often consigned to an auction house. So today, given the scarcity of natural gems elsewhere, the auction arena has become one of the most important sources of fine, natural gemstones. And the quest for natural gemstones is one of the major attractions for collectors and connoisseurs to attend auctions such as the "Magnificent" or "Important" jewelry sales held by major international auction houses. Here, among the jewels of royalty, among the jewels of the rich and famous, one has especially high hopes of finding the rarest and most exotic gems. But you must also keep in mind that even the rich and famous have been victims of unscrupulous jewelers through the ages. I have seen many treated gemstones, imitations, and synthetics among the "treasured heirlooms" of royalty. So, even if the provenance seems impeccable, don't assume the gems are, unless they are accompanied by appropriate documentation.

## Documentation Is the Key to Risk Reduction— For Buyers *and* Sellers

Major auction houses today are encouraging consignors of fine gems to obtain documentation from a respected laboratory. As a result, we are seeing more and more laboratory reports accompanying fine jewelry pieces. It has become almost routine. So, among important gems at auction, whether from a well-known estate or an unknown consignor, any piece containing a fine, rare gem with natural color and clarity will normally be accompanied by a gem-testing report verifying this. But this is not always the case. Sometimes there is no documentation because the consignor doesn't wish to undertake the expense; in such cases, the auction house may obtain the documentation, but often it does not. Also, jewelry pieces containing smaller stones are often overlooked and are not submitted to a laboratory for documentation, even if the value would be increased by so doing. So, sometimes you may get lucky and succeed in acquiring a rare, natural gemstone at a low price because no one bothered to verify whether the gem was natural or treated.

There are still bargains to be had, and this is one of the primary attractions to the auction arena. But when you are buying any expensive rare gem represented to be natural, be sure it is accompanied by a report from a respected gem-testing lab that verifies this fact. If there isn't any report, recognize that you are taking a risk; there is a strong possibility you will find out it is not natural. At auction, if there is no report and you cannot make the purchase contingent on verification from a respected laboratory, our advice is to bid low, or let it go.

***Sellers need to obtain documentation*** before *consigning.* If you are planning to sell a gemstone and think it might be natural, then obtaining a laboratory report from a respected lab *before consigning the piece to any auction* is also recommended. Don't make the mistake of turning to the auction house as the "expert" to advise you on the quality, value, and need for documentation; as we explained earlier, the auction house has a vested interest in having you consign the piece at the lowest possible reserve (see chapter 2). By taking the time to obtain proper documentation and laboratory certification before meeting with anyone at the auction house, you can negotiate a higher reserve and protect yourself from selling the piece for too little. Even more important, collectors and connoisseurs will bid higher prices for natural stones of fine quality when the stone is accompanied by a reliable lab report; the report provides assurance and greatly reduces the buyer's risk as well as your own. A stone that appears "natural" but that lacks documentation may be tempting, but the bidding will always be conservative because there is no assurance until the stone is thoroughly examined in a proper laboratory.

## AUCTIONS SELL MANY TREATED GEMSTONES

Although the auction arena has become an important source of natural gemstones, the vast majority of jewelry sold contains treated gems. There is nothing wrong with buying treated gemstones, as long as you are not misled into believing that they are natural or more rare and valuable than they are. Treated gemstones provide consumers with lovely pieces at affordable prices. The most important consideration, here as in all purchases of gemstones, is to know exactly what you are buying. But it is much easier to be sure about what you are buying and to protect yourself from misrepresentation when you buy colored gemstones from a traditional retailer; should you discover misrepresentation after purchasing a colored gemstone, the FTC requires the retailer to refund your money. More importantly, FTC rules require retailers to provide full disclosure about treatments—what type of treatment, whether or not it is permanent, special care requirements, and so on. But this is not the case when you buy at auction, and the auction house may not know the answers to questions you ask or be able to provide all of the relevant information. While the selling of treated gemstones is perfectly legitimate in most cases, fraudulent practices involving treated stones also exist. Although the assumption, unless otherwise stated, is that the gemstones sold at auction are treated, it is difficult to know by what means, whether or not the treatment is considered acceptable within the trade, or whether special care is required. So, before deciding where to buy, weigh the risk, ask the critical questions, make sure you are satisfied with the answers, and bid accordingly.

Even the most prestigious firms can offer "important" pieces that are not what they appear to be. A prominent auction firm offered what it described as an "important" diamond and ruby necklace; the estimate was $1.5 million to $2 million. It contained numerous large rubies, each with an accompanying lab report from an equally prestigious laboratory, stating that each ruby was of Burmese origin. None of the reports, however, provided any comment regarding whether or not the rubies had been enhanced in any way. What the buyer didn't know was that each of the rubies had been extensively treated. They all had serious cracks that were not noticeable because they had been filled with a glasslike filler. The color and clarity were also enhanced through extremely high heat, making the rubies much more fragile. The necklace was hardly the "important" piece it was represented to be. Fortunately, the auction house took back the necklace and rescinded the sale, explaining to the buyer that it had been unaware of the extent of the treatments and agreeing that the laboratory reports had created a misleading impression. The auction house did not have to cancel the sale, however; it did so simply in a gesture of good will. In this case, the buyer was very lucky.

How can you avoid this? Simply by asking the auction house pointed questions about treatments and enhancements (see chapter 24) and documenting their responses, or by retaining an expert to work with you in a consulting role. Most important, should you succeed in acquiring the piece you want, ask a qualified gemologist-appraiser or respected gem-testing laboratory to verify the representations made in the capitalized headings in the catalog. Also, remember that any representations made by any auction house representative—in response to your questions before the sale, for example—are not legally binding unless they are provided to you as guarantees in writing.

Here are some descriptions of the most common treatments used to enhance the color and clarity of gemstones.

## Heating

Subjecting certain gems to sophisticated heating procedures is a practice that is accepted within the jewelry industry as long as the change induced is permanent. Most sapphires and rubies are heated. The treatment may lighten, darken, or completely change the color and improve the clarity by melting some of the fine "silk" inclusions often present. A skilled gemologist or gem-testing laboratory can often determine whether or not the color of these gems has been altered by heating by examining the stone's inclusions under the microscope. Sapphire and ruby, for example, can withstand high temperatures, but often the heat causes small crystal inclusions inside the stone to melt or explode. These altered inclusions then provide the evidence of heating.

It may be easy to determine that a stone has been heated, but in rare instances it is impossible to know for certain that it has not been—that is, that its color is natural. Making this determination can require a high degree of skill and sophisticated equipment, often available only at a major laboratory, and even then it may not be possible to ascertain definitively. Gemologists must carefully examine the internal characteristics of the particular stone. Sometimes they see an unaltered inclusion that would lead to a determination that the color is natural; other times they see an altered inclusion that indicates treatment; and sometimes the inclusions, or changes and abnormalities in them, that enable a positive determination simply are not present. When there is nothing inside the gem to indicate whether it has or has not been heated, we cannot be sure.

Most rubies and sapphires sold since the 1960s have been heated to enhance their color and clarity. Other gemstones that are routinely heated today include amber, amethyst, aquamarine, pink beryl (morganite), carnelian, citrine, kunzite, tanzanite, pink topaz, several varieties of tourmaline, and zircon.

# Radiation

Radiation techniques are relatively new. Frequently used on a wide range of gemstones, radiation is sometimes combined with heating. The effect is permanent on some stones, and accepted in the trade; it is not acceptable on other stones because the color fades or changes back to its original color over a relatively short time. There are still some questions regarding radiation levels and the long-term effects on health. The Nuclear Regulatory Agency has been working to establish standards, and the Gemological Institute of America (GIA) Gem Trade Laboratory now has a facility with the capability to test gemstones for "acceptable" and "unacceptable" radiation levels.

Gemstones that are commonly irradiated to obtain color include blue topaz, deep blue beryl (called maxixe—this color will always fade), yellow beryl, diamond, kunzite, yellow or orange sapphire (not stable—will fade quickly), yellow and green topaz, and red, pink, and purple tourmaline.

# Diffusion Treatment

Diffusion is a newcomer to the world of treated gemstones and is already surrounded by controversy. Diffusion (sometimes called deep diffusion or surface diffusion) is a process that alters the color of a gem by exposing the surface to certain chemicals and heating it over a prolonged period of time. At present the procedure has been used successfully to produce "blue" sapphire, "ruby," and "green" topaz, but it could have application to other gemstone materials in the future.

The material being treated is usually colorless or very pale, and the beautiful color produced by the treatment is confined to the surface of the gem only. If you sliced one in half, you would see an essentially colorless stone with a very narrow rim of color along its perimeter. This could create a problem if the stone is ever badly chipped or nicked and needs to be recut or polished; the surface color might be removed in the recutting, leaving a colorless stone in its place. Should this happen, the treatment could be repeated to restore the original color. When repeated on a previously diffused stone, the process requires less time, and the restored color is virtually identical to the original.

It is possible that the process will be improved to produce a treatment in which color penetrates the entire stone. At this time, however, deep diffusion simply means that the color penetrates a little deeper than in the earliest diffused stones. The color is still confined to the surface. Diffusion treatment can also produce asterism (a star effect such as you sometimes see in sapphire and ruby), and light pink sapphire is now being transformed into the rare orangy-pink "padparadscha" sapphire using what may be a new diffusion technique. Be especially cautious when buying padparadsha sapphire at auction today.

Unfortunately, many surface-diffused blue sapphires have been found mixed in with parcels of nondiffused sapphires, and some may inadvertently have been set in jewelry and sold. Diffused sapphires have also entered the auction arena, without any disclosure. I've seen "important" sapphire pieces sold at prices that clearly reflected no one knew the stones were diffused. They can be easy to miss. A very fine auction house accepted an "important" sapphire and diamond necklace for an upcoming auction. The diamond necklace was designed to highlight at its center an enormous sapphire of very fine color. The necklace had already been photographed for the catalog before the senior gemologist noticed the very low reserve. She became suspicious because the piece—an estate piece—was consigned by a dealer who should have recognized its value. She reexamined the necklace and was shocked to discover that the sapphire was diffusion treated. It was withdrawn from the sale and returned to the dealer.

Where sapphire and ruby are concerned, we recommend double-checking for diffusion to avoid any unintentional misrepresentation. Ask the auction house whether it has the means to check for you; in many cases it is a simple, quick test with magnification and an immersion cell. If this is not possible, be sure to ask the auction house what its policy is regarding returning the piece for a full refund should you learn *after* purchase that it has been treated by diffusion techniques (and be sure to get the answer in writing).

Diffused stones offer beautiful choices at affordable prices. Just be sure you know whether or not the stone is diffused. If it is, pay the right price for it, and exercise some care in wearing and handling it, because these stones are somewhat more brittle than other stones.

## Fracture Filling

Fractures can interrupt light as it travels through a colored gemstone, creating a whitishness in the area of the fracture or, in some cases, reflecting back and making the fracture more noticeable. If a surface-reaching fracture is filled with the proper substance, the light will continue to pass through without blockage or reflection, so the color is not diminished and reflective fractures are much less noticeable because the reflectivity is greatly reduced. Certain gemstones, such as emerald, have more fractures than other gemstones because they form under extremely violent geological conditions. For this reason, emeralds are usually treated with fillers to reduce the visibility of fractures. The jewelry trade has always considered the oiling of emerald an acceptable practice, and it has been used routinely for many years. We don't know when the oiling of emerald began, but the practice was known during the Roman period, and we find many antique emerald pieces that still show traces of oil when examined with a microscope.

Today, gemstone treaters use various substances to fill fractures, including oil, wax, paraffin, glass, and various formulations of epoxy resin. Gemstones that may be treated with one of these substances include emerald, aquamarine, peridot, jade, turquoise, ruby, sapphire, and, in rare cases, alexandrite and garnet. Be especially alert to the possibility of fillers in ruby and sapphire; many rubies and sapphires from several new deposits contain reflective inclusions, so the use of oil and wax to improve their appearance is increasing.

A coloring agent can also be added to the filler to simultaneously improve a stone's overall color. This is a fraudulent practice. Selling such gems without disclosure is a violation of Federal Trade Commission practice.

## Dyed Stones

Gemstones have been dyed since earliest times. Gems that are frequently dyed include jade, opal, coral, lapis, and, to a lesser degree, poor-quality star rubies, star sapphires, and emeralds. Dyed material may be very stable, but it can also be very temporary. We've seen dyed lapis in which the "blue" came off with a cotton ball moistened in fingernail polish remover. Dyed gems may be genuine stones that have been dyed to enhance their color (as in dyeing pale green jadeite to a deeper green), or they may be different gems altogether.

## SYNTHETICS AND IMITATIONS: A WORLD OF DIFFERENCE

Scientific advances and new technology have resulted in a whole new world of synthetic gemstone materials, but it's important to understand what a synthetic is. First, a synthetic is *not* an imitation. Technically, the term *synthetic* indicates that the material is artificially made by using the same chemical ingredients found in natural products—in other words, using Mother Nature's recipe. This means that a synthetic gemstone will have essentially the same physical, chemical, and optical properties observed in natural gemstones. From a practical standpoint, this also means that they will respond to various gem-identification tests in the same way as do natural stones. This can make them difficult to distinguish from the natural gem.

An imitation is also artificially made, but not using "nature's recipe," so it is very different physically and chemically from the gem it is imitating, and it is very easy to distinguish it from the natural gem with standard gem-identification techniques. For example, a glass "gem" is an imitation. Red glass could imitate ruby. But it resembles ruby only in color; a quick examination with a simple jeweler's loupe (magnifier) would reveal telltale signs that it is glass and not ruby, and any gemological test would clearly corroborate this conclusion.

## NOT ALL SYNTHETICS ARE THE SAME

Synthetics have been on the market for many years. Good synthetic sapphires, rubies, and spinels have been manufactured commercially for almost one hundred years, and very good synthetic emeralds since the 1940s. While these early synthetics were attractive and popular because of their very low price, they didn't really look like natural stones. Most looked "too good to be true." They also had characteristics internally that made them easy for jewelers to spot with just a simple loupe.

Today, this is often not the case. In recent years, technological advances have enabled scientists to create environments that come much closer to duplicating what is found in nature. As a result, crystals can actually be "grown" in laboratories, creating a product that very closely resembles the natural gem. These new, sophisticated methods result in products that no longer possess the signature characteristics with which gem dealers and jewelers have long been familiar; instead, they often contain characteristics very similar to those of their natural counterparts.

The new generation of synthetics are often called *flux-grown* or *created*. They are fairly expensive to produce and cost much more than most other synthetics; in fact, the cost can be so high that consumers sometimes mistakenly conclude they are natural gemstones. But the real issue for the auction buyer is that they so closely resemble the natural that they can be easily misrepresented for the natural, both unintentionally and deliberately. Older techniques for producing synthetics are still used as well, and careless examination, especially of cabochons, can also result in misrepresentation.

Today it is very important to verify the genuineness of any fine, valuable gemstone because the new generation of synthetic products is so similar to the natural that the two can be easily confused without very careful gemological testing in a proper laboratory environment. Generally speaking, when you buy any gemstone or jewelry at auction, it must be genuine unless the capitalized heading description clearly states that it is synthetic. But even though it *should* be, it doesn't mean it *will be.*

## SYNTHETICS AND IMITATIONS AT AUCTION

The likelihood of encountering synthetic or imitation gemstones increases significantly when buying at auction. There are several reasons for this. First, many antique jewels are sold at auction, and what most people don't realize is that synthetics and imitations are frequently encountered in antiques. The common belief that "if it's old, it's the real thing" is a widespread myth. In fact, you are much more likely to find honest and reliable representations today than in yesteryear because of advances in the field of gemology. Nonetheless, auction houses also often make the mistake of assuming that gemstones in beautiful antique pieces are real, especially if consigned by a wealthy or prominent family. (For more on this subject, see the "Antique Jewelry" chapter in *Gem Identification Made Easy*).

As we mentioned earlier, traditional jewelry retailers are governed by Federal Trade Commission guidelines requiring that clear distinctions be made between natural, treated, synthetic, and imitation gemstones. At auction, however, especially in online auction sites, this is not always the case. Whether intentionally or unintentionally, synthetic gemstones and imitations have all too often been misrepresented as natural, and you cannot ignore the fact that some online auction sites have dishonest sellers who unscrupulously prey on unsuspecting buyers, selling synthetic and imitation stones that they portray as genuine.

Regardless of how the stone was represented, be sure to verify genuineness in order to protect yourself from intentional and sometimes unintentional misrepresentation. Should you discover the stone is synthetic or an imitation, there should be no problem getting your money back from any well-known auction firm. When you are buying from online vendors, however, it may be much more difficult. For this reason, we discourage buying gemstones at online sites unless you can arrange to verify all the facts before paying for the stone, or through an escrow arrangement.

*Beautiful old settings are often used to disguise synthetics and imitations.* Sometimes important gemstones are removed from their original settings because the owner wants a more contemporary design. What happens to the original setting? Often an inexpensive imitation or synthetic stone is set in the original, just to keep it in the family, and is subsequently passed on to another generation whose members don't realize that the stone is not genuine. More often than not, however, it is simply left with the jeweler, who may set another stone in the piece or sell the mounting to an estate dealer. Today many estate dealers seek old mountings and pay high prices for those with unusually fine workmanship, distinctive detailing, or an important maker's mark, such as Cartier. In some cases, a low-quality treated stone, synthetic, or imitation is set into an exquisite setting for the express purpose of creating a false impression as to the genuineness, quality, and value of the piece.

Here are some descriptions of the most common gemstone imitations.

## Simulated Stones

Glass simulations of all the colored stones, and glass and plastic simulated pearls, turquoise, and amber, are commonly misrepresented as genuine. They are frequently found in estate jewelry, sometimes mixed with natural gems in the same piece.

## Composite Stones

Composite stones are exactly what the term implies: stones composed of more than one part. Composites come in two basic types. *Doublets* are composite stones consisting of two parts, sometimes held together by a colored bonding agent. *Triplets* are composite stones consisting of three parts, usually glued together to a colored middle part.

Doublets are especially important to know about because they were widely used in antique jewelry before the development of synthetics and are still used today.

In antique pieces, the most commonly encountered doublet, often referred to as a false doublet, consists of a red garnet top fused to an appropriately colored glass bottom. With the right combination, any colored gem could be simulated by this method. Garnets were used for the top portion of these false doublets because they possessed nice luster and excellent durability and were readily available in great quantity, which made them very inexpensive.

Another form of the doublet is made from two parts of a colorless material, fused together with an appropriately colored bonding agent. An "emerald" (sometimes sold as *soudé emerald*) can be made, for example, from a colorless synthetic spinel top and bottom, held together in the middle (at the girdle) by green glue. Red glue or blue glue could be used to simulate ruby or sapphire. Opal doublets are also common, as are opal triplets.

Since some doublets are difficult to spot, especially when mounted, it is easy for one to be passed on to a customer unknowingly, especially when it is set in a sleek, modern bezel setting. There is nothing wrong with buying a doublet as long as you know what you are buying and pay a fair price. Just be careful not to buy a doublet unknowingly. Be sure to verify all the facts.

## Look-Alike Substitution

Another form of deception involves misrepresenting a more common, less expensive stone for a rarer, more expensive gem of similar color. Today, as more and more natural gemstones in a wide variety of colors enter the market, both deliberate and accidental misrepresentation can occur.

In some cases, more common stones are *altered* to look like rarer gems. Numerous examples of dyed chalcedony (an inexpensive variety of quartz) can be found in antique jewelry, imitating other gems. White opals can be *blackened* by introducing a chemical reaction (sugar-acid chemical reaction) that creates black carbon, making the white opal look like the rarer black opal. Cabochon (nonfaceted) transparent ("jelly") or semitransparent opals are also often "painted" to look like precious black opal. This process begins with putting the stone in a closed-back setting that has a high rim (bezel). A black cement or paint is spread on the inside of the setting so that when the opal is placed inside, the light entering it is trapped and reflected back, giving the opal the appearance of a fine black opal.

## Foil-Backed Stones

This technique is not frequently encountered in modern jewelry but is relatively common in antique jewelry, and anyone interested in antique jewelry should be aware of it. It is seen with both nonfaceted and faceted stones, set usually in a closed-back mounting. This technique involves lining the inside of the setting with silver or gold foil to add brilliance and sparkle (as with foil-backed glass imitating diamond) or with colored foil to change or enhance the color by projecting color into the stone. Always be apprehensive when considering a piece of jewelry that has a closed back.

Some exceptional foil-backed antique pieces from the Georgian period, containing lovely "colored" gems, are still desirable and are sought by collectors. Just keep in mind that the value of the gemstone component itself is lower than would be the case if the color were natural.

## A FINAL WORD OF CAUTION

In short, pieces containing treated, synthetic, or imitation gemstones often go undetected and the facts may be misrepresented. Even the best auction houses acknowledge that the conditions under which jewelry is usually consigned prevent comprehensive gemological testing, despite their best efforts. Unless the consignor agrees to obtain documentation from a respected gemological laboratory, auction houses cannot guarantee the gems except as stated explicitly in their catalogs.

# 18 ♦ Understanding Colored Gemstone Prices and What to Bid

WHEN YOU BUY COLORED GEMSTONES TODAY, YOU WILL FIND YOUR-self immersed in color—every hue, every shade of the spectrum. There has never been a more exciting time to search for a colored gem because there have never been so many alternatives. Whatever color you prefer, and whatever your budget, there is a sparkling natural gem awaiting your discovery. And the auction venue is one of the best sources.

In this chapter we provide guides to pricing natural gemstones as well as treated gemstones, and we present a sampling of prices brought at auction for some popular colored gemstones. In the following chapter gemstones are discussed individually.

## THE RAREST OF THEM ALL: THE NATURAL GEMS

There has been so much focus on the extensive use of treatments to enhance gems that it is easy to forget that there are also natural gems: those that have not been artificially enhanced in any way. Within every gemstone family there is the occasional beauty that is just as nature made it. Unfortunately, as we discussed earlier, sometimes we cannot distinguish what is natural from what is not. Such is the case with blue topaz, for example. Blue topaz does occur naturally, in lovely pastel shades. It is one of nature's rarest and loveliest gems, but alas, we do not yet have the means to definitively distinguish what is natural from what has been irradiated. Thus, regardless of its rarity and true preciousness (and value), it commands a very small price.

There are also natural rubies, sapphires, and emeralds. Many are exceptional in quality, and these often set record-breaking prices at important jewelry auctions, but not all "natural" rubies, sapphires, and emeralds are of top quality. Be careful not to overbid just because it's natural. Many people today are showing interest in natural stones in less rare qualities, especially in lighter shades of color, which can be very lovely at the right price. Fortunately, where ruby, sapphire, and emerald are concerned, it is usually possible to distinguish the natural from the treated, and as the natural stones become even rarer and rarer, prices are starting to reflect their preciousness.

There is yet another group of gems about which little has been said until recently: gemstones and gemstone families that are not routinely treated to alter color or clarity at this time. When you buy one of the gemstones in the following list, the color is generally natural, and in most cases these gemstones are not enhanced in any way. Included in this list are many beautiful choices in a rainbow of colors. If you are not familiar with them, there is more information in the following chapter. Whatever your color preference and budget, if you seek something truly "natural," you should be able to find the right gem from this list.

---

## GEMSTONES THAT ARE NOT ROUTINELY ENHANCED*

| | | |
|---|---|---|
| Alexandrite | Iolite | Tourmaline (rare |
| Andalusite | Moonstone | chrome green |
| Chrysoprase | Fire opal | variety and cat's-eye |
| Chrysoberyl | Peridot | tourmaline) |
| (all colors) | Spinel (all colors) | Zircon (brown and |
| Garnet (all colors) | Tanzanite (green) | green varieties) |
| Hematite | | |

*The color of these gems is normally natural. In rare instances, surface-reaching fractures or cavities may be filled with oil, wax, or resin.

---

## THE EFFECT OF TREATMENTS ON THE VALUE OF GEMSTONES

The following table provides an indication of price adjustment for *natural* versus *treated* ruby, sapphire, and emerald. Keep in mind that untreated sapphire and ruby from certain locations, such as Burma or Kashmir, command a premium greater than indicated here. Also, note that there are rare gems of exceptional quality above the extra-fine rating, and such stones will command a much greater premium if untreated.

## HOW TREATMENTS AFFECT PRICES OF COLORED GEMS*

| Emerald | GOOD | FINE | EXTRA FINE |
|---|---|---|---|
| Untreated | +10% to +25% | +25% to +50% | +50% and up |
| Slight treatment | 0% | 0% | 0% |
| Moderate treatment | −5% to −10% | −10% to −15% | −15% to −25% |
| Extensive treatment | −15% to −20% | −20% to −25% | −25% to −35% |
| Ruby | | | |
| Unheated | +5% to +20% | +20% to +35% | +35% to +50% and up |
| Moderate heat | 0% | 0% | 0% |
| High heat with slight glass residue | −5% | −5% to −10% | −10% to −15% |
| moderate glass residue | −5% to −10% | −10% to −15% | −15% to −20% |
| extensive glass residue | −15% to −20% | −20% to −25% | −25% to −35% |
| Glass-filled cavity | −10% to −50% | −10% to −50% | −10% to −50% |
| Sapphire | | | |
| Unheated | +5% to +10% | +10% to +20% | +20% to +30% and up |
| Heated | 0% | 0% | 0% |
| Oiled (no data; often goes undetected) | | | |

*The information presented above is based on information from several sources, including *The Guide* (Gemworld International) and *JCK Magazine.*

## POPULAR COLORED GEMSTONES SOLD AT AUCTION

Auction houses and internet auction sites offer a wide variety of colored gemstones at a broad range of prices, and fine auction houses have become the primary source of the finest natural gemstones, which are increasingly difficult to find in the traditional jewelry marketplace. The gemstones in the following chart are mostly extra fine in quality and their high prices reflect their rarity. The renowned Kashmir sapphire, for example, has not been mined for almost seventy-five years, and ruby sources in Burma are no longer producing top-quality gems. If you are considering buying a fine-quality natural gemstone, we strongly recommend taking extra steps to confirm its exceptional quality before purchase.

## A Sampling of Colored Gemstones Sold at Auction

| Gemstone | Shape | Carats | Origin | Report | Treatment | House | $/Carat | Total $* |
|---|---|---|---|---|---|---|---|---|
| Alexandrite | Cushion | 18.87 | Sri Lanka | AGL | None | Sotheby's | 5,167 | 97,500 |
| Alexandrite | Rectangular | 6.94 | n/a** | None | n/a** | Christie's | 9,244 | 64,155 |
| Alexandrite | Oval | 16.80 | n/a** | AGL | None | Christie's | 9,711 | 163,150 |
| Emerald | Emerald | 4.03 | Colombia | AGL | None | Sotheby's | 17,308 | 69,750 |
| Emerald | Square | 2.89 | Colombia | AGL | Oil | Christie's | 4,472 | 12,925 |
| Emerald | Square | 12.39 | Colombia | AGL | Oil | Christie's | 17,353 | 214,450 |
| Emerald | Emerald | 8.02 | Colombia | Gübelin | None | Christie's | 24,065 | 193,000 |
| Emerald | Emerald | 6.25 | Colombia | Gübelin | None | Phillips | 40,000 | 250,000 |
| Emerald | Rectangular | 12.80 | Zambia | Gübelin | Minor | Phillips | 1,953 | 25,000 |
| Emerald | Emerald | 19.04 | Colombia | AGL | Faint | Phillips | 5,252 | 100,000 |
| Ruby | Rectangular | 4.07 | Burma | AGL | None | Christie's | 6,351 | 25,850 |
| Ruby | Oval cabochon | 7.60 | Burma | GRS | None | Sotheby's | 2,520 | 19,150 |
| Ruby | Oval | 14.46 | Burma | AGL | None | Christie's | 2,275 | 32,900 |
| Ruby | Oval | 6.93 | Burma | SSEF | None | Christie's | 1,932 | 13,390 |
| Ruby | Oval | 7.06 | Burma | SSEF | None | Christie's | 1,932 | 13,640 |
| Ruby | Cushion | 4.12 | Burma | AGL | None | Christie's | 5,704 | 23,500 |
| Ruby | Oval | 4.27 | Burma | SSEF | None | Christie's | 16,464 | 70,300 |
| Ruby | Cushion | 18.39 | Burma | SSEF | None | Christie's | 10,495 | 193,000 |
| Ruby | Cut-cornered rectangle | 15.01 | Burma | Gübelin | None | Christie's | 42,905 | 644,000 |
| Ruby | Cushion | 7.13 | Malawi | Gübelin | None | Phillips | 4,123 | 29,400 |
| Ruby | Circular | 7.33 | Burma | Gübelin | None | Phillips | 3,520 | 25,800 |
| Ruby | Octagonal emerald cut | 8.59 | Burma | Gübelin | None | Phillips | 81,490 | 700,000 |

*Totals are rounded.
**Not available

(Chart continues on next page.)

# A Sampling of Colored Gemstones Sold at Auction, *continued*

| Gemstone | Shape | Carats | Origin | Report | Treatment | House | $/Carat | Total $* |
|---|---|---|---|---|---|---|---|---|
| Ruby | Oval | 4.07 | Burma | Gübelin | None | Phillips | 8,600 | 35,000 |
| Sapphire | Cushion | 46.32 | Sri Lanka | AGL | None | Christie's | 1,015 | 47,015 |
| Sapphire | Cushion | 2.43 | Kashmir | AGL | None | Christie's | 6,770 | 16,450 |
| Sapphire | Oval | 23.56 | Burma | None | n/a** | Christie's | 848 | 19,975 |
| Sapphire | Oval | 8.76 | Sri Lanka | AGL | None | Sotheby's | 959 | 8,400 |
| Sapphire | Cushion | 4.80 | Burma | AGL | None | Sotheby's | 2,500 | 12,000 |
| Sapphire | Cushion | 12.36 | Kashmir | AGL | None | Sotheby's | 9,810 | 121,250 |
| Sapphire | Cabochon | 10.44 | Sri Lanka | AGL | None | Sotheby's | 9,986 | 104,250 |
| Sapphire | Rectangular | 27.13 | Burma | Gübelin | None | Christie's | 2,252 | 61,100 |
| Sapphire | Cushion | 8.82 | Burma | AGTA | None | Christie's | 3,730 | 32,900 |
| Sapphire | Cushion | 8.60 | Kashmir | AGL | None | Christie's | 10,930 | 94,000 |
| Sapphire | Cushion | 43.91 | Sri Lanka | AGL | None | Christie's | 3,143 | 138,000 |
| Sapphire | Emerald | 62.02 | Burma | Gübelin | None | Christie's | 48,871 | 3,031,000 |
| Sapphire | Octagonal | 21.29 | Kashmir | SSEF/AGL | None | Christie's | 44,400 | 945,348 |
| Sapphire | Rectangular | 17.42 | Burma | SSEF | None | Phillips | 5,626 | 98,000 |
| Sapphire | Cushion | 21.75 | Sri Lanka | Gübelin | Yes | Phillips | 874 | 19,000 |

*Totals are rounded.
**Not available

# 19 ♦ Choices in Colored Gemstones

IN THIS CHAPTER, THE GEMSTONES ARE DISCUSSED INDIVIDUALLY, beginning with precious gems and followed alphabetically by the other popular gem families. It should be noted that the terms *precious* and *semiprecious* are discouraged today, since rubies, sapphires, and emeralds are only "precious" in rare qualities, and there are many "semiprecious" gemstones today that are rarer and more valuable than so-called precious gems.

## THE BIG THREE—EMERALD, RUBY, AND SAPPHIRE

### Emerald

Emerald is a green variety of the mineral beryl. One of the rarest members of the beryl family—only the red variety (sometimes called red emerald) is rarer—it is one of the most highly prized of all the gems.

Contrary to popular belief, emerald is *not soft*. It ranks 7½ to 8 on Mohs' scale—an internationally recognized standard that ranks hardness on a scale from 1 to 10, with 1 being the softest and 10 the hardest. It is more fragile than other varieties of beryl and other gems, however, because it is more brittle and under more stress from fractures resulting from the violent geologic conditions under which it formed. This is why it is important to exercise care when you are wearing and handling emerald.

The highest-quality emerald has the color of fresh young green grass—an almost pure spectral green, possibly with a very faint tint of blue, as in the finest emerald from Colombia, which is considered by connoisseurs to be the world's finest. Other sources include Brazil, Zambia, Pakistan, Afghanistan, Russia, and India. Flawless emeralds are rare, so their flaws have come to serve almost as fingerprints, while flawless emeralds are immediately suspect.

Because of emerald's popularity and value, imitations are abundant. Glass, manufactured complete with "flaws," and doublets or triplets, like "aquamarine emeralds" and "Tecla emeralds" (see chapter 17), are often encountered.

New products such as the "Lannyte emerald doublet" are also entering the market; when properly represented, they can make an interesting jewelry choice, but a second or third party may fail to mention that they are doublets.

Also, fine synthetic emeralds are being produced (see chapter 17) with nearly the same color, hardness, and brilliance as genuine emerald. These synthetics are not inexpensive themselves, except by comparison with genuine emeralds of equivalent quality.

Techniques to enhance color and reduce the visibility of flaws are also frequently used. A common practice is to fill surface-reaching cracks with oil (sometimes tinted green)—a practice that goes back to early Greek times. Today emeralds are oiled by use of a vacuum/heat technology. This is a widely accepted trade practice, since it is actually good for the stone in light of its fragile nature. Oiling hides some of the whitish flaws, which are actually cracks, filling the cracks so they become less visible. The oil becomes an integral part of the emerald unless it is subjected to some type of degreasing procedure. The development and use of the ultrasonic cleaner has brought to light the extensiveness of this practice. *Never clean emeralds in an ultrasonic cleaner.* (An ionic cleaner is fine for emeralds as well as for all other jewelry.)

Even though oiling is an acceptable practice, be sure the price reflects the actual quality of the stone. If necessary, most emeralds can be re-oiled.

Epoxy resin fillers are recent newcomers, but this treatment is gaining popularity and is now used on many emeralds mined in many parts of the world, including Colombia and Brazil.

As with all highly desired gems, the greater the value and demand, the greater the occurrence of fraudulent practices. Examples of almost every type of technique to simulate emerald can be found: color alteration by using green foil on closed backs; use of synthetics; substitution of less valuable green stones, doublets, or other composites, etc. Therefore, be especially cautious of bargains. Any very fine emerald purchased today should have a laboratory report or be submitted to a lab to obtain one.

## Ruby

Prized through the ages as, in the words of the Roman historian Pliny, the "gem of gems...surpassing all other precious stones in virtue," ruby is the red variety of the mineral corundum. Ruby has a color that ranges from purplish or bluish red to a yellowish red. The finest color is a vivid, almost pure spectral red with a very faint undertone of blue, as seen in Burmese rubies, which are considered the finest among ardent collectors. Other sources of fine ruby are Thailand, Vietnam, Cambodia, Kenya, Tanzania, and Azad Kashmir in Pakistan. The ruby is very brilliant and very hard, ranking 9 on Mohs' scale. Ruby is also very durable and wearable—characteristics that make it an unusually fine choice for any piece of jewelry.

Translucent varieties of ruby are also seen, and one variety exhibits a six-ray star effect when cut as a cabochon. This variety is called *star ruby* and is one of nature's most beautiful and interesting gifts. But, as with so many other beautiful gifts once produced only in nature, these lovely gems are now duplicated in synthetic star rubies, and numerous faked star rubies are also the products of human beings' attempts at mimicry.

Here again, remember that the greater the value and demand, the greater the use of techniques to "improve" or to simulate. Among rubies, as among other gemstones, examples of almost every type of deceptive technique can be found—color enhancement, synthesis, substitutes, doublets, triplets, misleading names, and so on. Be especially alert to diffusion treatment and oiling of reflective fractures. The newest laboratory-grown synthetic rubies, like those made by Ramaura and Chatham, are so close to natural ruby in every aspect that many are actually passing for genuine, even among gemologists. When you are getting a very fine, valuable ruby, be sure to verify genuineness with a gemologist who has both many years of experience in colored gems and an astute knowledge of the marketplace today. We would recommend having the gemologist also obtain a colored gemstone report from a major gem-testing laboratory.

Once again, be especially cautious of bargains, and have the purchase double-checked by a qualified gemologist-appraiser.

## Sapphire

The "celestial" sapphire, like ruby, is the mineral corundum. While we know it best in its blue variety, which is highly prized, it comes in essentially every color. As with ruby, sapphire is characterized by hardness (9 on Mohs' scale), brilliance, and availability in many beautiful colors, all of which make it probably the most important and most versatile of the gem families.

Blue sapphires can be among the most valuable members of the sapphire family—especially stones from Burma and Kashmir, which are closest to the pure spectral blue. Fine, brilliant, deep blue Burmese sapphires will surely dazzle the eye and the pocketbook, as will the Kashmir, which is a fine velvety-toned deep blue.

The Ceylon (Sri Lanka) sapphires are a very pleasing blue but are a less deep shade than the Burmese or Kashmir, instead tending to fall more on the pastel side.

We are also seeing many Australian sapphires, which are often a dark blue but with a slightly green undertone, as are those from Thailand; both sell for much less per carat. They offer a very affordable alternative to Burmese, Kashmir, or Ceylon sapphires and can still be very pleasing in their color. Blue sapphires also come from Tanzania, Brazil, Africa, and even the United States. Montana sapphires are very collectible because of their unusual shades of color and because many are of a *natural* color—that is, not subjected to any treatment. For those who want a gem that is truly natural, Montana sapphire may be the choice for you.

With sapphire, origin can have a significant effect on price, so if you are purchasing a Kashmir, Burmese, or Ceylon sapphire, that should be noted in the description.

Like ruby, the blue sapphire may be found in a translucent variety that may show a six-rayed star effect when cut into a cabochon. This variety is known as *star sapphire,* of which there are numerous synthetics (often referred to in the trade as Linde, pronounced Lin´dee).

In addition to blue sapphire, we are now beginning to see the appearance of many other color varieties in the latest jewelry designs, especially yellow and pink (Madagascar has recently emerged as an important source of pink sapphires) and, in smaller sizes, some beautiful shades of green. These are known as *fancy* sapphires. Compared with the costly blue sapphire and ruby, these stones offer excellent value and real beauty.

A beautiful and rare variety called *padparadscha* (a type of lotus flower) is also in demand. *The true padparadscha should exhibit pink and orange colors simultaneously.* Depending on the richness of color, brilliance, and size, these can be very expensive. A lovely but more common and more affordable variety, available today, is really a rich orange color. It is often sold as padparadscha, but the rarer and more costly gem will always exhibit a strong pink with the orange. Inexpensive pink sapphire from Madagascar is also being transformed into the much more costly "padparadscha" sapphire by new diffusion techniques. Be very cautious when buying one at auction, unless the stone is accompanied by a laboratory report or the auction house will rescind the sale if subsequent gemological testing reveals it is not a true padparadscha.

Many sapphires today tend to be too dark, however, because of the presence of too much black and poor cutting (cutting deep for additional weight), but the deep blues can be treated to lighten the color. Inevitably, evidence abounds of every technique known to improve the perceived quality and value of the sapphire—alteration of color, synthesis, composites, and misleading names. Be especially alert to the new, treated "padparadscha" sapphire and diffusion-treated blue sapphire, which is blue on the surface only. Note that oil is being used increasingly to conceal fractures and reflective inclusions. Also, watch out for the doublets flooding the market. As always, we urge you to be especially cautious of bargains.

## OTHER POPULAR COLORED GEMS

### Alexandrite

Alexandrite is a fascinating transparent gem that appears grass green in daylight and raspberry red under artificial light. It is a variety of chrysoberyl reputedly discovered in Russia in 1831 on the day Alexander II reached his majority, hence the name.

Unlike other stones, which have been known and admired for thousands of years, alexandrite is a relatively recent gem discovery. Nonetheless, it has definitely come into its own and is presently commanding both high appeal and high prices. Alexandrite is a hard, durable stone (8½ on Mohs' scale) and is normally cut in a faceted style, but some cat's-eye–type alexandrites, found in Brazil, are cut as a cabochon to display the eye effect. These are usually small; the largest we've seen was approximately three carats.

While alexandrite is fairly common in small sizes, it has become relatively scarce in sizes over two carats. A fine three-carat stone can cost $45,000 today in a jewelry store. For people interested in fine alexandrite, the auction market is one of the best sources because fine alexandrites, even in very large sizes—ten carats and above—are frequently seen at important gem and jewelry auctions, at very attractive prices.

Synthetics are frequently encountered as well, so you must be especially careful to buy from a reputable firm. Before 1973, there were no good synthetic alexandrites. While some varieties of synthetic sapphire and synthetic spinel were frequently sold as alexandrite, they really didn't look like alexandrite to anyone who was familiar with genuine alexandrite. But since so few people had ever seen one, they bought them unknowingly. Such is still the case; they are still being made and still being misrepresented. We've seen large "genuine alexandrites" from private estates, with documentation from the stores where they were purchased, which upon closer examination proved to be inexpensive synthetic color-change corundum. Such stones are often sold to tourists in Mexico, Egypt, and Asia as "alexandrite." In Mexico several years ago, at a "government-controlled store" I saw such stones everywhere; when I asked if they would provide a guarantee that the stones were genuine alexandrite, they were more than happy to oblige! Most of the large "alexandrite" purchased while people are traveling abroad is not alexandrite but inexpensive, synthetic color-change sapphire.

Fortunately, these synthetics are easy for a gemologist to spot. In 1973, however, a very good synthetic alexandrite was produced that was *not* easy to differentiate from natural stones. While a good gemologist today can identify these synthetic stones, when they first appeared on the market many were mistaken for the real thing. Be especially careful to verify the authenticity of your alexandrite, since it might have been mistakenly identified years ago and passed along as authentic to the auction house, and from there to you. Remember that if a stone is described *in the capitalized headings* as "alexandrite," then it must be genuine alexandrite, or the auction house can be held liable and must rescind (cancel) the sale or refund your money. However, you must be sure to double-check with an experienced gemologist to make sure; never assume that just because it is described as alexandrite that it *is* genuine alexandrite. When you are buying anything described by online vendors as alexandrite, the risk is much higher, so be sure to take the precautions we recommend in chapter 3.

## Amber

Amber is not a stone but rather amorphous fossilized tree sap. It was one of the earliest substances used for personal adornment. Modestly decorated pieces of rough amber have been found in Stone Age excavations and are assumed to have been used as amulets and talismans—a use definitely recorded throughout history before, during, and since the ancient Greeks. Because of its beautiful color and the ease with which it could be fashioned, amber quickly became a favorite object of trade and barter and personal adornment. Amber varies from transparent to semitranslucent and from yellow to dark brown; occasionally it's seen in reddish and greenish brown tones. In addition, amber can be dyed in many colors. Occasionally, one can find "foreign" fragments or insects that were trapped in the amber, which usually increases its value because of the added curiosity factor.

Plastics are the most common amber imitations. But real amber, which is the lightest gem material, may be easily distinguished from most plastic when dropped into a saturated salt solution: amber will float, while plastic sinks. One other commonly encountered "amber" type is "reconstructed" amber—amber fragments compressed under heat to form a larger piece. An expert can differentiate this from real amber under magnification.

Amber can be easily tested by touching it in an inconspicuous place with a hot needle held by tweezers. The whitish smoke that should be produced should smell like burning pine wood, not like medicine or disinfectant. If there is no smoke, but a black mark occurs, then it is *not* amber. Another test is to try to cut a little piece of the amber with a sharp pointed knife, at the drill hole of the bead; if it cuts like wood (producing a shaving), it is *not* amber, which would produce a sharp, crumbly deposit.

With the exception of those pieces possessing special antique value, the value of amber fluctuates with its popularity, which in part is dictated by the fashion industry and the prevalence of yellow and brown in one's wardrobe. Nonetheless, amber has proved itself an ageless gem and will always be loved and admired.

## Amethyst

Amethyst, a transparent purple variety of quartz, is one of the most popular of the colored stones. Available in shades from light to dark purple, amethyst is relatively hard (7 on Mohs' scale), fairly brilliant, and overall a good, versatile, wearable stone, available in plentiful supply even in very large sizes (although large sizes with deep color are now becoming scarce). Amethyst is probably one of the most beautiful stones available at a moderate price; buyers should be careful, however, because "fine" amethyst is being produced synthetically today. Most synthetics can be identified by a skilled gemologist.

Amethyst may fade from heat and strong sunshine. Guard your amethyst from these conditions, and it should retain its color indefinitely. We are hearing stories from customers across the country, however, complaining of newly purchased amethyst jewelry fading over just a few months, from deep purple to light lavender. This should not happen and may result from an unacceptable color treatment.

## Aquamarine

Aquamarine is a member of the important beryl family, which includes emerald, but aquamarine is less brittle and more durable than its green counterpart (7½ to 8 on Mohs' scale). Aquamarine ranges in color from light blue to bluish green to deep blue, the latter being the most valuable and desirable. It is a very wearable gem, clear and brilliant, and unlike emerald is available with excellent clarity even in very large sizes, although these are becoming scarce today. Aquamarines are still widely available in sizes up to fifteen carats, but ten-carat sizes with fine color and clarity are becoming scarce and are more expensive. Long considered a beautiful and moderately priced gem, aquamarine is now entering the "expensive" classification for stones in larger sizes with a good deep blue color.

Several words of caution for those interested in this lovely gem. First, you may want to think twice before buying a pale or shallow-cut stone, since the color will become paler as dirt accumulates on the back. These stones need constant cleaning to keep them beautiful. Second, be careful not to mistake blue topaz for aquamarine. While topaz is an equally beautiful gem, it is usually much less expensive, since it is usually treated to obtain its desirable color. For those who can't afford an aquamarine, however, blue topaz is an excellent alternative as long as it is properly represented and priced. Finally, note that many aquamarine-colored *synthetic* spinels are erroneously sold as aquamarine, especially in antique jewelry and jewelry from earlier periods.

## Beryl (Golden Beryl, Red Beryl, Morganite)

Beryl is an important gem that comes in a variety of colors, with wonderful clarity (except for emerald), brilliance, and durability (7½ to 8 on Mohs' scale; again with the exception of emerald).

Most people are familiar with the blue variety of beryl, aquamarine, and the green variety, emerald. Few as yet know the pink variety, morganite, and the beautiful yellow to yellow-green variety, referred to as golden beryl. These gems have only recently found their place in the jewelry world but are already being shown in fabulous pieces made by the greatest designers. Beryl is also found in lilac, salmon, orange, sea green, and colorless. Some orange varieties are heated to produce the popular pink color and then sold as morganite.

The rarest color is red, which is even more rare than emerald and is comparable in cost. Until recently, it was known only to serious collectors and was called bixbite after the man who discovered it. The gem variety of red beryl was discovered in Utah, still its only known source. But thanks to the discovery of a new deposit, we are now beginning to see this exciting gemstone in the jewelry market. It faces a major problem, however: what to call it. Some dealers are calling it *red emerald* because it is the same basic material as emerald and because it is truly comparable to emerald in rarity, beauty, and value. Whatever the name by which it is called—red "emerald," red beryl, or bixbite—it is a beautiful gem that should be loved and cherished by anyone lucky enough to own one.

## Bloodstone (Heliotrope)

Bloodstone is a more or less opaque, dark green variety of quartz with specks of red jasper (a variety of quartz) spattering red throughout the dark green field. Particularly popular for men's rings, bloodstone is most desirable when the green isn't so dark as to approach black and the red flecks are roundish and pronounced. It is moderately durable (7 on Mohs' scale) and is fairly readily available and inexpensive.

## Chrysoberyl and Cat's-Eye

The chrysoberyl family is very interesting because all three of its varieties (alexandrite, cat's-eye, and chrysoberyl), while chemically alike, are quite distinct from one another in their optical characteristics and bear no visible resemblance to one another.

Chrysoberyl in its cat's-eye variety (8½ on Mohs' scale) is a hard, translucent gem ranging in color from a honey yellow or honey brown to yellowish green to an almost emerald green. It has a velvety or silklike texture and, when properly cut, displays a brilliant whitish line of light right down the center, appearing almost to be lighted from inside. Genuine cat's-eye should not be confused with the common quartz variety, which is often brown and is called tiger's-eye; the latter has a much less striking eye and weaker color altogether. This phenomenon is produced only in cabochons.

To see the effect properly, the stone should be viewed under a single strong light source, coming if possible from directly overhead. If the line is not exactly in the center, the stone's value is reduced. The line does shift from side to side when the stone is moved about—probably another reason ancient people believed it capable of seeing all and guarding its wearer.

The stone called chrysoberyl, on the other hand, is a brilliant, transparent, very clear, and very durable stone (8½ on Mohs' scale), found in yellow, yellow-green, and green varieties. This is another stone that still offers excellent value. It's a real beauty, very moderately priced, and just beginning to be appreciated and used in contemporary jewelry.

## Chrysoprase and Carnelian

Chrysoprase is an inexpensive, highly translucent, bright, light green to dark green variety of quartz. While its color is often very uniform and can be very lovely in jewelry, for many years these gems have been dyed to enhance their color, where necessary. Chrysoprase is another stone that is usually cut in cabochon style. It has become very popular for jewelry as a fashion accessory. Do not confuse it with jade, however. It is sometimes called Australian jade and is sometimes misrepresented as real jade.

Carnelian is a reddish orange to brownish orange variety of quartz. A moderately hard (7 on Mohs' scale), translucent to opaque stone, it is a favorite because of its warm uniform color and fair durability. It is often found in antique jewelry and lends itself to engraving or carving, especially in cameos. It is still a relatively inexpensive stone, with great warmth and beauty, and offers an excellent choice for jewelry to be worn as an accessory with today's fashion colors.

## Coral

Coral lost its popularity for a while but has been steadily gaining in popularity in recent years. It is a semitranslucent to opaque material, formed from a colony of marine invertebrates, that is primarily a skeletal calcium carbonate gem. The formations as seen in the water look like tree branches. Coral occurs in a variety of colors: white, pink, orange, red, and black. One of the most expensive varieties, very popular in recent years and used extensively in fine jewelry, is angel-skin coral. This is a whitish variety highlighted with a faint blush of pink or peach. Today the rarest variety, and the most expensive, is blood coral, also called noble or oxblood coral. This is a very deep red variety and shouldn't be confused with the more common orangy red varieties. The best red comes from the seas around Italy, the whites from Japanese waters, the blacks (which we personally don't find very attractive, and which are also different chemically) from Hawaii and Mexico.

Coral is usually cabochon cut, often carved, but is also fairly frequently found in jewelry fashioned "in the rough" (uncut) in certain countries where the belief persists that coral's magical powers are lost with cutting. It is a fairly soft stone (3½ on Mohs' scale), so some caution should be exercised when wearing. Also, because of its calcium composition, you must be careful to avoid contact with acid, such as vinegar in a salad that you might toss with your hands.

Also, be a cautious buyer for this gem as for others; glass and plastic imitations are commonplace.

## Garnet

The garnet family is one of the most exciting families in the gem world. One of the few gems not routinely treated, it is moderately hard (ranging from 6½ to 7½ on Mohs' scale), durable, and brilliant. It is available in many colors (greens, reds, yellows, oranges) and offers far greater versatility and opportunity for the jewelry trade than has yet been capitalized on. Depending on the variety, quality, and size, lovely garnets are available for under $40 per carat or more than $5,000 per carat. Garnet can also be mistaken for other, usually more expensive, gems. Green garnet (tsavorite) is one of the most beautiful, and all but a few would assume it was an emerald of the finest quality. In fact, it is clearer, more brilliant, and more durable than emerald itself. There is also a rarer green garnet, called demantoid, which costs slightly more than tsavorite but which, although slightly softer, has more fire. While still rare, expensive gems themselves, these garnet varieties are far less expensive than emeralds of comparable quality. Garnet also occurs in certain shades of red that have been taken for some varieties of ruby, and in yellow it has been confused with precious topaz.

Garnet is found in almost every color and shade, including a rare color-change variety that appears red in incandescent light and blue (the only color not normally seen in garnet) in daylight or fluorescent light. It is best known in a deep red variety but is commonly found in orangish brown shades and brilliant wine red shades as well. Other colors include orange (the new Mandarin garnet being an intense fiery red-orange), red-purple, violet, and pink. A nontransparent variety, grossularite, resembles jade and may be mistaken for jade in cabochons and carvings.

A star garnet found in the United States is a reddish to purple variety that displays a faint four-rayed or six-rayed star, similar to the six-rayed star ruby but not as pronounced.

## Hematite and Marcasite

Hematite is an iron oxide (like iron rust), a metallic, opaque stone found in iron-mining areas. It takes a very brilliant, metallic polish that can look almost like silver, or almost pure black, or gunmetal blue. It was and is popular for use in carving hollow cameo portraits known as intaglio.

Marcasite, the tiny, glittering stone with a brassy-colored luster often seen in old belt buckles and costume jewelry, is a relative of hematite. Most "marcasite" seen in jewelry is not marcasite but pyrite (fool's gold)—another brassy-colored metallic mineral.

## Iolite

This is a transparent, usually very clean, blue gem, ranging from deep blue to light gray-blue to yellowish gray. It is sometimes called dichroite, and in its sapphire blue color is sometimes referred to as *water sapphire* or *lynx sapphire*. It is a lovely, brilliant stone but is not as durable as sapphire (7 to 7½ on Mohs' scale). We are just beginning to see this stone in jewelry, and it is still a good value. It is abundant, still very low priced, and one of the most attractive jewelry options for the near future.

## Jade

Jade is a very tough, although not too hard, translucent to opaque gem, often seen in jewelry and carvings. There are two types of jade—jadeite and nephrite—which are really two separate and distinct minerals differing from each other in weight, hardness, and color range. Both are called jade.

Jadeite, the more expensive and more desirable variety, was the most sought after by the Chinese after 1740. It is not found in China, however, but in Burma. Some fine jadeite also comes from Guatemala. It is found in a much wider range of colors than nephrite: green, mottled green and white, whitish gray, pink, brown, mauve, yellow, orange, and lilac. In fact, it occurs in almost every color. But with the exception of green, which comes in shades that vary from light to a beautiful emerald green, colored jade is usually pale and unevenly tinted. The most desirable color is a rich emerald green, sometimes referred to as imperial jade. Smooth, evenly colored pieces of this jadeite are highly prized and, in fact, can be classed as precious stones today. The mottled pieces of irregular green, often seen carved, are less valuable but are still more rare and valuable than nephrite jade.

Nephrite jade, the old and true Chinese jade, resembles jadeite but is slightly softer (jadeite is 7 on Mohs' scale; nephrite, 6½, yet slightly tougher and thus less easily broken) and has a much more limited range of color. Usually fashioned in cabochon cut, or round beads, or in carvings, it is regularly seen in dark green shades sometimes so dark as to look black—hence, black jade. Nephrite green is a more sober green than the apple green or emerald green color of good jadeite. It is closer in color to a dark sage green or spinach green. Nephrite may also be a creamier color, as in mutton-fat jade. Any fine Chinese carving that is more than 230 years old is carved from nephrite (jadeite was unknown to the Chinese before 1740).

Nephrite has been found in many countries, including the United States, where Chinese miners panning for gold in California in the late nineteenth century discovered large boulders of nephrite jade that they sent back to China to be cut or carved. It is also common in Wyoming, Alaska, and British Columbia.

Nephrite jade is much more common than jadeite and is therefore much less expensive. But it is a lovely, popular stone, used extensively in jewelry and carvings.

One must be careful, however, in purchasing jade. You will often see "imperial" jade that is nothing more than a cheap jade that has been dyed, or dyed quartz. Much jade is treated with polymers or dyed to enhance its value. The dyeing, however, may be very temporary. Black jade is either dyed or very dark green nephrite that looks black. There are also numerous minerals that look like jade and are sold as jade under misleading names, such as "Korean jade," which is serpentine, a soft, green stone similar in appearance to some varieties of jade. In fact, much of the intricately and beautifully carved jade is actually serpentine, which can be scratched easily with a knife.

Soapstone may also look like jade to the amateur, especially when it is beautifully carved. This stone is so soft that it can easily be scratched with a pin, a hairpin, or the point of a pen. It is much less expensive than comparable varieties of jade, as well as softer and less durable.

Jade is a wonderful stone, and imperial jade is breathtaking; no wonder it was the emperor's stone! But jade has long been "copied"—misrepresented and altered. Just be sure you *know* you are buying what you *think* you are buying.

## Lapis Lazuli

Genuine lapis is a natural blue opaque stone of intense, brilliant, deep blue color. It sometimes possesses small, sparkling gold-colored or silver-colored flecks (pyrite inclusions), although the finest quality is a deep, even blue with a purplish tint or undertone and no trace of those flecks. Occasionally it may be blue mottled with white.

Don't confuse genuine lapis with the cheaper "Swiss lapis" or "Italian lapis," which aren't lapis at all. These are natural stones (usually quartz) artificially colored to look like lapis lazuli. Genuine lapis is often represented as "Russian lapis," although it doesn't always come from Russia. The finest lapis comes from Afghanistan.

Lapis has become very fashionable, and the finest-quality lapis is becoming more rare and more expensive. This has resulted in an abundance of lapis that has been "color improved." It is often fashioned today with other gems—pearls, crystal, coral—that make particularly striking fashion accessories.

Sodalite is sometimes confused with the more expensive, and rarer, lapis and is used as a substitute for it. However, sodalite rarely contains the silvery or golden flecks typical of most lapis. It may have some white veining, but more commonly it just exhibits the fine lapis blue without any markings. The lapis substitutes transmit some light through the edges of the stone; lapis does not, since it is opaque.

Dyed chalcedony (quartz), glass, and plastic imitations are common. One quick and easy test to identify genuine lapis is to put a drop of hydrochloric acid on the stones; this will immediately produce the odor of a rotten egg. This test should be administered only by a professional, however, since hydrochloric acid can be dangerous.

## Malachite and Azurite

Malachite is popular today because of the exquisite color and a softness (3½ on Mohs' scale) that makes it very popular for carving. Malachite is a copper ore that comes in a brilliant kelly green, marked with bands or concentric striping in contrasting shades of the same basic green. It is opaque and takes a good polish, but it is soft and should not be worn in rings. This softness, however, makes it a favorite substance for use in carved bases, boxes, beads, statues, spheres, and so on. It is also used in pins, pendants, and necklaces (usually of malachite beads).

Azurite is also a copper ore, but it occurs in a very vivid deep blue, similarly marked. Occasionally one will come across both the green and the blue intermingled in brilliant combinations of color and striking patterns. Both malachite and azurite make beautiful jewelry and lovely carvings.

*A particular note of caution:* Never clean malachite or azurite with any product containing ammonia. In seconds the ammonia will remove all the polish, which will significantly reduce the stone's beauty.

## Moonstone (Orthoclase Feldspar)

The name *moonstone* is probably derived from the myth that one can observe the lunar month through the stone—that a small white spot appears in the stone as the new moon begins and gradually moves toward the stone's center, growing always larger, until the spot finally takes the shape of a full moon in the center of the stone.

Moonstone is a member of the feldspar family (6 to 6½ on Mohs' scale). It is a transparent, milky white variety in which can be seen a floating opalescent white or blue light within the stone's body. It is a popular stone for rings because as the hand moves the effect of the brilliant light color is more pronounced. The bluer color is the finer and more desirable, but it is becoming rare in today's market, particularly in large sizes.

There are some glass imitations of moonstone, but compared with the real thing they are not very good.

## Onyx

Onyx is a lovely, banded, semitranslucent to opaque quartz. It comes naturally in a variety of colors—reds, oranges, reddish orange, apricot, and shades of brown from cream to dark, often alternating with striking bands of white. The banding in onyx is straight, while curved bands occur in the variety of quartz known as agate. Onyx is used extensively for cameo and other carving work. It is also frequently dyed.

The "black onyx" that is commonly used in jewelry isn't onyx at all and isn't naturally black. It is chalcedony (another variety of quartz) dyed black. It is *always* dyed and may be banded or solid black.

Do not confuse the quartz variety of onyx with cave onyx, which is found in the stalactites and stalagmites of underground caves. Cave onyx is a different material altogether. It is much softer, lacks the color variety, and is much less expensive than quartz onyx.

## Opal

When we try to describe the opal, we realize how insufficient the English language is. It is unique among the gems, displaying an array of very brilliant miniature rainbow effects, all mixed together.

Its most outstanding characteristic is this unusual, intense display of many colors flashing out like mini-rainbows. This effect is created by opal's formation process, which is very different from that of other gems. Opal is composed of hydrated silica spheres. The mini-rainbows seen in most opals result from light interference created by these spheres. The arrangement of the spheres, which vary in size and pattern, is responsible for the different colors.

Opal is usually cut flat or in cabochon, since there is no additional brilliance to be captured by faceting. In opals, color is everything. The more brilliant the color, the more valuable the gem. It is probably truer of opal than any other stone that the more beautiful the stone and its color, the more it will cost. But it is fairly soft (5 to 6½ on Mohs' scale), so opals should be treated with care.

The finest of all is the black opal. Black opals are usually a deep gray or grayish black with flashes of incredibly brilliant color dancing around within and about the stones as they are turned. One must be careful when purchasing a black opal, however, to ensure that it is not a doublet or triplet: a stone composed of two or three parts of some material fused or glued together.

There are many such doublets on the market because of the black opal's rarity, beauty, and extremely high cost; a black opal the size of a lima bean could cost $25,000 today. The black opal doublet provides an affordable option to one who loves the stone but can't afford a natural, but it also provides another opportunity for misrepresentation that can be very costly to the consumer.

Generally speaking, purity of color, absence of dead spots (called trueness), flawlessness, and intensity or brilliance of color are the primary variables affecting value. Opals with an abundance of red are usually the most expensive; those strong in blue and green are equally beautiful but not as rare, so their price is somewhat less. Some opals are very transparent and are classified as jelly, semi-jelly, or water opals. One of the rarest is the harlequin opal, which displays color patterns resembling a checkerboard.

While there are imitations and synthetics, for the most part their quality is such that they are not yet worth considering. The synthetic opal, nonetheless, is being used extensively. Also, since the color of black opals can be improved by treatment, treated opals are encountered frequently. So the usual precautions are in order: make sure you know what you are getting, and before buying, shop around at auction firms and online auctions. This holds truer for opal, perhaps, than for any other stone.

One word of caution must also be offered: opals require special care because some tend to dry and crack. Avoid exposure to anything that is potentially drying, and immerse your opal in water for several hours periodically to help preserve it. *Never immerse opals in oil;* soaking some opals in oil for only a few hours can cause them to lose some or nearly all of their fire. *Note:* It was once thought that wiping the surface of an opal regularly with oil would protect it. *This is not true and will damage most opals.*

## Peridot (Olivine)

Peridot is popular today for its lovely shade of green. While peridot is not particularly brilliant, the richness of its color can be exceptional. It comes in shades of yellowish green to darker, purer green colors. Unfortunately, because of its rarity most people never see peridot in the deeper, purer green color that is so prized.

Peridot is still widely available in small sizes, but larger stones are becoming scarce, so prices are now fairly high for good-quality material in higher-carat weights.

Some caution should be exercised in wearing peridot. It is moderately hard (6½ to 7 on Mohs' scale) but can chip and scratch easily. Also, some stones—like green sapphire or green tourmaline—can look like peridot and be mistaken or misrepresented.

## Quartz

The most versatile of any of the gem families, quartz includes among its members more variety and a larger number of gems than any other three mineral families together. In the gem trade, the old saying "If in doubt, say quartz" still holds true.

The quartz minerals, for the most part, are relatively inexpensive gems that offer a wide range of pleasing color alternatives in both transparent and nontransparent varieties, from translucent to opaque. They are reasonably hard stones (7 on Mohs' scale) and, while not very brilliant in the transparent varieties, still create lovely, affordable jewelry.

Some of these gems have been discussed in separate sections, but we will provide a list here with brief descriptions of most of the quartz family members.

***Transparent varieties.*** *Amethyst* (see pages 219–220) is lilac to purple in color.

*Citrine* is often called quartz topaz, citrine topaz, or topaz, all of which are misleading. The correct name for this stone is citrine. It is yellow, amber to amber brown. This is the most commonly seen "topaz" in today's marketplace and is, unfortunately, too often confused with precious topaz because of the careless use of the name. While a pleasing stone in terms of color and fairly durable, citrine is slightly softer and has less brilliance than precious topaz. It also lacks the subtle color shading—the pinker yellow or pinkish amber shades—that lends to precious topaz a distinctive color difference. Much citrine is made by heating pale amethyst.

Citrine is much less expensive than precious topaz. It should never be represented as topaz, which technically is "precious" or "imperial" topaz. Unfortunately, it often is. For example, "topaz" birthstone jewelry is almost always citrine (or a worthless synthetic). So the question to ask the seller is, "Is this citrine or precious topaz?" Get the answer in writing if you are told "precious topaz."

Citrine is plentiful in all sizes and can be made into striking jewelry, especially in very large sizes, for a relatively small investment, while precious topaz of fine quality is scarce in sizes over seven carats and is very expensive.

*Ametrine* is a lovely, unusual bicolor quartz in which amethyst and citrine are both present in the same stone. The name is derived by taking the first three letters of amethyst and the last five letters in citrine. Bolivia is the source of natural ametrine, although "ametrine" can also be created in the laboratory.

*Praseolite* is a pale green transparent variety produced by heating amethyst.

*Rock crystal* is water clear. It was used in old jewelry for rondelles, a type of small bead resembling a doughnut. Faceted crystal beads were also common in older jewelry. Today, however, *crystal* usually refers to glass.

*Rose quartz* is light to deep pink. This stone has been very popular for many years for use in carved pieces—beads, statues, ashtrays, fine lamp bases, and pins and brooches. Rarely clear, this stone is usually seen in cabochon cuts, rounded beads, or carvings rather than in faceted styles. Once very inexpensive, it is becoming more costly, particularly in the finer deep pink shades. But the color of rose quartz is especially pleasing and offers an excellent choice for use in fashion accessory jewelry.

You must be somewhat cautious with rose quartz, however, because it tends to crack more easily than most other varieties of quartz if struck or exposed to a blow. The inclusions or internal fractures that are also responsible for the absence of clarity in this stone cause it to be slightly brittle.

*Smokey quartz* is a pale to rich smokey brown variety, sometimes mistaken for or misrepresented as smokey topaz or topaz. It is also very plentiful and is becoming popular for use in very large sizes for beautiful brooches, large dinner rings, and so forth.

**Translucent to opaque varieties.** *Agate* and *chalcedony* are found in all colors, and all varieties of markings are seen in this wonderful ornamental gem. Among them you'll find, to mention a few, banded agate; moss agate, a fascinating white or milky agate that looks as though it actually has black, brown, or green moss growing within; eye agate, which has an eyeball effect; or plume agate, which looks as if it's filled with beautiful feather plumes. The colors and "scenes" in agate are infinite. While agate is usually an inexpensive stone, some varieties or special stones with very unusual scenes or markings can be quite expensive.

*Carnelian, sard,* and *sardonyx* are reddish, orange, apricot, and brown varieties of chalcedony and are often seen in cameo or other carving work.

Black onyx is a dyed chalcedony; chrysoprase is green chalcedony, often dyed green. They are often seen in antique jewelry as well as in contemporary pieces. One must be careful, however, to exercise some caution in wear to protect the stone from knocks, as some varieties are more fragile than others. Also, agate is frequently dyed, so it is important to ask whether the color is natural and to be sure that it is not another less valuable stone, dyed to look like a special variety of agate.

*Aventurine* is a lovely pale to medium green semitranslucent stone with tiny sparkling flecks of mica within. This stone makes very lovely cabochon or bead jewelry at a very affordable price. It is occasionally misrepresented as jade; although the mica flecks are sometimes so small that they cannot be seen easily, they provide an immediate and reliable indicator that the material is aventurine quartz. Be aware, however, that there are some fairly good glass imitations in the marketplace.

*Bloodstone* (see page 221) is dark green with red spots.

*Cat's-eye* is a pale yellowish green stone that when cut in cabochon style produces a streak of light down the center, creating an eye effect. This stone has a weaker center line, a paler color, and a much lower cost than true cat's-eye from the chrysoberyl family.

*Chrysocolla*—the true chrysocolla—is a very soft copper mineral, too soft for jewelry use. However, quartz that has been naturally impregnated or stained with chrysocolla has good hardness and the same brilliant blue-green, highly translucent color. Chrysocolla is becoming a very popular stone for jewelry.

*Chrysoprase* (see page 222) is a bright light to dark green, highly translucent stone, often of very even color. It is sometimes misrepresented as or confused with jade.

*Jasper* is opaque red, yellow, green, and brown (or sometimes gray). It is usually strongly marked in terms of the contrast between the green and other colors in an almost blotchlike or veinlike pattern. The red and green combination is the most popular, although there are more than fifty types of jasper of various colors and patterns. Jasper offers interesting color contrast and variety and was a favorite in bygone eras.

*Petrified wood* is sections of trees or limbs that have been replaced by quartz-type silica and transformed into a mineral after centuries of immersion in silica-rich water under extreme pressure. It is usually red, reddish brown, or brown and is not often seen in jewelry.

*Tiger's-eye* is a golden, yellowish, reddish, and sometimes bluish variety of quartz that produces a bright shimmering line (or lines) of light, which when cut in a cabochon will produce an eye. The eye will move when the stone is turned from side to side. It is popular for men's cufflinks and rings.

## Serpentine

Serpentine derives its name from its similarity to the green speckled skin of the serpent. It is often used as a jade substitute. It is a translucent to semi-translucent stone occurring in light to dark yellowish green to greenish yellow. One variety is used for decorative wall facings and table and counter surfaces, but some of the more attractive green varieties so closely resemble jadeite or nephrite jade that they are used in carvings and jewelry and are often misrepresented as jade. Common serpentine is also sometimes dyed a jade-like color. One lovely green variety, williamsite, which is a very pleasing deep green, often with small black flecks within, is often sold as "Pennsylvania jade." It is pretty, but it is not jade. Another variety of serpentine, bowenite, is also sold today as "Korean jade" or "new jade." Again, it is pretty, but it is not jade. Serpentine is softer than jade, less durable, and much more common, which its price should reflect.

## Sodalite

This stone has already been discussed under "Lapis." It is a dark blue semi-transparent to semitranslucent stone, used frequently as a substitute for the rarer, more expensive lapis. While it may have some white veining, it does not have the golden or silver flecks that are characteristic of lapis. If you do not see these shiny flecks, suspect that the stone is probably sodalite.

## Spinel

Spinel is one of the loveliest of the gems, but it has only recently begun to enjoy the respect and admiration it deserves. It is usually compared with sapphire or ruby rather than being recognized for its own intrinsic beauty and value. There is also a common belief that spinel (and similarly zircon) is synthetic rather than natural, when in fact it is one of nature's most beautiful—and truly natural—creations. This misconception probably arose because synthetic spinel is seen frequently on the market, whereas genuine spinel is not often seen.

Spinel is one of the few gems not routinely treated or enhanced. It occurs in red-orange (flame spinel), light to dark orangy red, light to dark slightly grayish blue, greenish blue, grayish green, and dark to light purple to violet. It also occurs in yellow and in an opaque variety: black. When compared with the blue of sapphire or the red of ruby, the color is usually considered less intense (although some red spinel can look very much like some ruby on the market now), yet its brilliance can be greater. If you appreciate these spinel colors for themselves, they are quite pleasing. The most popular are red (usually a more orange-red than ruby red) and blue (sometimes resembling a strong Bromo-Seltzer–bottle blue).

Spinel may be confused with or misrepresented as one of many stones—ruby, sapphire, zircon, amethyst, garnet, synthetic ruby/sapphire, or synthetic spinel—as well as glass. The synthetic is often used to make composite stones such as doublets. Spinel is a hard (8 on Mohs' scale), fairly durable stone, possessing a nice brilliance, and is still a good value.

## Spodumene (Kunzite and Hiddenite)

Spodumene is another gem relatively new to widespread jewelry use. The most popular varieties are kunzite and hiddenite.

*Kunzite* is a very lovely brilliant stone occurring in delicate lilac, pinkish, or violet shades. Its color can fade in strong light, so it has become known as an "evening" stone. Also, while basically hard (6 to 7 on Mohs' scale), it is nonetheless brittle and can break easily if it receives a sharp blow from certain directions. It is not recommended for rings for this reason unless set in a protective mounting. But it is a lovely gem, whose low cost makes it attractive in large sizes, and is an excellent choice for lovely, dramatic jewelry design.

*Hiddenite* is rarer. Light green or yellow-green varieties are available, but the emerald green varieties are scarce. As with kunzite, it is hard but brittle, so care must be exercised in wear.

Spodumene also occurs in many other shades of color, all pale but very clear and brilliant. Only blue is currently missing—but who knows what may yet be discovered in some part of the world? Spodumene is still fairly inexpensive and is an excellent choice for contemporary jewelry design. Be careful, however, as it can be confused with and sold as more expensive topaz, tourmaline, spinel, or beryl. Also, synthetic corundum or spinel can be mistaken for this gem.

# Topaz

True topaz is one of nature's most wonderful and least-known families. The true topaz is rarely seen in jewelry stores. Unfortunately, most people know only the quartz (citrine) topaz, or glass, and in the past almost any yellow stone was called topaz. A very beautiful and versatile stone, topaz is a hard, brilliant stone with a fine color range, and it is much rarer and much more expensive than the stones commonly sold as topaz. It is also heavier than its imitators.

Topaz occurs not only in the transparent yellow, yellow-brown, orangy brown, and pinky brown colors most popularly associated with it, but also in a very light to medium red now found naturally in fair supply, although many are produced through heat treatment. It also is found in a very light to medium deep blue, also often as the result of radiation treatment, although blue does occur naturally on a fairly wide scale. Other topaz shades include very light green, light greenish yellow, violet, and colorless. Diffusion-treated topaz is also available in medium to deep green and blue-green.

Blue topaz has become very popular in recent years, most of it treated; unfortunately, there is no way yet to determine which stones have been treated and which are natural. The blue form closely resembles the finest aquamarine, which is very expensive today, and offers a very attractive and much more affordable alternative to it. Some of the fine, deeper blue treated topazes have been found to be radioactive and, according to the Nuclear Regulatory Commission, may be injurious to the wearer. In the United States, all blue topaz must be tested for radiation levels; the Gemological Institute of America now provides this service to the jewelry trade. However, be very careful when buying blue topaz outside the United States. If you do, you may be wise to have it tested when you get home.

There are many misleading names to suggest that a stone is topaz when it is not, for example, "Rio topaz," "Madeira topaz," "Spanish topaz," and "Palmeira topaz." They are types of citrine (quartz) and should be represented as such.

The true topaz family offers a variety of color options in lovely, clear, brilliant, and durable stones (8 on Mohs' scale). This family should become more important in the years ahead.

## Tourmaline

Tourmaline is one of the most versatile of the gem families. It is available in every color and in every tone, from deep to pastel and even with two or more colors appearing in the same stone, side by side. There are bicolored tourmalines (half red and half green, for example) and tricolored (one-third blue, one-third green, and one-third yet another color). The fascinating "watermelon" tourmaline looks just like the inside of a watermelon: red in the center surrounded by a green "rind."

One of the most exciting gemological discoveries of this century was the discovery of a unique variety of tourmaline in Paraiba, Brazil. These particular beauties, referred to as Paraiba, have colors so intense and come in such a wide range of green, blue, and lilac shades that they are referred to as the neon tourmalines. Unfortunately, demand has been unprecedented for these particular tourmalines, and the supply has dwindled. The result is that many of the finest Paraibas are very expensive, and some rival the finest sapphires in price. Occasionally they appear at auction, selling at prices way below the current market value. Many imitations are now on the market as well, and we have found apatite, a common, inexpensive stone that occurs in similar colors but is too soft for most jewelry use, being sold as "Paraiba" tourmaline.

It is indeed surprising that most people know of tourmaline simply as a common "green" stone. Nothing could be more misleading. Today, we are finally beginning to see other lovely varieties of this fascinating gem in the jewelry market. In addition to the exciting new Paraiba, other popular varieties include the following:

- Chrome—a particularly rare green hue
- Indicolite—deep indigo blue, usually with a green undertone
- Rubellite—deep pink to red, as in ruby

While many tourmalines are very inexpensive, the chrome, indicolite, and rubellite varieties are priced (depending on size and quality) anywhere from $300 to $1,000 per carat or more. And the incomparable Paraiba varieties can sell for $12,000 to $15,000 per carat for a top-quality one-carat stone and up to $25,000 per carat for a five-carat stone, if you can find one. So much for the "common and inexpensive" myth!

Tourmaline is a fairly hard (7 to 7½ on Mohs' scale), durable, brilliant, and very wearable stone with a wide choice of colors. It is also still available in large sizes. It is a stone that without question will play a more and more important role in jewelry in the years ahead.

## Turquoise

Turquoise is an opaque, light to dark blue or blue-green stone. The finest color is an intense blue, with poorer qualities tending toward yellowish green. The famous Persian turquoise, which can be a very intense and pleasing blue, is considered a very rare and valuable gem. The United States (Arizona and New Mexico) is also an important source of fine turquoise and is now the major source of turquoise used in jewelry worldwide.

All turquoises are susceptible to "aging," turning greenish or possibly darker with age. Also, care must be taken to avoid contact with soap, grease, or other materials that might discolor it and to protect it from abuse, since turquoise scratches fairly easily (6 on Mohs' scale).

But you should exercise caution when buying turquoise. This is a frequently simulated gem. Very fine glass imitations are produced that are difficult to distinguish from the genuine. Enhanced, coated, and "stabilized" stones, and reconstructed stones (from turquoise powder bonded in plastic), saturate the marketplace, as does synthetic turquoise. There are techniques to quickly distinguish these imitations or treated stones, so, if in doubt, check it out (and get a complete description on the bill of sale: "genuine, natural turquoise").

## Zircon

Zircons are very brilliant, transparent stones available in several lovely colors. Unfortunately, many consumers suffer from a strange misconception that zircon is a synthetic or artificial stone rather than a lovely natural creation. Perhaps this belief is based on the fact that they are frequently color treated, as in the blue zircons so often seen. Zircons also occur naturally in yellow, brown, orange, and red.

Many might mistake the colorless zircon for diamond because of its strong brilliance, which, coupled with its very low cost, makes colorless zircon an interesting alternative to diamonds as a stone to offset or dress up colored stones. But care needs to be exercised because zircon is only moderately hard

(6½ to 7½ on Mohs' scale), and it is brittle, so it will chip or abrade easily. For this reason, zircon is recommended for earrings, pendants, brooches, or rings with a protective setting.

## Zoisite (Tanzanite)

Zoisite was not considered a gem material until 1967, when a beautiful rich, blue to purple-blue, transparent variety was found in Tanzania (hence tanzanite). Tanzanite can possess a rich, sapphire blue color, possibly with some violet-red or greenish yellow flashes. A gem green variety has recently been discovered, which is being called green tanzanite or chrome tanzanite. The green can be a very lovely shade, ranging from a slightly yellowish green to gray-green to a bluish green. The supply is still limited, so time will tell whether or not this green variety will be readily available to the public.

Tanzanite has become one of the most popular gems in the marketplace. As a result, many imitations are being produced. Double-check the identity of any fine tanzanite with a gemologist-appraiser. However, while it is hard (8½ on Mohs' scale), it is brittle and can chip easily, so we do not recommend tanzanite for rings (unless set in a very protected setting) or for everyday wear in which it would be exposed to knocks and other abuse.

# 20 ◆ PEARLS

*The richest merchandise of all, and the most sovereign commodity throughout the whole world, are these pearls.*

—G. Plinius Secundus (Pliny the Elder), Roman historian and writer, from *Natural History,* 77 A.D.

NEXT TO THE DIAMOND, THERE IS NO GEM MORE FASCINATING THAN the pearl. The oldest known natural pearl necklace is more than four thousand years old.

Today, the auction market has become a primary source for rare, *natural* pearls. While the finest are rarely seen on the auction block today and can command stellar prices, natural pearls can still be found at very attractive prices by comparison to the cost of cultured pearls. When seeking pearls at auction, whether rare natural pearls or cultured, you must keep in mind that they run the gamut in quality, rarity, and price. To recognize the rarest and most valuable, and to avoid overpaying for something inferior, you must understand how to judge variations in characteristics and quality. Here, we will provide some of the most essential information to help you understand pearls better.

## WHAT IS A PEARL?

A pearl is the gem produced by saltwater oysters (the nonedible variety) or by freshwater mollusks. In either case, a small foreign object (such as a tiny sea parasite from the ocean floor) finds its way into the shell and then into the tissue of the mollusk. If the intruder becomes trapped, and the oyster can't rid itself of it, the foreign body becomes an irritant. To ease the discomfort created by this irritant, the mollusk takes defensive action and produces a blackish substance called conchiolin, over which another substance, a whitish substance called nacre, is secreted. This is the lustrous pearly coating for which the pearl is prized. The nacre is composed of microscopic crystals, each crystal aligned perfectly with the others so that light passing along the axis of one is reflected and refracted by the others to produce a rainbowlike glow of light and color. The pearl is the result of the buildup of layer after layer of this nacre. The thicker the nacre, the more beautiful the pearl.

Most pearls sold today are cultured pearls, produced by saltwater and freshwater mollusks in specially controlled environments created by trained technicians. Natural pearls—or "Oriental" pearls, as they are sometimes called—are rarer today than ever before in history.

The finest cultured pearls are also rare and expensive, but they are much more affordable than fine natural pearls. As a result of pearl culturing, many more people can enjoy pearls than would otherwise have been possible.

One way to understand the difference between a natural pearl and a cultured pearl is to think of the natural pearl as a product of the oyster working alone, and the cultured pearl as a product of humans *helping* nature. In the natural pearl, the irritating intruder that starts the whole process is a very tiny intruder—often microscopic—such as a parasitic worm that bores its way through the shell into the oyster tissue. In the cultured pearl, humans surgically *implant* the intruder. In *round* saltwater and freshwater cultured pearls, this implant is a round mother-of-pearl bead, accompanied by a piece of mantle tissue; in freshwater cultured pearls, the implant may be mantle tissue alone. The mantle tissue carries the cells that start the actual production of conchiolin and nacre; placing it next to the round bead assures that the *bead* will be nacre-coated to become a nice, *round* pearl. Freshwater pearls produced from only mantle tissue are *not* round but elongated and asymmetrical in shape. The implant, whether a bead and mantle tissue implant or mantle tissue alone, is called the nucleus; the nucleus then causes an irritation that the mollusk eases by secreting nacre, which ultimately becomes the pearl.

After the initial implantation, the process by which the cultured pearl is produced is very similar to that in the natural pearl: the oyster begins to produce conchiolin and nacre to coat the irritating nucleus, layer after layer building up to produce the pearl. It is the *oyster* that produces the nacre; it is the *oyster* that produces the pearl; *it is the oyster and nature that determine what the quality of each pearl will be.*

In the case of natural pearls, scientists estimate that depending upon conditions such as water temperature and food supply, it can take *ten to fifteen years,* or longer, for an oyster to produce a seven-millimeter pearl. With cultured pearls, the cultivation period normally ranges from less than a year to under two years from the time of the implant. The shorter the cultivation period, the thinner the nacre; the longer the cultivation period, the thicker the nacre.

At one time, pearls remained in the oyster for much longer periods: up to five years. For cultured pearl growers, however, escalating production costs and the ever-present natural risks to the oyster crop are reduced by shortening the cultivation period. Growers have also learned that apart from nacre thickness, longer cultivation periods can adversely affect other factors determining the beauty of the pearl, especially shape and surface perfection. The nucleus inserted into the oyster, for example, is round at the start, but the longer it remains in the oyster, the more out-of-round it can become as the nacre builds up. Furthermore, the longer the nucleus is in the oyster, the more spotted its surface can become. In other words, earlier harvesting results in rounder pearls with more perfect surfaces.

## How Much of the Pearl Is Really "Pearl"?

The primary physical differences between natural and cultured pearls are related to the thickness of the actual pearl substance: the nacre. In natural pearls, the thickness of the nacre affects size, shape, beauty, and how long the pearl will last.

In cultured pearls, the size of the *nucleus* dictates the size of the pearl; in cultured pearl production, larger pearls are produced by inserting a larger nucleus, smaller pearls by implanting a smaller nucleus. While it takes several years to raise the oyster and produce a fine cultured pearl, natural pearls take *many* years, even for very small pearls. With natural pearls, the pearl is essentially all nacre, with no nucleus at its core. The process that creates the natural pearl is usually started by a very small intruder, so the size of the pearl is an indication of the number of years the pearl has been in the oyster rather than the size of the implant. Small natural pearls have normally been in the oyster for a shorter time; larger pearls a much longer time.

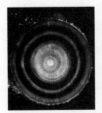 

*Left:* Cross section of *natural* pearl showing concentric rings of nacre; *Right:* Cross section of *cultured* pearl showing large nucleus

## CULTURED OR NATURAL, FINE PEARLS IN LARGE SIZES ARE RARE AND COSTLY

Large natural pearls of fine quality are among the rarest of earth's treasures. Keep in mind that among all the pearl-producing oysters, only a very small percentage ever experience that unique set of natural circumstances that result in the creation of the pearl. Furthermore, in nature there are more variables affecting the quality and beauty of the pearl—not all natural pearls are of fine quality; not all are beautiful and desirable. The larger the pearl, the less likely it will be fine and beautiful; as in cultured pearls, the longer the pearl remains in the oyster, the greater the likelihood that there will be defects in its shape, surface perfection, nacre crystallization, and so on. Last but not least, natural pearl-producing oysters have never been conveniently located for easy access, and diving for natural pearls has always been very perilous, often ending in death. Divers have spent entire lifetimes diving for pearls, only to end up with little more than a handful of small pearls for their work. Among all the known natural pearls, including famous historic pearls, fine large pearls are few and far between.

Diving for natural pearls continues today in various parts of the world, but for the most part, the oyster beds known for fine natural pearls have been killed by pollution. Discovering so rare a treasure as a large, fine, natural pearl holds a powerful allure to some, but for most the discovery will never be more than a dream. Fine natural pearls are rarer today than ever before, and large natural pearls are rarer still.

Fine large cultured pearls are also rarer than smaller cultured pearls. A very fine fifteen-millimeter round cultured pearl is not as rare as the natural, but it is still a costly treasure. Whether cultured or natural, the larger the pearl, the rarer and costlier. In cultured pearls, cultivators insert several different size nuclei into oysters, producing a variety of pearl sizes at harvest. But as the size of the implant increases, the number of fine-quality pearls actually harvested decreases. As the size of the nucleus increases, fewer oysters survive the implant operation, and more oysters reject the nucleus, so fewer pearls are actually harvested. Furthermore, as we've already discussed, the larger the nucleus, the more difficult it becomes for the oyster to produce a fine-quality pearl. So there are fewer pearls, and far fewer *fine* pearls. This is why larger cultured pearls of fine quality are rarer, and why they cost so much more than comparable smaller cultured pearls.

## CLUES TO SPOTTING NATURAL PEARLS

The major difference between natural and cultured pearls lies in the percentage of the pearl that is truly "pearl"—that is, nacre. The natural pearl is all pearl, or all nacre, while most cultured pearls consist of a nucleus coated with nacre.

Very few people can *see* any difference between a very fine cultured pearl *with thick nacre* and a very fine natural pearl. Both will exhibit a rich, deep, intense lustrousness accentuated by a beautiful, soft iridescent "play of color"—sometimes referred to as "orient"—that can be seen moving across the surface of the pearl as it moves in the light. As a result, the only way to distinguish an exceptionally fine cultured pearl with thick nacre from a rare natural pearl is by submitting it to a gem-testing laboratory for x-ray analysis.

Generally speaking, however, there are some visual clues that might suggest whether a pearl is natural or cultured.

- *Matching.* Because of their scarcity and limited supply, matching of natural pearls was often ignored, especially as the size increased, so necklaces often contain pearls with marked differences in size, color, and shape.
- *Color.* In terms of color, natural pearls are usually *creamier* than today's finest cultured pearls, and in necklaces and bracelets, there may be subtle variations in color throughout the strand.
- *Shape.* In terms of shape, natural pearls are rarely truly "round," and necklaces often seem to contain pearls that seem *out-of-round* to today's pearl buyer. Occasionally we find the rare exception, but finding an appreciative buyer for such a rare beauty may be rarer than the pearls themselves.

In nature there is really nothing that is truly perfect—a fact that, where gems are concerned, was more fully appreciated and accepted in days gone by. Natural pearls are just that: natural. As such, differences abound, and given their rarity to begin with, there was often no choice about what was available to use. With cultured pearls there are much larger quantities of pearls from which to choose, so it is easier to find and carefully match them.

Since cultured pearls now dominate the market, we have come to expect a certain "look" in pearls—a look rarely found in natural pearls: uniformity, whiteness, roundness, and much larger sizes than are normally seen in natur-

A natural pearl necklace given to Empress Eugénie by Napolean III. The size and shape of the pearls are irregular, and differences in color are present. Even so, it was a rare and precious gift, fit for royalty.

al pearls. Ironically, this has had a negative impact on natural pearls. While much rarer than cultured pearls, a strand of small natural pearls will have a perceived value of much *less* than a larger strand of cultured pearls.

I recently witnessed an example of this: a magnificent natural pearl necklace containing exceptionally fine, well-matched, bright, lustrous, round pearls. This very rare necklace was about thirty-six inches long and contained pearls ranging from over 6.8 millimeters to just under 8.0 millimeters (most being over 7 millimeters), giving the impression of a uniform necklace—another rarity in natural pearls of this size, number, and quality. This necklace was truly one of nature's rarest creations. For natural pearls, the pearls were very large. Compared with cultured pearls, however, they were small. At $65,000, the price was not small! Today, it is difficult to sell such a necklace because few will guess what it is or appreciate its importance.

Before this era of cultured pearls, such a necklace would have found an immediate home in some illustrious setting and would have been treasured and cherished by its owner. But today, it is so fine—so white and so well matched—that ironically, it could be confused with a fine cultured pearl necklace, and perceived to have a much lower value (one-tenth its real worth)! While people may have some idea of how much a large, "important" cultured pearl necklace might cost, very few understand the value represented in a natural pearl necklace, especially one that appears to be so modest in size. And let's face it—most buyers spending a large sum on a piece of jewelry want others to recognize its value. Only a connoisseur would pay such a price for a necklace of this size, one that could be confused with a cultured pearl necklace of much less value; only a connoisseur could appreciate it for the priceless, rare, and magnificent natural treasure that it is. I've never seen another natural pearl necklace that was comparable in terms of overall quality, matching, and size. Nor can I imagine when or where another of comparable beauty might be found.

In a market so totally dominated by cultured pearls, the unknowledgeable can easily confuse exceptionally fine natural pearls for fine cultured pearls. To make matters worse, part of the evaluation of cultured pearls includes an evaluation of how well matched all the pearls are within the strand; we've come to expect precise matching in a fine strand, and ignore pearls that lack this characteristic. Natural pearls rarely exhibit precise matching. So in this cultured pearl market, a strand of rare natural pearls is not only assumed to be cultured but is often mistaken for *poor-quality* cultured pearls!

It is important to understand this when buying natural pearls at auction. First, it explains why natural pearls can still be had at bargain prices. But it also illustrates why it may be difficult to find a buyer who can appreciate their rarity and value—and you must bid accordingly. At least for now. This is starting to change (which you will note if you track natural pearl pieces that have sold at auction over the past ten years).

## Other Tips on How to Tell the Natural from the Cultured Pearl

Appreciation for natural pearls is increasing as people learn more about them and how they compare with cultured pearls, and as interest in heirloom jewelry, antiques, and estate pieces increases. Strengthening prices for natural pearls at auction and among fine estate dealers seems to indicate that they are a collectible with a lustrous future. Here is how one can determine whether a pearl is cultured or natural:

1. *Examine the drill hole.* If a pearl has been drilled, a jeweler or gemologist can usually identify a cultured pearl very easily; with experience, even the novice can learn to spot cultured pearls. By examining several pearls, looking into the drill hole carefully with a loupe, you may see the line of demarcation between the shell nucleus and the layer of conchiolin, sometimes appearing as a darker line. It may not be visible in all pearls, and you may see only a portion of the line in a given pearl. If the strand is tightly knotted, as in a newly strung necklace, you may have to try several pearls before finding enough space between the pearl and the knot to be able to use the loupe. *When this dark line is visible, and you can see where it covers the shell bead, you can be sure you have a cultured pearl.* Note: Many cultured pearls have been bleached to remove the brownish conchiolin line. Also, it won't be seen in cultured pearls with extremely thick nacre. When you can't see this brownish layer, you must test further.

2. *Check the size of the drill hole.* This is sometimes an important indicator. Very small drill holes may indicate a natural pearl. Since natural pearls are

valued in part by weight, great care was taken to keep the hole as small as possible to minimize loss of weight and maintain maximum value.

3. ***Examine with an ultraviolet lamp, using long-wave ultraviolet radiation*** (an inexpensive "black light" is all you need). Examination with ultraviolet light is often helpful with pearls that don't show any line of demarcation, when it's difficult to view the drill hole, or in cases where the pearl is undrilled. It can be especially useful with necklaces or bracelets. When examined under ultraviolet light, cultured pearls normally have a strong, milky, bluish white appearance. In the case of cultured pearl strands, this response will be *uniform throughout;* in a natural strand, there will be variations from pearl to pearl in the intensity of color seen. Natural pearls may also appear to be a *tan* or *yellowish* color when viewed under ultraviolet light.

4. ***Examine with a strong penlight or fiberoptic light.*** View the pearl from

Cross section of cultured pearl showing *parallel banding* of the nucleus. In poor-quality, thin-nacre pearls, this parallel banding can sometimes be seen when the pearl is examined in strong light.

several different directions while holding a strong light in direct contact with it, slowly moving it around the pearl's surface without losing contact. If viewed in this manner, it is sometimes possible to see *dark, parallel lines from the shell nucleus* showing through the nacre (especially in cultured pearls with very thin nacre). These dark, parallel lines always indicate a cultured pearl. With a strong light, viewed in this way, you might also notice some orangy colored, irregularly shaped spots, some large and some small. This is an indication of cultured pearls.

5. ***X-ray examination.*** Cultured pearls can often be identified as cultured by the above tests. However, such tests may be inconclusive on undrilled pearls and cultured pearls with extremely thick nacre. In these cases, pearls must be x-rayed.

If you think you may have a strand of natural pearls but aren't sure, submit them to a reliable gem-testing laboratory for documentation. *Natural pearls must be x-rayed to confirm their authenticity.* If you are buying pearls represented to be natural, make sure there is an accompanying identification report from a reliable lab, or bid as though they were cultured pearls. If you are bidding sight unseen, from an online seller, be sure the seller is willing to permit you to have them tested before making payment.

Fine natural pearls are rare and valuable, and always have been. Never take anyone's word that pearls are natural, even inherited pearls. Most of the time these inherited heirlooms turn out *not* to be natural, or even cultured, but *fake*. Imitation pearls have been around for centuries. Even Queen Elizabeth I, the Duchess of Windsor, and Mrs. Harry Winston wore fake pearls on occasion. Of course, they also had real pearls in the safe, to be worn on very special occasions.

## How Does an Imitation Pearl Differ from a Cultured Pearl?

Natural pearls and cultured pearls are produced in rivers, lakes, and bays by living mollusks and can be very similar in appearance. Imitation pearls—also called faux, simulated, and most recently, semicultured—are not created by any living creature. They should not be referred to in any way as genuine or cultured. Imitation pearls have never seen the inside of an oyster. They are entirely artificial, made from round glass or plastic beads dipped in a bath of ground fish scales and lacquer, or one of the new plastic substances.

Imitation pearls have been sold as cultured pearls at auction, even at the very best auction houses. In the Duchess of Windsor sale at Sotheby's, a strand of imitation pearls was described in the catalog, in the capitalized headings, as cultured. Sotheby's discovered the error and printed a correction next to the necklace during viewing, and made an announcement at the start of the session in which they were sold. This is a classic example of assuming that pearls were cultured because of the reputation of the person to whom they had belonged. It never even occurred to the gemologist to test them, and he gave them little more than a cursory glance!

If major auction houses can mistakenly represent imitation pearls as cultured, it can happen anywhere. And at the cost of fine pearls, cultured as well as natural, you don't want to pay for getting stuck with overpriced fakes.

## Use the Tooth Test to Spot the Fake

Some fine imitations today can be very convincing. Some have actually been mistaken for fine cultured pearls. An easy, reliable test in most cases is the tooth test. Run the pearl gently along the edge of your teeth (the upper teeth are more sensitive, and also be aware that the test won't work with false teeth). The genuine pearl will have a mildly abrasive or gritty feel (think of the gritty feeling of sand at the seaside—real pearls come from the sea), while the imitation will be slippery smooth (like the con artist, slippery smooth signifies a fake!). Try this test on pearls you know are genuine, and then on known imitations, to get a feel for the difference. You'll never forget it!

The tooth test may be unreliable for amateurs when applied to the imitation Majorica pearl, but close examination of the surface with a loupe will reveal a fine, pinpoint surface that is very different from the smooth surface of a cultured or natural pearl. An experienced jeweler or gemologist can quickly and easily identify the Majorica for you.

## THE SIX FACTORS THAT AFFECT PEARL QUALITY AND VALUE

Regardless of the type of pearl, or whether it is natural or cultured, the following factors must be evaluated to determine whether or not it is a fine pearl that will give you lasting beauty. But keep in mind that there is less uniformity in natural pearls, and greater tolerance for differences. It takes experience to judge natural pearls accurately.

1. *Nacre thickness and quality.* This is the most important factor in terms of beauty and, with cultured pearls, in knowing how long they will last! For this reason, we consider it the most important factor. Nacre thickness determines the pearl's longevity. The thicker the nacre, the longer the life of the pearl; the thinner the nacre, the shorter its life. Nacre quality determines how the light travels through the layers. Sometimes pearls with thick nacre fail to exhibit the intensity of luster or orient that is expected because the nacre layers didn't crystallize properly. The crystals may lack transparency, the layers may not be uniform, or the layers may not be properly aligned. The result is a pearl with lower luster. To have a lustrous, iridescent pearl, the nacre must be thick, and it must also have good crystallization. There are pearls with thick nacre that aren't lustrous because of how the layers crystallized, but any pearl that exhibits a rich lustrousness is one that must have thick nacre. So always look for a pearl with high luster because this provides a visual indication of thick nacre—your guarantee of lasting beauty.

2. *Luster and orient.* This is the sharpness and intensity of the images reflected from the pearl's surface (luster) and the underlying iridescent play of colors (orient) that distinguish the pearl from all other gems. The degree of luster and orient is one of the most important factors in determining the quality and value of the pearl. The higher the luster and orient, the finer the pearl. When judging luster and orient, look at the shadow area of the pearl, not the shiny, reflective area (don't confuse "shine" with the deep iridescent glow created by the combination of luster and orient).

3. *Color.* Color is usually considered the most important factor affecting value and cost. Two elements are involved in evaluating color: body color and overtone. The body color is the basic color, i.e., white, yellow, black. The overtone is a secondary color (its tint), such as the pinkish overtone in fine white pearls. Color refers to the combination of the body color and overtone. Very white pearls with a rose-colored overtone (tint) are the rarest and the most expensive. The creamier the color becomes, the less costly they are. However, today the rose tint is often imparted to the pearl through artificial means. If you use a loupe to examine the drill hole, you may be able to detect the color enhancement if you can see the line of demarcation between the mother-of-pearl nucleus and the nacre; if the pearl has been tinted, the line will show a pinkish coloration.

Cultured pearls are available in many colors—gray, black, pink, blue, gold—but often these colors have been produced by surface dyes or irradiation techniques. White pearls that have been drilled for jewelry use (as in a necklace) and then tinted or dyed can usually be detected easily by a qualified gemologist. With rare black pearls it may be necessary to send them to a gem-testing laboratory with sophisticated equipment in order to be sure.

4. *Cleanliness* (surface texture or perfection). This refers to the pearl's freedom from such surface blemishes as small blisters, pimples, spots, or cracks. Imperfections may also appear as dark spots, small indentations, welts or blisters, or surface bumps.

5. *Shape.* Shape in pearls is divided into three categories: spherical, symmetrical, and baroque. The rarest and most valuable are the spherical or round pearls; these are judged on their degree of sphericity, or roundness. While perfectly round pearls are extremely rare, the closer to perfectly round, the finer and more expensive the pearl. Button pearls and pear-shaped pearls are symmetrical pearls and are judged on evenness

and good symmetry—that is, whether they have a nice, well-proportioned shape. Symmetrical pearls are less expensive than round pearls but much more expensive than baroque pearls, which are irregularly shaped.

6. *Size.* Natural pearls are sold by weight. They are weighed in grains, four grains being equal to one carat. Cultured pearls are sold by millimeter size (1 millimeter equals approximately ⅟25 inch): their measurement indicates the number of millimeters in the diameter of the pearl. Two millimeter dimensions—length and width—may be given if the pearl is not round. The larger the pearl, the greater the cost.

Another factor affecting the value of any pearl item that has been strung, as in a necklace, is the precision that went into the matching of the pearls; this is called the make. Consider how well matched the strand's pearls are in size, shape, color, luster, and surface texture. Graduated pearls also require careful sizing. Failure to match carefully will detract from both the appearance of the item and its value.

## AUCTIONS PROVIDE AN IMPORTANT SOURCE OF THE BEST PEARLS: NATURAL AND CULTURED

Natural pearl earrings sold by Christie's, New York, April 1998, for $409,000

Auctions are the major source of natural pearls available today. The oyster populations that produced natural pearls are virtually extinct, and although some natural pearl-producing ventures are under way in various parts of the world today, there is no reliable modern source. Today, if you seek these rare treasures, you are most likely to find them at auction among pieces consigned from private estates.

As we discussed in the first chapter, important historic pearls can fetch impressive prices at auction and can capture lots of media attention—as we saw with La Peregrina, which Richard Burton bought at auction for Elizabeth Taylor. The following chart shows the *top twenty record prices* brought at auction for *natural pearl lots.*

Auctions are also an important source of the finest cultured pearls, especially those produced many years ago, which have much thicker nacre coatings and look so much more like the natural. Some cultured pearls of exceptional quality bring very high prices at auction, especially if they are large or well matched in size and color.

# Top Twenty Natural Pearl Lots Sold at Auction

| Date | House | Description | No. of Pearls | Size/Weight | Color | Total $ |
|---|---|---|---|---|---|---|
| 11/99 | Christie's | Barbara Hutton single-strand necklace | 41 | 8.50–16.35 mm graduated | white | 1,476,345 |
| 5/00 | Christie's | Cartier & Janesich two single-strand necklaces | 130 | 4.70–14.40 mm | black | 1,044,153 |
| 11/97 | Christie's | Nina Dyer triple-strand necklace | 151 | 5.20–13.95 mm | black | 913,320 |
| 5/88 | Christie's | La Régente | 1 | 302.68 grains* | | 859,100 |
| 11/99 | Sotheby's | Double-strand necklace | 82 | 7.40–13.90 mm graduated | | 781,840 |
| 4/87 | Sotheby's | Cartier Windsor necklace | 28 | 9.20–16.80 mm graduated | | 733,333 |
| 5/92 | Sotheby's | Barbara Hutton single-strand necklace | 40 | 8.70–16.30 mm | | 579,700 |
| 4/99 | Christie's | Pair of pearl and diamond ear pendants | | *gray:* 12.95–13.15 x 15.80 mm *white:* 13.40–13.50 x 16.00 mm | gray and white | 531,700 |
| 2/78 | Sotheby's | Triple-strand necklace of Persian Gulf pearls | | | | 632,600 |
| 5/86 | Sotheby's | Van Cleef & Arpels triple-strand necklace | 111 | 9.20–14.70 mm | | 516,575 |
| 11/01 | Christie's | Triple-strand necklace | 161 | 6.30–10.70 mm | | 515,908 |
| 5/89 | Christie's | Double-strand necklace | | | | 510,400 |
| 11/98 | Christie's | Single-strand necklace | 63 | 6.80–11.15 mm graduated | | 471,691 |
| 5/92 | Christie's | Sara Pearl drop-shaped pearl | 1 | 292 grains* | gray | 470,600 |
| 10/96 | Sotheby's | Single-strand necklace | 63 | 6.80–11.10 mm graduated | | 464,500 |
| 5/87 | Christie's | La Pelegrina | 1 | 133.16 grains* | | 463,800 |
| 5/98 | Sotheby's | Pearl and diamond necklace, brooch, and pair of earrings, circa 1910 | | | | 448,220 |
| 4/98 | Christie's | Pair of white and black pearl and diamond ear pendants | | 16.50 x 14.50 mm and 16.50 x 13.40 mm | white and black | 409,500 |
| 10/83 | Christie's | Single-strand necklace | 32 | 10.20–15.20 mm graduated | | 374,000 |
| 10/96 | Sotheby's | Pair of pearl and fancy pink diamond ear clips | | | | 343,500 |

*4 grains equals 1 carat

| Necklace of round, natural, black-colored Tahitian cultured pearls and diamonds sold by Christie's, New York, April 1990, for $797,500 | Florence Gould necklace, with well-matched pear-shaped cultured South Sea pearls, sold by Christie's, New York, April 1984, for $990,000 | Important pair of earclips with large cultured button pearls (each measuring approximately 18.1 by 16.8 mm) sold by Sotheby's, New York, April 1989, for $176,000 |

When seeking pearls at auction, whether rare natural pearls or cultured pearls, remember that there is a wide range of quality, rarity, and price. While fine-quality natural pearls often command high prices, this is not always the case. Sometimes natural pearls are sold as "cultured" because no one obtained laboratory documentation to the contrary. Beautiful older cultured pearls can also sometimes be had at bargain prices, because they are often ignored when estates are consigned to the auction house.

Although bargains can still be found, it is more common to overpay for something inferior, so it is important to know exactly what you are buying. There have been many new developments in the field of pearl culturing, and more nations than ever before are now culturing pearls, so the quality of cultured pearls varies greatly. It is not possible to adequately cover all aspects of pearls in the space allocated here. For those with a special interest in pearls, refer to *The Pearl Book: The Definitive Buying Guide, Second Edition,* which provides comprehensive information about all types of pearls from every country, including the latest in treatments and enhancements.

# 21 ◆ Gemstone Investment:
## Not for the Casual Investor

GEMS MAY OFFER AN EXCITING, SPARKLING, AND VERY ENJOYABLE AREA for investment if you take the time to become knowledgeable about the gem industry; are interested in a long-term investment (over five years); and are willing to locate, retain, and work with a knowledgeable, reputable gem consultant. But entered casually, without knowledge of the industry and the risks, and without the ability to accurately determine value, this investment may lose its sparkle quickly.

## Colored Gemstones May Offer an Unusual and Timely Opportunity

Fine-quality colored gemstones may offer an unusual—even unique—investment opportunity at this time. But keep in mind, *high quality* is the key here, as it is in any investment piece.

Increasingly, rare and natural gemstones are hard to locate, and since there is a limited source of natural gems, they are likely to continue to go up in value. Furthermore, with the wide selection available at auction today, you have a good chance of discovering a high-quality gemstone at a price near or below wholesale, making it more attractive as an investment.

Once again, we stress that colored gemstones are not for the casual investor because of the complexities involved in judging quality, the widespread use of routine treatments to enhance their appearance, and the high incidence of fraud and misrepresentation. Nonetheless, colored gemstones offer a unique situation today that merits a serious investor's attention.

As we have discussed, most colored gemstones have been enhanced in some way to improve their appearance; treatment techniques have been used routinely since the late 1960s and early 1970s. Truly natural gems have never been rarer than they are today—but their prices are not yet reflecting this. The reason is really not difficult to understand if we take a moment to examine the history of treatment disclosure.

Until recently, consumers were totally unaware that most gemstones were treated and were under the impression that all gemstones were natural because no one in the jewelry trade was telling them anything to the contrary. The subject of treatments was kept secret. As a result, jewelers couldn't ask a premium price for a natural gemstone because this would have meant divulging the fact that most of the gems they were selling had been treated. No one wanted to open this can of worms, and they rationalized that the prices were "right" for the treated gems they were selling (prices for sapphires and rubies, for example, had dropped significantly since the 1960s, reflecting the constantly increasing supply of the pretty treated material).

Over the years, as more and more treated material came into the market, we witnessed an interesting twist of fate. While jewelers could ask a *little* more for natural stones—justifying it by suggesting that one stone (the natural) might have had a richer or more saturated color—they couldn't ask for prices that reflected their true rarity and preciousness. The net result was that *the cost of rare, fine-quality, natural gems was kept artificially low for over thirty years!*

While I discussed treatments in my first book in the early 1980s, it has only been in the last few years, following several media exposés, that information about treatments has reached the general public. The jewelry industry now requires full disclosure, and gradually people are becoming more and more aware that there are really two categories of gemstones: natural and treated. Most people, however, still don't realize this. And so, while prices have strengthened over the past two years, prices may increase to a much greater degree as more and more people become aware of the situation, and more people begin to demand natural stones.

It is for this reason, and this unique situation, that natural-colored gemstones may offer unusual investment opportunities. As wealthy collectors and connoisseurs, unaware until now that they were buying treated gems, begin to demand the natural, we predict that prices will rise dramatically over the next few years as demand increases and supplies decrease.

Here are some gemstones that might offer especially good opportunities at this time:

- *Natural blue sapphire.* Especially those from Kashmir and Burma, because they are among the rarest of all gems.

- *Colombian emerald* and chromium-rich emerald from other localities. There is a particularly good opportunity now because emeralds have suffered severely in the heat of recent exposés about oiling and resin treatments, and the market is very soft. While there is still controversy about the use of epoxy resins, fine emeralds accompanied by laboratory reports that indicate either "no clarity enhancement" or "light to moderate clarity enhancement—*oil* only" (a treatment that has been around for centuries) are very desirable. As more and more people understand how emerald forms in nature, why oil has been routinely used, and how that has been factored into the valuation of the stone, they have no problem accepting oil, and the emerald market will rally.

- *Ruby.* Especially from Burma, one of the rarest of all gems, but natural rubies of fine color and clarity from all sources, since there will be increased demand as the scarcity of Burmese rubies increases.

- *Lesser-known gemstones.* Tsavorite garnet, chrome tourmaline, and red and blue spinel are gemstones for which demand will increase as more people seek natural alternatives to fine-quality emerald, ruby, and sapphire. For those who want a natural gem and can't afford natural emerald, ruby, and sapphire in the quality they seek, other natural gemstones in comparable colors will become attractive alternatives.

So it is clear there may be some unusually sparkling investment opportunities for the person willing to follow the advice we've offered throughout the book. Just be sure to seek expert advice before purchasing any rare gemstone for investment. And keep in mind that for every rare gem, there are many imitations, synthetics, and scams that can delude even the most savvy.

And last, but not least, remember the words of the Roman historian G. Plinius Secundus, in the year 77 A.D.:

*To tell the truth, there is no fraud or deceit in the world which yields greater gain and profit than that of counterfeiting gems.*

Some things never change!

# PART 5

# DESIGN AND STYLE: GREAT JEWELRY

# 22 ◆ GOLD AND PLATINUM:
## TIMELESS CHOICES

THE AUCTIONS ARE AN EXCELLENT SOURCE OF GOLD AND PLATINUM jewelry. Beautiful, distinctive gold necklaces, earrings, bracelets, and rings from every period can be found at auction, usually at very low prices compared with what you normally pay in jewelry stores. You can discover everything from ancient to modern, from geometric Art Deco designs to the architectural style of 1940s Retro pieces to the bold and graphic jewelry of the 1960s and 1970s.

It is very important to understand gold and the differences that affect price, in order to avoid confusion about the wide range of prices that seems to pervade the market for what may appear to be the same thing. As with gems, wherever there are significant price differences there are usually quality differences. The key to getting good value in gold is understanding what accounts for differences in quality and price.

Here we will discuss gold and platinum, but remember that there are other metals that can look like gold or platinum but are not. Be sure to confirm the metal, and the content of precious metal. Any reliable gemologist-appraiser can test the metal for you.

## WHAT IS GOLD?

Gold is one of the world's most precious metals. It is so soft and workable that one ounce can be stretched into a wire five miles long, or hammered into a sheet so thin that it could cover a hundred square feet. It is one of our rarest metals, and since pure gold doesn't rust or corrode, it can last forever.

### Most Gold Used in Jewelry Is an Alloy

Gold is the most popular metal used for jewelry today. But pure gold is very soft, so it is usually mixed with other metals to make it stronger and prevent it from bending too easily. When two or more metals are mixed together, we call the resulting product an alloy. Most gold used in jewelry is an alloy—and the metals added to the gold are also called alloys.

## WHAT IS A KARAT? OR IS IT CARAT?

In jewelry, the term *carat* (or *karat*) has a double meaning: carat is used as a measurement of weight for gemstones, with one carat weighing ⅕ of a gram; *carat* is also used in countries around the world to indicate the amount of pure gold in a piece of gold jewelry. Jewelry should always be marked to indicate how much pure gold it contains. In the United States, when the word is used to indicate gold content rather than gemstone weight, it is spelled with a K—hence karat—to avoid confusion. In some countries outside the United States it is spelled with a "c."

In the United States, a karat mark, abbreviated to K or KT, indicates the amount of pure gold present in the metal. A 24-karat mark (24K or 24KT) indicates pure gold.

To understand the concept, imagine that "pure gold" is a pie divided into 24 equal slices, or parts. Each karat equals one part of the pie. So, 24K would mean that 24 parts (out of a total of 24) are gold. In other words, 24K would be 100 percent gold, or pure gold. In 18K gold jewelry, 18 parts are pure gold and 6 are another metal (or, $18/24 = \frac{3}{4} = 75$ percent pure gold), and so on.

In some cultures, 24K gold jewelry is required for certain jewelry pieces, but it's generally agreed that 24K (pure) gold is too soft for jewelry use. In some parts of the world, 18K or 20K is preferred because of its brighter yellow color and because it is considered "purer" and more precious. In the United States, 14K or 18K gold is preferred because it is more durable than higher-karat gold.

## ANTIQUE PIECES ARE NOT ALWAYS "HIGH-KARAT" GOLD

Keep in mind that antique jewelry, especially English pieces from the late 1800s and early 1900s, were often fashioned in 9K gold. Depending upon the age, who made it, and the design, such pieces can still command a high price, but don't assume just because they are "antique" and represented to be "gold" that they are high-karat gold; they are often low-karat gold. I bought two beautiful Victorian period necklaces from a small auction house, one in gold with citrines and seed pearls, the other in gold with aquamarine and seed pearls. The workmanship is beautiful and delicate, and I love wearing them because of all the compliments I receive, but the gold content in both is 9K. Knowing this didn't affect my desire to own them, but when I bid, I bid accordingly.

The following table shows how different international gold markings correspond to one another.

## GOLD MARKS

| American Marking (Karatage) | Pure Gold Content (Fineness in Percent) | European Marking |
|---|---|---|
| 24K | 100 | 1,000 |
| 22K | 91.6 | 916 |
| 20K | 83 | 833 |
| 19K (used in Portugal) | 79.2 | 792 |
| 18K | 75.0 | 750 |
| 15K (seen in antiques) | 62.5 | 625 |
| 14K | 58.3 | 585 |
| 12K | 50.0 | 500 |
| 10K | 41.7 | 417 |
| 9K | 37.5 | 375 |

## TO BE CALLED GOLD, WHAT IS THE MINIMUM GOLD CONTENT?

Many countries have established minimum standards that must be met for items to be legally called gold. The laws governing the actual content of gold required in a piece of jewelry, however, vary. In the United States, to be called gold, the item must be at least 10K; in England and Canada, 9K; in Italy and France, 18K. *This is important to anyone buying at auction. At an auction in the United States, if the capitalized heading description in the catalog says "gold," don't assume it is 14K or 18K; it can be as low as 10K. In England, it can be as low as 9K. In France or Italy, however, if the catalog says "gold," it must be at least 18K.*

*A word about Russian marks:* Old timepieces made in Russia were marked to indicate the content based on its equivalent to a zolotnik. A piece marked 96 contained as much gold as 96 zolotniks, which equals pure gold; 72 equals 18K (750); 56 equals 14K (585).

## THE MANY COLORS OF GOLD

Pure gold is always yellow. But because pure gold is too soft for most jewelry use and must be mixed with other metals (alloys) to increase its hardness, the color can also be modified by adding varying amounts of these other metals. Those usually added to gold for use in jewelry include copper, zinc, silver, nickel, platinum, and palladium (a metal in the platinum family). Depending on which alloys are used, a variety of colors can be produced. Another practice is to plate 14K gold jewelry with 18K for an 18K look—that is, a stronger yellow color. White gold is also frequently plated with rhodium, a rare and more expensive metal from the platinum family, to create a whiter, brighter finish.

Using some combination of one or more of the metals shown below will result in various colors.

---

### HOW ALLOYS AFFECT COLOR

| Color | Composition |
|---|---|
| Yellow gold | Gold, copper, silver |
| White gold | Gold, nickel,* zinc, silver, platinum, palladium |
| Green gold | Gold, silver (much more than in yellow gold), copper, zinc |
| Pink (red) gold | Gold, copper (sometimes a small amount of silver is used) |

* Note: some people are allergic to nickel and should not wear white gold containing nickel. For this reason, a white gold alloyed with palladium is being used by some manufacturers. White gold that contains palladium will be more expensive than yellow gold or white gold containing another alloy, but it is still less expensive than all platinum.

---

## DETERMINING VALUE REQUIRES MORE THAN A SCALE!

- **Weight** is one factor that goes into determining the value of a piece of gold jewelry. Gold is usually sold by weight, in grams or pennyweights. The weight may be given in auction catalogs in pennyweights, abbreviated DWT, or in grams. There are 20 pennyweights to one ounce; if you multiply grams by 0.643, you will have the number of pennyweights, or if the weight is given in pennyweights, divide by 0.643 to convert to grams. Weight is important because it is an indication of the actual amount of pure gold in the piece. But it is not the only factor, or the most important; it is just one factor.

- *Design and construction* are important not only because of the piece's finished look but also because specific details in the overall design and construction affect comfort, wearability, and ease in putting the piece on or taking it off. Good design requires excellent designers as well as extra care and attention to small mechanical details. This adds to the cost of any piece of jewelry. You can feel and see the difference, especially with the loupe.

  In looking at a piece of gold jewelry, you must also consider the type of construction necessary to create a particular design or look. Is the construction simple or complex? Did the piece require extensive labor or minimal labor? Did it require special skill, talent, or equipment?

  In addition, jewelry design is also becoming recognized as art, and jewelry designers as artists. Some award-winning designers command top dollar, as do top painters, sculptors, and other artists. A piece of gold jewelry made by a fine designer, especially if it is a one-of-a-kind or limited-edition piece, will sometimes sell for much more than another piece of mass-produced gold jewelry of the same weight and gold content.

  To ignore the design and construction factors and assign a value to a piece of gold jewelry based on gold content (i.e., 14K, 18K) and weight alone would be equivalent to placing a value on a painting based on the cost of paint and canvas alone.

- *Production* can affect price significantly. Is the piece produced by machine or by hand? The type of construction required to create a particular design may require that it be made entirely or in part by hand, while others can be completely made by machine. Some designs may be produced either way, but those done by hand will have a different look, feel, and cost.

- *Finish* is where we take into account the care and labor costs associated with the actual finishing of the piece. For example, special skills or techniques are required to put on the final touches that make the piece distinctive, such as engraving, milgraining, hammering, or granulation. Here we also need to note whether or not the piece has been carefully polished to remove rough edges that might be abrasive or catch or snag on fabric. Consider whether the item was hand polished or machine polished; some pieces are machine made but finished by hand. We must also take into consideration any special finishes to the metal itself, such as a florentine, matte, or sand-blasted finish. Each step in the process, and each special step or skill required, adds—sometimes dramatically—to the cost.

## Adding It All Up

All these factors help explain why a piece of 18K gold jewelry from an important jewelry house such as Cartier or Bulgari will command a higher price at auction than another piece of 18K gold jewelry of the same "weight" in grams. While the "name" contributes, remember that the "name" stands for something: the overall quality that is associated with it and, where gold is concerned, outstanding design, construction, production, and finish.

Vintage, estate, and period designs that bring top dollar at auction also reflect the influence of these factors. Those that fetch the highest prices do so not only because of rarity but because they reflect the best in the design, construction, and finish seen in jewelry of their period.

Many pieces of gold jewelry look alike at first glance. When they are examined carefully, however, it often becomes clear where the differences lie, both in quality and in cost. Compare various pieces at auction, and ask questions. Only after carefully evaluating all these factors can you appreciate gold jewelry and recognize cost differences and real value.

## NOT ALL THAT GLITTERS IS GOLD

Not all that glitters at auction is gold. Common base metals with a heavy gold overlay—heavy *gold-plated* jewelry—can look like the real thing. At auction

there is a higher risk of buying gold-plated jewelry or underkarated gold. Beware of underkarating, which is a serious problem around the world. If a piece of gold jewelry is underkarated, it means that the jewelry is marked to indicate a certain gold content but actually contains less than is indicated. Needless to say, sell-

*Above, left:* Antique gold filigree ear pendants (nineteenth century) (sold: $1,700)
*Above, right:* Retro gold bracelet (estimate: $4,500–$5,000)

ers who knowingly sell underkarated gold jewelry create the impression that they are giving you a bargain because their prices are so low, but if there is actually less gold (and more alloy, so the piece would have a weight comparable with that of others you might be considering), you aren't getting any bargain. We know of people who bought gold jewelry marked 14K or 18K and found out later that it was only 8K or 10K—or less!

Fine, expensive gold jewelry should always be tested. Any gemologist-appraiser can usually detect any underkarating that is serious enough to affect the value of a specific piece of jewelry and the price paid.

## PLATINUM—RAREST AND MOST PRECIOUS

Platinum, which has been used in jewelry since the turn of the past century, became especially popular during the Edwardian period because its malleable character made it a natural for the intricate and lacelike style of the day. Fine auction houses offer some of the world's most beautiful platinum designs from bygone eras.

Platinum is frequently used in the finest jewelry and to set the most valuable gems because it's more workable and the prongs or setting can be moved more easily around the stone, thereby reducing the risk of accidental damage to it.

*Nothing is purer than platinum.* Platinum is even more rare and valuable than gold. The platinum family is composed of six elements: platinum, palladium, iridium, osmium, rhodium, and ruthenium. These six silvery white metals are generally found together in nature, with platinum and palladium the most abundant and osmium, rhodium, and ruthenium the rarest.

Platinum is rarer and heavier than other precious metals. As the purest, it's sometimes referred to as the noblest. Most platinum jewelry also contains small amounts of the rarer and more expensive elements iridium or ruthenium for added strength.

Because platinum is so pure, it rarely causes allergic reactions. This is greatly appreciated by sensitive people who experience allergic reactions to alloys such as nickel, which is one of the alloys used to create white gold. Platinum is also somewhat stronger than other precious metals.

Platinum is not identified by karat marks. In the United States, the abbreviations PT or plat indicate platinum. In Europe, the numerical marks 950 or PT950 indicate platinum. The finest jewelry often uses platinum mixed with 10 percent iridium or ruthenium for added strength. This costs more, since these are rarer and costlier metals.

## Rhodium

Rhodium, another member of the platinum family, is the brightest and most reflective of all the platinum metals. Rhodium is also harder and whiter than platinum and, because it is so durable, doesn't wear off quickly, as does gold plating. As a result, it is often used to coat gold and platinum jewelry.

Rhodium plating should be considered especially for people who have allergic reactions to 10K or 14K gold, since it can help eliminate reaction to the alloys.

# 23 ♦ What's in a Name:
## Great Jewelry Periods and
## Great Jewelers

AUCTIONS ARE ONE OF THE BEST SOURCES FOR BEAUTIFUL *PERIOD* JEW-elry. While any piece of well-made, well-designed jewelry will sell for more than mediocre mass-produced jewelry, certain periods and styles are more highly sought than others, especially among collectors. It's important to become knowledgeable about the periods of antique jewelry and other collectible periods that result in higher prices for both buyers and sellers.

The best way to learn about fine period jewelry, and how to spot some of these exquisite treasures, is to start going to exhibitions where you will see the best. Christie's auction house in New York City, for example, auctioned off one of the world's finest collections of Art Nouveau jewelry by a famous master of the period, Lalique. It provided an excellent opportunity to see exemplary work from this period by a master artist. By examining it carefully, noting its feel, paying attention to particular details, seeing where and how each piece was signed, and so on, you could learn a tremendous amount. And then you could better appreciate why each piece sold at prices soaring above the estimates; when and where would such pieces ever come on the market again?

By taking the time to view fine pieces from various periods, and to note overall design characteristics, the use of particular materials, small details such as the type of clasp, closures, enameling techniques, style of the prongs, and so on, you can quickly hone your skills at identifying a particular period. Examining pieces carefully, comparing pieces side by side, and asking the jewelry specialist to explain what makes certain pieces more valuable than others will be the best way to learn. In this way you can also learn which pieces are especially rare, and why, and factor that into the prices they fetch. There are also many excellent books on jewelry from specific periods that can provide invaluable information. Our space here is limited, but we will give you an introduction to some of the most collectible periods at this time, and some of the most famous jewelers whose names add significantly to value. The rest is up to you.

Here is a brief look at the various jewelry periods. Keep in mind that many periods overlap and that dates are approximate. You will find many inconsistencies in the dates given for the span of any particular period, but nonetheless, they provide a useful guide.

## GEORGIAN PERIOD (APPROXIMATELY 1714–1830)

The Georgian period covers most of the eighteenth century into the early nineteenth century: a period when Great Britain was ruled by the four "Georges." Jewelry of this period was all handmade and designs consisted primarily of themes from nature—birds, flowers, leaves, insects—and also "ribbon and bow" motifs. Along with a very delicate design, you will find jewelry *en tremblant* (with moving parts that would "tremble" as the wearer moved). A new and important discovery of diamonds in Brazil in the eighteenth century resulted in the creation of jewelry that combined many diamonds with colored gemstones such as pink topaz and aquamarine—and lots of foil-backing was done in this period.

Georgian (George IV) brooch and ear pendants (sold: $12,000)

During the mid-eighteenth century, paste (glass), rhinestones, cut steel, and marcasites became extremely popular. A gold look-alike, known as *pinchback,* was produced from copper and zinc, and it replaced gold in less expensive jewelry.

In the second half of the eighteenth century, intaglios and carved gemstones became popular, and the style became more sentimental, as evidenced by the increased use of hearts, doves, and bows.

French influence can be seen in the beginning of the nineteenth century as Greek mythological subjects, foliate designs, and scrolls entered the design of the day. Cameos and mosaics, along with amethysts and pearls, were also popular, and pieces "paved" with diamonds (pavé) reached a peak.

Pieces from this period are very rare and very expensive.

## VICTORIAN PERIOD (APPROXIMATELY 1837–1901)

This period began with the reign of Queen Victoria in 1837, and the jewelry we see covers a range of styles. Jewelry from the early Victorian period (the Romantic period) was light in feel and used small, inexpensive colored stones and seed pearls. Designs consisted of a lot of scrollwork, floral spray designs, and multicolored gold. The 1850s ushered in the Gothic Revival movement, which brought with it a rebirth of the art of enameling, and exquisite pieces returned to the jewelry scene after a long dormant period. In the mid-1850s we also find much greater use of gemstones in all sizes, shapes, and colors, but larger was definitely better. We find massive suites of jewelry with colored gemstones in heavy gold. Diamonds were worn in abundance. Gold necklaces and brooches with festoons and fringe also became popular, with and without gemstones.

Victorian bracelet
(sold: $3,000)

After the death of Prince Albert in 1861, "mourning" jewelry was worn. Usually made from jet or black onyx, sometimes with seed pearls, the design was somber. Heavy silver jewelry also came into fashion for daytime wear.

While most Victorian jewelry is associated with England, the finest Victorian period jewelry was made in France. These pieces were of much finer quality overall; they were lighter, more delicate, more finely engraved, and enameled.

Among the great names of the Victorian period you will find Castellani, Carlo Giuliano, Fontenay, Hancock, Falize, Fabergé, and, at the end of the period, Boucheron and Tiffany.

## ARTS AND CRAFTS MOVEMENT (APPROXIMATELY 1885–1923)

A movement known as Arts and Crafts occurred in reaction to the increase in mass-produced jewelry among those who feared the loss of the fine workmanship of high-quality craftsmen. Jewelers who belonged to this movement made each piece by hand, from beginning to end. Although gold was sometimes used, perhaps as a decoration upon silver, they worked mostly in inexpensive and less glamorous materials such as silver, beaten copper, and aluminum, and they used inexpensive cabochon-cut or uncut stones. Diamonds were never used, and faceted stones rarely. Opals and moonstones were

especially popular, along with small, asymmetrical baroque pearls. There was little use of prong settings, the craftsmen preferring bezel or collet settings, and connecting elements by wire or by slipping flaps through slits and bending the metal. Color was important, and many designs also incorporated bright enamel.

Arts and Crafts sterling silver, moonstone, and labradorite necklace by Georg Jensen (sold: $7,475)

Leading figures in the Arts and Crafts movement include Arthur Gaskin, C.R. Ashbee, Fred Partridge, Edgar Simpson, Bernard Cuzner, Henry Wilson, John Paul Cooper, Alexander Fisher, Nelson Dawson, Archibald Knox, Edward Spencer, and Omar Ramsden.

## ART NOUVEAU PERIOD (APPROXIMATELY 1890–1915)

A French jeweler named Oscar Massin set the tone and paved the way for the Art Nouveau period with his designs from 1860 to 1880. His work inspired designers at the end of the nineteenth century, looking toward the new century, to abandon the restraints of the day and start the new century with a fresh burst of creative energy. They took a bold new approach and were concerned more with the overall impression created by each jewel than with the use of valuable gemstones. Using free-flowing designs, they focused on detailing in the metalwork, using unusual stones, incorporating other materials, and using enamel to create works of art that were unique in every aspect.

This period was one of great experimentation. Designers were uninhibited and used new materials such as horn and ivory, unusual stones such as moonstone and natural "wing" pearls, and enamel in unusual combinations that had never before been done. The prevailing themes were taken from nature: flowers, insects, leaves, intertwined vines, and elusive, whimsical feminine figures prevailed. But their subjects were out of the ordinary; they used flowers such as large irises, and insects such as butterflies and dragonflies captured in flight. The softly flowing movement and the more abstract character of Art Nouveau jewelry created a feeling of peace and serenity, an almost dreamlike quality.

French designers moved to center stage during this period, the main stars being names such as René Lalique, Henri Vever, Georges Fouquet, Joe Descomps, Boucheron, Phillipe Wolfers, Plisson and Hartz, and Lucien Gaillard, but Peter Carl Fabergé was an Art Nouveau master as well. In America, Louis Comfort Tiffany created a sensation with jewelry in the Art Nouveau style. Other American names of

Art Noveau *plique-a-jour* enamel and diamond choker by Lucien Gaillard (sold: $127,000)

the period include Theodore Dreicer; J.E. Caldwell; Shreve & Company; Peacock & Company; Bailey, Banks & Biddle; Black, Starr & Frost; Marcus & Company; Spaulding & Company; and T.B. Starr.

## EDWARDIAN AND BELLE EPOQUE PERIOD (APPROXIMATELY 1901–1914)

The Edwardian period coincides with the Belle Epoque (the French term that means "beautiful era"). During this period we find new styles of diamond cutting entering the scene, creating greater brilliance and sparkle and providing designers with new incentives to show them off to best advantage. Designers turned to platinum because its strength and malleability allowed for innovation in the design of settings, including ways to set diamonds in which the settings became virtually invisible. Platinum settings of this period, referred to as "marvels of engineering," are so delicate and lacelike that one wonders how they did it, and how the settings have survived generations of wear.

Jewelry from the Edwardian and Belle Epoque period is ornate but incredibly light, with a soft, feminine, romantic feel. It is characterized by very delicate lacelike open work, sometimes incorporating garlands and swags, and other times being somewhat more geometric. The preferred metal of the period was platinum, but gold was also used. Natural pearls, seed pearls, and diamonds were the preferred gems of the period. Some of the most exceptional pieces were created by stringing small natural pearls on platinum and

*Above:* Belle Epoque diamond and seed pearl "dog collar choker" (sold: $11,000)   *At left:* Edwardian imperial topaz and diamond pendant (sold: $17,200)

weaving them into delicate patterns for use in necklaces, bracelets, and even watch bands. Tassels, sautoirs—especially pearl sautoirs, "negligee" pendants (a necklace at the center of which were two drops of unequal length, suspended from a single stone, all on a slim chain), and pearl chokers were favorites of the Edwardian period as well.

Among the masters of this period you will find the names Tiffany, Cartier, Van Cleef & Arpels, LaCloche, Mauboussin, and Boucheron.

## Art Deco Period (approximately 1920–1935)

The jewelry of the Art Deco period reflects the new order of things after World War I—the Roaring Twenties. The early Art Deco jewelry continued the Art Nouveau style, characterized by highly ornamental floral designs in bright colors. Gradually this changed, moving away from flowing, curving lines toward stronger lines and geometrical patterns

While platinum and diamonds were used extensively, we see much greater use of colored gemstones, including—in addition to ruby, emerald, and sapphire—gemstones such as citrine, peridot, aquamarine, and garnet, which were available in large sizes and which were typically cut in geometric shapes: square and rectangular emerald cut. We also find extensive use of jade, coral, and black onyx. The Art Deco period also made use of unusual diamond shapes—trapezoid, square, triangle, and half-moon—to use with larger diamonds or to incorporate into intricate geometric patterns.

Another innovation in the Art Deco period was the use of colored gemstones to create or augment geometric patterns. You will often see rows of black onyx, or small *calibré*-cut colored gemstones—small square or rectangular step-cut stones—to create interesting patterns within the overall design. And it seemed to matter little whether they were natural or synthetic. Since it was often too difficult and time consuming to find rubies, sapphires, and emeralds that were perfectly matched in color, only the finest jewelers insisted on all natural gemstones; some of the manufacturers of less costly jewelry would substitute synthetics. Given their small size and inconsequential total weight, the gemstone component was an insignificant factor in the overall value of the piece, but one must never assume they are natural, regardless of the genuineness of the diamonds and the use of platinum. The small calibré-cut stones found in many pieces of period Art Deco jewelry sold at auction as "genuine" have turned out to be synthetic.

The Art Deco period cannot be mentioned without the name of the House of Cartier because of the influence of Cartier's designers on the entire Art Deco period. Cartier's designers were influenced by many factors and events that were then incorporated into their jewelry designs. Cartier's most important designer of the period, Charles Jacqueau, is considered one of the great pioneers of the Art Deco period. His influence affected not only the work of Cartier but that of all the great jewelers of the period: his interest in Persia and China can be seen in the dominant "oriental" themes of the period; his intense interest in the Ballet Russes—and their dramatic use of color in their costume design—inspired his strong use of color; his love of India and the influence of the maharajahs, from whom Cartier acquired many fine gemstones, inspired the fruit basket style now known as Tutti Frutti; and his love of Egyptian history and art resulted in what came to be known as Egyptian Revival, which was perhaps the crowning glory of his contributions, and which received an enormous impetus after the discovery of the tomb of Tutankhamen in 1922.

Among the masters of the Art Deco period you will find the names of Cartier, Van Cleef & Arpels, Boucheron, Chaumet, Mauboussin, Boivin, Belperron, Mellerio, Georg Jensen, LaCloche, Templier, Tiffany, Marchak, J.E. Caldwell, and Fouquet.

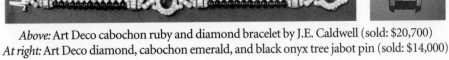

*Above:* Art Deco cabochon ruby and diamond bracelet by J.E. Caldwell (sold: $20,700)
*At right:* Art Deco diamond, cabochon emerald, and black onyx tree jabot pin (sold: $14,000)

## RETRO PERIOD

Retro jewelry is a modern style that emerged after World War II. The style is very distinctive and recognizable, and you will quickly develop an eye for it. Gold was the preferred metal, and rose gold was very popular. You often see two-tone pieces combining yellow and rose gold. The goal was wearability. These pieces are not overly ornate or formal. The jewelry tends to be larger and very architectural in feel, often set with large, affordable, colored gemstones such as citrine, aquamarine, topaz, and peridot. One can also find diamonds, sapphires, rubies, and emeralds, often set in a pavé style, in designs

where the metal seems to fold over and meld into itself; you'll find horn shapes, paved inside and out with stones, and three-dimensional comet shapes.

Retro period jewelry is just coming into its own and offers excellent value and a very wearable, distinctive choice. All of the major jewelry houses, including Cartier, Bulgari, Tiffany, and Van Cleef & Arpels, made beautiful jewelry in this period, but so did other firms that are less well known, including American firms such as J.E. Caldwell and Black, Starr & Frost.

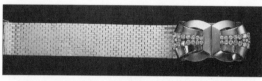

Retro bracelet (estimate: $10,000–$12,000)
and earrings (sold: $2,600)

## WHAT'S IN A NAME?

Signed pieces have added value. The primary reason for this is that artists want to sign their work when they create something beautiful, and they don't want to put their names to something that isn't fine, so a signature usually means high quality. While even the most prestigious jewelry houses have created some dogs, when a piece is signed by Cartier, Tiffany, Harry Winston, Van Cleef & Arpels, and so on, it gives buyers assurance and confidence that the piece is well designed, well made, and rarer than other jewelry because these houses don't mass-produce thousands of pieces. As a result, buyers will normally bid higher, and sellers can usually expect to get better prices.

Geneva-based Antiquorum Auctioneers, in partnership with the French auction house Etude Tajan, produced a once-in-a-lifetime auction, entitled

*The Magical Art of Cartier,* that featured only Cartier jewels, watches, and clocks. Each piece was authenticated by Cartier. On average, the pieces sold for seven to ten times more than their estimates. What we saw here was in part the impact of the name of Cartier. But it was much more. Each piece was a masterpiece, reflecting the finest workmanship and quality ever to come out of the workshops of Cartier over its entire history. They included the rarest of gems—workmanship that even Cartier would find difficult and cost-prohibitive to try to produce today—and reflected the finest design. Each of these factors affected the price. And in some cases, the piece was also owned by a celebrity, adding even greater allure.

The Merle Oberon necklace, made by Cartier in 1938 with twenty-nine baroque emerald drops (sold: $2,112,000)

Even when a piece is signed, however, you must examine it carefully and learn to recognize the type of workmanship and quality found in pieces by important jewelry firms. *Never rely on a signature alone.* There have been numerous cases where auction houses have represented—in the capitalized headings—that a piece was by a firm such as Cartier or another well-known jewelry house, and it was not. In documenting pieces submitted for the Cartier sale, for example, it was learned that in some cases the piece had been altered significantly and was so different from the original that it could no longer be called Cartier despite the presence of a Cartier signature on some part of the jewel. In other cases, the mounting was created by Cartier, but the original jewel had been replaced with something far inferior in quality. Finally, other pieces were simply fakes.

Major firms such as Sotheby's are very explicit where attribution to specific makers or signatures are concerned. Here is what Sotheby's states in its catalog:

- **Capitalized Heading:** When the maker's name appears in Capitalized Heading in the catalog description, in Sotheby's qualified opinion, the piece is by the named jeweler.
- **Name of Jeweler:** When we state the name of a maker in the catalog description below the Capitalized Heading, we mean that, in Sothe-

by's qualified opinion, although unsigned, the piece is by the named jeweler.

- **Mounting by:** When we state in the catalog description below the Capitalized Heading "Mounting by_____" we mean that, in Sotheby's qualified opinion, the mounting is by the jeweler, but either the gemstones have been replaced or the piece has been altered in some way after its manufacture.

If you are considering bidding on a piece that bears the name of an important jeweler or jewelry house, be sure that the name is stated in the capitalized heading. If it is not, then either there is no signature, or the piece may not contain the original stones or may have been altered significantly since it was originally made. If a signature is indicated in the capitalized heading, be sure you contact the jewelry house if possible to verify authenticity if you are the successful bidder. Most important jewelry houses will verify the authenticity of a piece for a nominal fee. This is not possible on antique pieces where the makers or firms no longer exist; if such is the case on a piece in which you are interested, be sure to check the quality of the workmanship to make sure it is as fine as you would expect. Also, check for signs of repair or alteration.

Keep in mind that sometimes, for whatever reason, a piece is not signed, or the signature is too worn to read. While it won't have the same value that it would if you could document the maker, it may still offer an exceptionally fine, beautiful piece of jewelry that you can get for a much lower price.

Contemporary jewelry designers and houses are also moving into the limelight. There are many books that provide extensive information on great jewelers and designers—information that can help you recognize their work, signatures, marks, and fakes. We have provided the names of some excellent books in our "Selected Readings" list in the appendix, and your local library can provide a wealth of additional sources.

## IMPORTANT JEWELERS

The following list of jewelers or jewelry houses includes names that have shown strong interest among collectors at auction. When jewelry is attributed to one of these firms, bidding may be stronger than for comparable jewelry with no attribution or for pieces made by a less well-known firm. Also keep in mind that despite the name, some designs stand the test of time, while others do not and simply look outdated and out of style; outmoded pieces or trendy pieces will bring less than those with a more timeless look.

Bailey, Banks & Biddle
Belperron
Black, Starr & Frost (period pieces)
Boivin
Boucheron
Buccellati
Bulgari
J.E. Caldwell & Company (period pieces)
Cartier
Castellani
Chanel
Chaumet
Joe Descomps

Theodore Dreicer
Peter Carl Fabergé
Falize
Flato
Fontenay
Georges Fouquet
Fred
Lucien Gaillard
Garrard
Gautrait
Carlo Giuliano
Hammerman Brothers
Hancock
Oscar Heyman & Brothers
Georg Jensen

LaCloche
Lalaounis
René Lalique
Lambert Brothers
Marcus & Company
Marchak
Masriera
Massoni
Mauboussin
Mellerio
Nardi
Peacock & Company
Plisson and Hartz
Rubel Frères
Ruser
Schlumberger
Seaman Schepps

Shreve & Company
Spaulding & Company
T.B. Starr
Sterlé
Tiffany & Company
Torrini
Trabert and Hoeffer
Van Cleef & Arpels
Verdura
Henri Vever
David Webb
Harry Winston
Phillipe Wolfers
Raymond Yard

# PART 6

# IMPORTANT ADVICE BEFORE BUYING OR SELLING AT AUCTION

# 24 ◆ Important Questions to Ask Before Buying or Selling at Auction

TO BECOME MORE KNOWLEDGEABLE ABOUT THE GEMSTONES AND JEW-
elry you are thinking about buying, and to protect yourself from costly mistakes, you must ask the right questions. This can help you become more
knowledgeable not only about what you are buying in a specific auction, but
for the future. Asking the right questions can transform the exhibition experience from one in which you are just looking at pretty jewelry and deciding
whether or not you like it, into an experience where you can actually gain valuable knowledge and build your expertise.

Asking the right questions is also important because buying at auction differs from other sources in two very important ways. First, a bid is a legally
binding agreement that you will purchase the item for the agreed-upon price.
Second, there is little or no recourse once you have successfully bid on an item,
even when the stone is not accurately described in the fine print (that is, whatever is not in the capitalized headings). Remember that the auction house
guarantees only what is listed in the capitalized headings in the catalog, which
oftentimes is brief, ambiguous, or lacking in important information. By asking the right questions, buyers can:

- Eliminate misunderstandings about the terms and conditions under
  which they are buying.
- Clarify information provided in the catalog descriptions.
- Obtain important information that has been omitted, for a variety of
  reasons, from the catalog.
- Evaluate the reliability of the auction house or seller.

## THE BASIC QUESTIONS TO ASK AT AN AUCTION HOUSE

Even before beginning to consider specific lots, be sure to clarify the terms under which you are buying. In general, the most important questions to ask at the very start are these:

1. Do you have a gemologist on staff? If not, on what are you basing descriptions?
2. What are you actually *guaranteeing* on each lot? Also ask this question for each specific lot in which you are interested.
3. Do you guarantee that stones are the quality indicated on accompanying documentation?
4. Do I have any recourse if I purchase something and discover subsequently that any substantive information—such as color of gemstones or gold karatage—provided in the small print is not accurate?
5. Do I have any recourse if I purchase something and discover subsequently that important information was omitted, such as fracture-filling of a diamond, which is a *temporary* treatment and thus differs from *permanent* treatments described in many auction catalogs as "routinely" used?

Sometimes you can obtain additional assurances that limit your risk. For example, if you ask whether the auction house would be willing to "guarantee" the validity of the information on a Gemological Institute of America (GIA) report accompanying a lot, there is a good chance it would be willing to do so if it has double-checked and is confident that everything is accurate. If so, get a statement to this effect, in writing, before the auction. *Just be sure you are dealing with a person who has the legally binding authority to make such a guarantee.* Then, after the sale, confirm everything with a gemologist-appraiser or gem-testing laboratory. If it doesn't check out, you would have the ability to ask that the sale be rescinded (canceled), and you would be released from your obligation to pay for the piece; when the payment has already been made, you would be entitled to a refund.

## THE MOST IMPORTANT QUESTION TO ASK
## WHEN BUYING FROM AN ONLINE AUCTION SITE

Be especially cautious, regardless of what you are told, when buying at an online auction site because the identity of the seller can easily be concealed.

It can be very difficult, costly, and time-consuming to track down a fraudulent seller once you have purchased jewelry on-line.

The most important question to ask online sellers at the very start is this:

- If I am the successful bidder, are you willing to agree to an escrow arrangement, or other means, whereby the sale will not be concluded, nor payment received by you, until all representations have been verified by an independent gemologist-appraiser or gem-testing laboratory, agreeable to both of us?

The answer to this must be yes unless you are willing to make a costly mistake. You may need to incur the costs involved in setting up an escrow account, or find another way to ensure that no money changes hands until you have seen the item firsthand and have been able to verify representations. Don't accept excuses regarding "unreliable" appraisers; if both parties are acting in good faith, there are always ways to find a gemologist acceptable to them. Or, depending on the location of buyer and seller, it may be possible to meet at the office of a gemologist or gem-testing lab to complete the transaction more quickly. But whatever the case, if you fail to ask *this* question, or if you pay first, verification may come too late.

Another important question to ask online sellers is this:

- What is the return policy?

Carefully read the fine print regarding terms and conditions covering any sale from an online auction site. Most large firms have strict policies, but some smaller firms or independent online sellers might be more flexible. You never know unless you ask.

## IMPORTANT QUESTIONS TO ASK REGARDING SPECIFIC GEMS AND JEWELRY

We emphasize the importance of asking good questions, but keep in mind that the reliability of the answers will depend on the competence of the person you are asking. Where gems and jewelry are involved, always direct your questions to one of the house gemologists, or to the head of the jewelry department.

Never rely on the information provided by staff people who lack gemological training. This is the case with most of the people who help you during the exhibitions, and they can give you wrong or misleading information.

If you recall the earlier case of the woman who purchased the "pink topaz" necklace, she had observed several people working behind the showcase who were looking at the necklace and discussing how rare pink topaz was. While she didn't ask explicitly, their conversation reinforced her impression that the topaz was pink topaz rather than colorless topaz backed with pink foil. If she had only asked a knowledgeable person at the auction house about the color of the topaz—the jewelry specialist or gemologist—the story would probably have ended differently. She would probably have been told about the foil backing that created the pink color—information with which she could have made a more *informed* decision about whether or not to bid, and how much.

## What to Ask When Buying a Diamond

You should obtain as much specific information as possible before purchasing any fine diamond, especially stones weighing one carat or more. For small stones, it is usually not possible to obtain accurate information when they are mounted, since settings make it much more difficult to grade them, but you should be able to obtain the information you need on stones weighing one-half carat or more. Indeed, some laboratories now provide grading reports for diamonds as small as one-half carat, or smaller.

Here are the basic questions to ask. Remember that the responses are not necessarily guarantees, and the answers provided may not offer any legal protection, but asking them can still be useful. Just by *asking,* you may be better able to judge the knowledge of the people you're dealing with. If they can't or won't answer important questions, this is important to know and should signal the need for caution. As we've said before, bid low or let it go. If they do answer them, note what you've been told alongside the lot in your catalog; if you succeed in acquiring the lot and then everything checks out when verified by a gemologist-appraiser or gem-testing lab, you can begin to place confidence in the seller's knowledge and reliability. If it doesn't, you'll know not to rely on what they tell you in the future.

To sum up, whatever you are told, and whatever guarantees the seller is willing to make, be sure to verify your purchases with a respected gemologist-appraiser or gem-testing laboratory. And whether you come away disappointed or ecstatic, you'll know for tomorrow.

1. *Is this stone accompanied by a diamond grading report or certificate?* If so, ask to see a copy of it, and ask the jewelry specialist or house gemologist if they have double-checked to confirm what's on it. If not, ask if they could do it for you.

2. *What is the exact carat weight?* (See chapter 5.)

3. *What is its color grade?* (See chapter 8.)

4. *Is the color natural?* (See chapter 12.) If not, how was it altered?

5. *If natural, what was done to ascertain and confirm the color is natural?*

6. *Does the stone show any fluorescence, and if so, does it have any negative effect on the stone's appearance?* (See chapter 8.) Remember that showing fluorescence can be a benefit, not a negative. Just make sure the stone is not one of the rare exceptions in which extreme fluorescence creates a less brilliant stone with an oily or murky character.

7. *What is its clarity (flaw) grade?* (See chapter 9.)

8. *Has this stone been clarity enhanced?* Be sure to ask whether or not the diamond has been laser treated or fracture-filled. (See chapter 12.) If it is accompanied by a GIA report, the report will indicate lasering, if present. However, the GIA won't issue a report on a fracture-filled stone. *If there is no GIA report, be sure to ask explicitly.*

9. *Is it well cut for its shape?* How would the make be graded (ideal, excellent, good, and so on)? (See chapter 7.)

## What to Ask When Buying a Colored Gemstone

As with diamonds, it's very important to ask the right questions to help you understand the differences in gems you may be considering. Asking the following questions should help you to gain a greater understanding of the differences, especially if you are simultaneously comparing several stones side by side; determine what's right for you; and have greater confidence in your decision.

1. *Are you sure the stone is genuine?* What has been done to ensure it isn't a synthetic? (See chapter 17.)

2. *Is the color natural or enhanced?* (See chapter 17.) If not enhanced, what was done to ascertain it is natural? If enhanced, by what method? Remember that stones such as lapis will not retain their color if they have been dyed. See information on specific gems (chapters 17 and 19) to determine whether or not this is an important question for you to ask.

Be especially cautious when buying any blue sapphire; *make sure you ask whether or not the stone has been checked for diffusion treatment and oiling.* Ask explicitly what the policy of the firm is if the stone proves to have been diffusion treated.

3. *How would you rank this stone's color, on a scale of one to ten, in terms of the ideal for the particular type of gemstone?* While this is a subjective question, it can provide some general parameters within which to make comparisons, especially if you ask this same question about several stones you may be considering.

4. *Does this stone show any fluorescence under either longwave or shortwave?* If the answer is yes, be sure to examine it carefully in different lighting conditions to make sure the color doesn't change noticeably, and if it does, whether or not you see it in all lighting conditions. (See chapter 16.)

5. *Clarify names with qualifiers.* For example, Rio topaz or Korean jade. Ask explicitly what any "qualifier" means; ask specifically whether or not the stone is a genuine stone of whatever the name suggests. Rio topaz is not topaz; Korean jade is not jade. Ask why the qualifier is being used. Burma sapphire means sapphire from Burma, but Burma-type sapphire or Burma color means the stone does not come from Burma, only that the color resembles that of sapphires from Burma.

6. *Where would you rank this stone's clarity, on a scale of one to ten, in terms of the ideal for the particular type of gemstone?* Again, while subjective, this can help you learn what is typical or exceptional for the type of gem you seek.

7. *Are there any flaws, inclusions, or natural characteristics in this stone that might make it more vulnerable to breakage with normal wear?* This is a particularly important question when you are considering colored stones such as emerald and ruby. (See chapter 19.) While visible inclusions are more common in colored gems than in diamonds, and their existence has much less impact on value than it has on diamond value, value is nonetheless reduced if the inclusions or blemishes affect the stone's durability, or are so numerous that they mar its beauty.

8. *Has there been any clarity enhancement?* If the answer is no, ask what has been done to verify that. If the answer is yes, ask how and to what extent.

9. *Are there any glass fillings or oil in fissures, or other fillers?* If the answer is no, ask what has been done to verify that. If the answer is yes, ask how and to what extent.

10. *What are the colorless stones?* In a piece of jewelry where a colored stone is mounted with colorless stones, ask, "What are the colorless stones?" Do not assume they are diamonds. They may be diamonds, zircons, artificial diamond imitations such as cubic zirconia (CZ) or yttrium aluminum garnet (YAG), or synthetic white spinel (spinel is frequently used in the Orient).

## Special Tips to Remember When Buying a Colored Stone

*View colored gemstones through the side as well as from the top.* Also, turn them upside down on a flat white surface so they are resting on the table facet and you can look straight down through the stone from the back. Look for evenness of color versus color zoning—shades of lighter or darker tones that create streaks or planes of differing color.

Remember that color is the most important consideration. If the color is fine, flaws or inclusions don't detract from the stone's value as significantly as with diamonds. If the overall color or beauty is not seriously affected, the presence of flaws should not deter a purchase. But, conversely, flawless stones may bring a disproportionately higher price per carat because of their rarity, and larger sizes will also command higher prices. In pastel-colored gems, or stones with less fine color, clarity may be more important.

*Be sure to check the stone's color in several different types of light*—a spotlight, sunlight, fluorescent light, or lamplight—before making any decision. Many stones change color—some just slightly, others dramatically—depending on the light in which they are viewed. Be sure that the stone is a pleasing color in the type of light in which you expect to be wearing it most.

If you are considering a stone with rich, deep color—especially if it is for special occasions and likely to be worn mostly at night—be sure it doesn't turn black in evening light. Some stones, like sapphire, can look like black onyx in evening light.

## WHAT TO ASK WHEN BUYING JEWELRY ATTRIBUTED TO AN IMPORTANT MAKER

If a piece is being represented as being made by a famous designer or house (Van Cleef & Arpels, Tiffany, J.E. Caldwell, Cartier, etc.) regardless of the estimate shown, make no assumptions. It is important to ask the following questions:

1. *Why have you attributed this piece to this particular jewelry house or jeweler?*

2. *Has it been documented or authenticated by the jewelry house or jeweler?* This may not be possible if the jeweler is deceased or the firm is out of business.

3. *Can you tell me if the piece was made by the jeweler named, or does it just carry the name of the firm? Does it affect value? How can one distinguish between them?* Some rare jewelry pieces, for example, carry a mark attributing them to Louis C. Tiffany, or to a period when he was personally overseeing production. Such pieces command a much higher price than pieces made by Tiffany & Company in more recent history. The same can be said for pieces by David Webb and other important names.

4. *Does this piece show any repair or alteration? How serious is it?*

5. *Can you assure me this is not a "marriage" piece?* (Such a piece is made by assembling several pieces of old jewelry together, often with one part carrying the mark of an important maker.)

## What to Ask When Buying Jewelry Attributed to a Particular Period

When jewelry is represented to have been made during a particular period, make no assumptions, regardless of estimates shown. It is important to ask the following questions:

1. *Can you give me an approximate date when this piece was made?* (Keep in mind that to be represented as "antique" the piece must be at least one hundred years old.)

2. *Why do you attribute this piece to this particular period?* Answers to this question can help you learn to recognize particular design elements or production methods that will help you recognize other jewelry from the same period.

3. *Are there any marks that would confirm an age consistent with this period?* This can be very important. Sometimes hallmarks provide the necessary confirmation (see "Selected Readings" for guides to hallmarks and related dates).

4. *Is there any sign of repair or alteration?* A loupe can be helpful in double-checking what the expert tells you. Spotting a sloppy solder mark, for

example, would provide evidence of repair or alteration, or spotting an area where the color of the gold doesn't match well (remember that different alloys create different colors; not all "yellow" gold is the same exact color).

5. *Are you sure this is not a marriage piece? Why?*

## DON'T BUY ONLINE WITHOUT THIRD PARTY VERIFICATION

When dealing with online sellers, ask if you can arrange for verification of what you have been told before payment. You may need to establish an escrow account so that you can view the stone while keeping the money safely with a third party until the quality is confirmed. If both parties are acting in good faith, there are always ways to find a gemologist acceptable to them. Or, depending upon the location of buyer and seller, it may be possible to meet at the office of a gemologist or gem-testing lab.

## IMPORTANT QUESTIONS FOR SELLERS TO ASK

While much of the information provided below has been covered in greater detail in previous chapters, here we provide some additional questions that some people overlook. This provides a succinct guide to important questions sellers should be asking. The focus is on questions that should be asked by sellers who are consigning gems or jewelry to a traditional auction house, or to online sites to which goods might be delivered for exhibition purposes (such as Sotheby's special online auctions).

1. *Can I withdraw what I've consigned before the auction? Up to, and including, the day of the sale? Will I incur any costs to do so?* Some unforeseen event may create a situation in which it would be in your best interest to withdraw your lot. Make sure you know beforehand what this might entail.

2. *Will my piece do best at this location, or would it be better to consign it for an upcoming sale in a different location such as Europe or Asia?* Some types of jewelry sell better in foreign markets than in the United States, and vice versa.

3. *Will my piece do best at the upcoming sale, or do you have any special or "theme" sales planned, at which mine might do better? Or will it do better*

*at a different time of year?* If you have a piece of jewelry made by a contemporary American designer, for example, it might bring a higher amount at a "theme" sale focusing on jewelry by American designers because the audience would include those with a serious interest in this particular segment of the jewelry marketplace. There is also a seasonality to certain types of jewelry. Coral, for example, often sells better in a spring sale, when fashion-conscious women are thinking "pastel," while amber often brings more in the fall, when earthy colors are more popular.

4. *Will you cover the cost of getting laboratory documentation?* If you have been advised by a gemologist before consigning your piece, and realize that laboratory documentation could result in stronger bidding, you might want to speak to the auction house before obtaining the documentation, just in case it is willing to cover the cost. While it is usually the responsibility of the consignor, if the piece contains an exceptional gemstone, the auction house may agree to pay for documentation or to share responsibility for the cost.

5. *If the piece sells, how quickly can I expect to receive payment? What assurance can you provide that this will occur? What penalty will you incur if I am not paid punctually?* This may or may not be covered in the terms and conditions of the firm. If not, make sure you get statements covering payment terms. There may be no penalty clauses, but try to negotiate something that provides an incentive not to be late, especially on major pieces where a large sum of money might be involved.

6. *If my piece does not sell, what costs do I incur?* This is usually stipulated in the terms and conditions of sale, but it is also a point you can try to negotiate so that you pay a smaller fee or no fee at all, especially if you have an especially rare or beautiful piece that will add excitement or draw the attention of prospective buyers.

7. *What insurance coverage do you provide while my property is in your possession? Is it covered under all conditions and in all locations?* Ask to see proof of insurance, and make sure it is current.

# 25 ◆ How to Find a Reliable Gemologist-Appraiser— And Why You Need One

FOR THE AUCTION BUYER, WHETHER YOU HAVE BOUGHT A DIAMOND, colored gemstone, pearls, gold, or jewelry from a particular period or by a famous maker, it is essential to find someone who can verify your purchase, along with finding out whether or not you got the "bargain" you think you did. But it can also serve other important purposes. The primary reasons to seek a reliable gemologist-appraiser include these:

- Verifying all representations made about the piece you obtain, whether or not they were guaranteed (this is especially critical today because of the abundance of new synthetic materials and treatments).
- Finding out whether or not you really got a bargain.
- Obtaining adequate insurance to protect against theft, loss, or damage.
- Obtaining adequate information to legally claim lost or stolen jewelry recovered by police.
- Ensuring replacement of lost or stolen items with items of comparable quality by having an appraisal that provides a thorough and accurate description.

For sellers, it is critical to know the value of your piece *before* you consign anything to an auction house. You need to know the true identity of the gemstones and materials used in a piece of jewelry—heirlooms and gifts are often not what you think they are—along with the quality, condition, desirability, and rarity of a piece. This is the only way you can learn the true value of what you have and protect yourself against selling your piece for less than it's really worth. And this is the primary reason to retain the services of a reliable gemologist-appraiser.

A respected gemologist-appraiser can perform these services:

- Determine the value of what you have.
- Explain ways to go about selling what you have, and which avenue might be most appropriate for selling it within your timetable.
- Estimate what you should expect to get for it, and where you might get the most.
- Advise you on the right auction venue—major international house, regional house, online site—and provide useful information on specific auction houses that might be best for your piece.
- Advise you on what would be a reasonable reserve price should you decide to consign to an auction house.
- Advise you on whether or not any diamond or colored gemstone warrants getting a laboratory report from a major gem-testing laboratory. If so, they can also oversee submitting the stone to the appropriate lab and getting the appropriate type of report.

Armed with this information, you can negotiate a much better deal for yourself at the auction house. In some cases, the gemologist-appraiser might accompany you to the auction house, or act as your agent and consign the piece on your behalf.

If selling on-line, having an appraisal from a gemologist-appraiser with respected credentials increases your credibility with prospective buyers.

## How to Find a Reliable Gemologist-Appraiser

There are essentially no officially established guidelines or legal requirements governing who can represent themselves as gemologist-appraisers. Anyone can represent himself or herself as an appraiser. Auction houses are also in the "appraisal" business. However, they have a vested interest that should not be ignored by prospective sellers, or buyers, as we explained in chapter 2. We strongly recommend obtaining the services of an independent gemologist.

It is essential that you select a gemologist-appraiser, but it is also very important to understand that not all "gemologists" are equally reliable. While there are many highly qualified professionals in the field, there are also many who lack the requisite training, fully equipped laboratories, or sufficient experience to do what needs to be done today. Some adhere to higher professional and ethical standards than others.

We emphasize the importance of selecting an appraiser with care and diligence. To help you find a reliable gemologist-appraiser in your own area, here is a list of organizations that award highly respected designations to qualifying members (a list of internationally respected gem-testing laboratories is provided in the appendix):

The American Society of Appraisers
PO Box 17265, Washington, DC 20041
(703) 478-2228

- Ask for a current listing of *Master Gemologist Appraisers.*

The American Gem Society Laboratory (AGSL)
8881 W. Sahara Ave., Las Vegas, NV 89117
(702) 255-6500

- Ask for a list of *Certified Gemologist Appraisers* or *Independent Certified Gemologist Appraisers.*

The Accredited Gemologists Association
888 Brannan St., Ste. 1175, San Francisco, CA 94103
(415) 252-9340

- Ask for a list of *Certified Gem Laboratories* or *Certified Master Gemologists.*

The National Association of Jewelry Appraisers
PO Box 6558, Annapolis, MD 21401-0558
(410) 897-0889

- Ask for a list of *Certified Master Appraisers* or *Certified Senior Members.*

Some fine gemologists and appraisers lack these titles because they do not belong to the organizations awarding them, but these titles currently represent the highest awards presented in the gemological appraisal field. Anyone holding these titles should have fine gemological credentials and adhere to high standards of professional conduct.

# APPENDIX

## INTERNATIONALLY RESPECTED LABORATORIES ISSUING REPORTS USED BY MAJOR AUCTION HOUSES

American Gemological Laboratory (AGL)
580 Fifth Ave., Ste. 706
New York, NY 10036

American Gem Trade Association (AGTA)
  Gemological Testing Center
18 E. 48th St., Ste. 1002
New York, NY 10017

CISGEM-External Service for
  Precious Stones
Via Ansperto, 5
20123 Milano
Italy

Gemmological Association and Gem
  Testing Laboratory of Great Britain
27 Greville St.
London EC1N 8SU
England

Gemological Association of All Japan
Katsumi Bldg., 5F, 5-25-8
Ueno, Taito-ku
Tokyo 110
Japan

Gemological Institute of America
  Gem Trade Laboratory (GIA-GTL)
580 Fifth Ave.
New York, NY 10036
  and
5345 Armada Dr.
Carlsbad, CA 92008

German Foundation for
  Gemological Research
Gemological Laboratory
Prof.-Schlossmacher-Strasse 1
D-55743 Idar-Oberstein
Germany

Gübelin Gemmological Lab
Maihofstrasse 102
CH-6006 Lucerne 9
Switzerland

Hoge Raad voor Diamant (HRD)
Institute of Gemmology
Hoveniersstraat 22
B-2018 Antwerp 1
Belgium

Swiss Gemmological Institute
  SSEF—Schweizerische Stiftung für
  Edelstein-Forschung
Falknerstrasse 9
CH-4001 Basel
Switzerland

## Online Auction Sites

Below are some websites that currently offer live, online auctions. However, auction houses and their online capabilities are constantly changing, so be sure to check with individual auction houses regarding the services provided online.

- www.antiquorum.com (online viewing and online bidding during live auction sales)
- www.auctionsmart.com
- www.butterfields.com (through eBay Premier)
- www.dickeranddicker.com
- www.eBay.com
- www.ice.com (through yahoo! and eBay)
- www.realbidder.com
- www.sothebys.com
- www.yahoo.com

## A Selected List of Auction Houses

Provided here is a list of some of the major auction houses. All of these offer online information; some have online absentee bidding forms that you can send in before the start of a traditional auction at an auction house; others provide the capability of bidding on-line, in real time (indicated by asterisk), for items being sold at the auction house; and a few offer special internet-only auctions. For a list of websites that offer live, online auctions, see below.

Alderfer's
501 Fairgrounds Rd.
Hatfield, PA 19440
(215) 393-3000
Fax: (215) 368-9055
www.alderfercompany.com

Antiquorum Auctioneers*
609 Fifth Ave., Ste. 503
New York, NY 10017
(212) 750-1103
Fax: (212) 750-6127
www.antiquorum.com*

Antiquorum Auctioneers*
2 rue du Mont-Blanc
1201 Geneva, Switzerland
(41) 22-909-2850
Fax: (41) 22-909-2860
www.antiquorum.com*

Bloomington Auction Gallery
  (formerly Joy Luke
  Auctioneers)
300 E. Grove St.
Bloomington, IL 61701-5232
(309) 828-5533
Fax: (309) 829-2266
www.joyluke.com

Bonham's & Brooks
101 New Bond St.
London, UK W15 15R
(44) 020-7468-3900
Fax: (44) 020-7393-3905
www.bonhams.com

Frank H. Boos Gallery
420 Enterprise Ct.
Bloomfield Hills, MI 48302
(248) 332-1500
Fax: (248) 332-6770
www.boosgallery.com

Bunda Auctioneers
608 Fifth Ave., #701
New York, NY 10020
(212) 489-6553
Fax: (212) 459-9068
www.jewelry-time.com

Bunte Auction Services
755 Church Rd.
Elgin, IL 60123
(847) 214-8423
Fax: (847) 214-8801
www.bunteauction.com

Butterfields
220 San Bruno Ave.
San Francisco, CA 94103
(415) 861-7500
Fax: (415) 861-8951
www.butterfields.com

Christie's
20 Rockefeller Plaza
New York, NY 10020
(212) 636-2000
Fax: (212) 636-2399
www.christies.com

Christie's
1 Darling St.
South Yarra, Victoria
Australia 3141
(61) 03-9820-4311
Fax: (61) 03-9820-4876
www.christies.com

Christie's
2203-5 Alexandra House
16-20 Chater Rd.
Central Hong Kong
(852) 2521-5396
Fax: (852) 2845-2646
www.christies.com

Christie's
8 King St.
St. James, London, UK,
   SWIY 6QT
44-20-7839-9060
Fax: 44-20-7839-1611
www.christies.com

Christie's
8 Place de la Taconnerie
1204 Geneva, Switzerland
(41) 22-319-1766
Fax: (41) 22-319-1767
www.christies.com

Dicker & Dicker Jewelers
24001 Chagrin Blvd.
Beachwood, OH 44122
(216) 464-0400
Fax: (216) 595-3824
www.dickeranddicker.com

William Doyle Galleries
175 E. 87th St.
New York NY 10128
(212) 427-2730
Fax: (212) 369-0892
www.doylenewyork.com

Joseph DuMouchelle
   International Auctioneers
5 Kercheval Ave.
Grosse Pointe Farms, MI
   48236-3601
(800) 475-4367
Fax: (313) 884-7662
www.dumouchelleauction.
   com

Dupuis Jewellery
   Auctioneers
94 Cumberland St., Ste. 908
Toronto, ON, Canada
   M5R 1A3
(416) 968-7500
Fax: (416) 968-7739
www.dupuisauctions.com

Freeman Fine Arts
1808 Chestnut St.
Philadelphia, PA 19103
(215) 563-9275
Fax: (215) 563-8236
www.freemansauction.com

Bob Koty Professional
   Auctioneers
PO Box 625
Freehold, NJ 07728
(732) 751-0504
Fax: (732) 751-9190
www.kotyauctions.com

Northeast Auctions
93 Pleasant St.
Portsmouth, NH 03801
(603) 433-8400
Fax: (603) 433-0415
www.northeastauctions.com

Phillips, de Pury &
   Luxembourg
3 W. 57th St.
New York, NY 10019
(212) 940-1290
Fax: (212) 688-0732
www.phillips-auctions.com

Phillips, de Pury &
   Luxembourg
9 rue Ami-Lévrier
1201 Geneva, Switzerland
(41) 22-738-0707
Fax: (41) 22-731-6644
www.phillips-auctions.com

Ritchie's Auctioneers &
  Appraisers
228 King St. East
Toronto, ON, Canada M5A
  1K4
(416) 364-1864
Fax: (416) 364-0704
www.ritchies.com

Skinner, Inc.
63 Park Plaza
Boston, MA 02116
(617) 350-5400
Fax: (617) 350-5429
www.skinnerinc.com

Sloan's
4920 Wyaconda Rd.
North Bethesda, MD 20852
(301) 468-4911
Fax: (301) 468-9182
www.sloansauction.com

Sloan's
2516 Ponce de Leon Blvd.
Coral Gables, FL 33134
(305) 447-0757
Fax: (305) 444-2944
www.sloansauction.com

Barry S. Slosberg, Inc.
2501 E. Ontario St.
Philadelphia, PA 19134
(215) 425-7030
Fax: (215) 425-7039
www.bssauction.com

Sotheby's
1334 York Ave.
New York, NY 10021
(212) 606-7000
Fax: (212) 606-7014
www.sothebys.com

Susanin's
138 Merchandise Mart
Chicago, IL 60654
(312) 832-9800
Fax: (312) 832-9311
www.auctionsmart.com

Tepper Galleries, Inc.
110 E. 25th St.
New York, NY 10010
(212) 677-5300
Fax: (212) 673-3686
www.teppergalleries.com

Treadway/Toomey Gallery
818 North Blvd.
Oak Park, IL 60301
(708) 383-5234
Fax: (708) 383-4828
www.treadwaygallery.com

Waddington's
111 Bathurst St.
Toronto, ON, Canada
  M5V 2R1
(416) 504-9100
Fax: (416) 504-0033
www.waddingtonsauctions.
  com

Weschler's
905-9 E St., NW
Washington, DC 20004
(202) 628-1281
Fax: (202) 628-2366
www.weschlers.com

## WHERE TO GET ADDITIONAL INFORMATION

### Selected Readings

Arem, Joel E. *Color Encyclopedia of Gemstones.* New York: Van Nostrand Reinhold, 1987.

Becker, Vivienne. *Antique and Twentieth Century Jewellery.* London: N.A.G Press, 1987.

Blauer, Ettagale. *Contemporary American Jewelry Design.* New York: Van Nostrand Reinhold, 1991.

Bronstein, Alan. *Forever Brilliant: The Aurora Collection of Colored Diamonds.* New York: Ashland Press, Inc., 2000.

Downing, Paul B. *Opal Identification and Value.* Tallahassee, Fla.: Majestic Press, 1992.

Farn, Alexander E. *Pearls: Natural, Cultured and Imitation.* Oxford: Butterworth-Heinemann Ltd., 1991.

Gübelin, Edward, and J.L. Koivula. *Photoatlas of Inclusions in Gemstones.* Zurich: ABC Editions, 1986.

Hill, Gerald, ed. *Fabergé and the Russian Master Goldsmiths.* New York: Hugh Lauter Levin Associates, Inc., 1989.

Hofer, Stephen C. *Collecting and Classifying Colored Diamonds.* New York: Ashland Press, 1998.

Keller, Peter C. *Gemstones and Their Origins.* New York: Van Nostrand Reinhold, 1989.

Keverne, Roger, ed. *Jade.* New York: Lorenz Books, 1996.

Matlins, Antoinette. *Colored Gemstones: The Antoinette Matlins Buying Guide—How to Select, Buy, Care for & Enjoy Sapphires, Emeralds, Rubies and Other Colored Gems with Confidence and Knowledge.* Woodstock, Vt.: GemStone Press, 2001.

———. *Diamonds: The Antoinette Matlins Buying Guide—How to Select, Buy, Care for & Enjoy Diamonds with Confidence and Knowledge.* Woodstock, Vt.: GemStone Press, 2001.

———. *The Pearl Book: The Definitive Buying Guide—How to Select, Buy, Care for & Enjoy Pearls.* 2nd ed. Woodstock, Vt.: GemStone Press, 1999.

Matlins, Antoinette L., and A.C. Bonanno. *Gem Identification Made Easy: A Hands-On Guide to More Confident Buying & Selling.* 2nd ed. Woodstock, Vt.: GemStone Press, 1997.

Miller, Anna M. *The Buyer's Guide to Affordable Antique Jewelry.* New York: Citadel Press, 1995.

———. *Cameos Old & New.* 2nd ed. Woodstock, Vt.: GemStone Press, 1998.

———. *Gems & Jewelry Appraising: Techniques of Professional Practice.* 2nd ed. Woodstock, Vt.: GemStone Press, 1999.

———. *Illustrated Guide to Jewelry Appraising: Antique, Period, and Modern.* 2nd ed. Woodstock, Vt.: GemStone Press, 1999.

Nassau, Kurt. *Gemstone Enhancement.* Woburn, Mass.: Butterworth's, 1983.

Raulet, Sylvie. *Art Deco Jewelry.* New York: Rizzoli, 1985.

Sataloff, Joseph. *Art Nouveau Jewelry.* Bryn Mawr, Pa.: Dorrance & Company, Inc., 1984.

Scarisbrick, Diana, ed. *The Jewelry Design Sourcebook.* New York: Van Nostrand Reinhold, 1989.

Schumann, W. *Gemstones of the World.* Translated by E. Stern. New York: Sterling Publishing Co., 1977.

Snowman, A. Kenneth, ed. *The Master Jewelers.* New York: Harry N. Abrams, Inc., 1990.

Sofianides, Anna S., and George E. Harlow. *Gems and Crystals.* New York: Simon & Schuster, 1991.

Webster, R. Revised by B.W. Anderson. *Gems.* 4th ed. London: Butterworth & Co., 1990.

Zeitner, June C. *Gem and Lapidary Materials: For Cutters, Collectors, and Jewelers.* Tucson: Geoscience Press, 1996.

Zucker, Benjamin. *Gems and Jewels: A Connoisseur's Guide.* New York: Thames and Hudson, Inc., 1984.

### References for Hallmarks and Makers' Marks

Burton, Eric. *Hallmarks & Date Letters on Silver, Gold and Platinum.* London: NAG Press, Ltd, 1977.

DiViš, Jan. *Guide to Gold Marks of the World,* Twickenham, UK: Tiger Books International, 1998.

*Explorer Trade Marks.* Altavilla, Italy: Edizioni Gov, s.n.c., 2000. Order from Via Retronr 39, 360777, Altavilla VI, Italy (tel. [0]4-444-520847).

Pickford, Ian, ed. *Jackson's Silver and Gold Marks of England, Scotland & Ireland.* Wappingers Falls, N.Y.: Antique Collectors Club, 1987.

Sataloff, Joseph. *Art Nouveau Jewelry*. (See "Selected Readings.")

Tardy, L. *International Hallmarks on Silver*. Paris: Tardy, 1993.

————. *Poinçons D'Or et de Platine*. Paris: Tardy, 1988. Currently available only in French. Order both from 6 Rue Milton, 75009, Paris, France (tel. (1) 42-81-44-97).

## Auction Market Publications

*Auction Market Resource for Gems and Jewelry*. Published twice yearly by Gail Brett Levine, PO Box 7683, Rego Park, NY 11374 (tel.: 718-897-7305). By subscription: $195 in the US, $250 overseas. Comprehensive information on jewelry pieces sold at auction houses in the United States. Includes description, black-and-white photographs, summary of accompanying laboratory reports, and prices at which lots sold (online auction sites are not included).

*Palmieri Market Monitor*. Published monthly by Gemological Appraisal Association, Inc., 580 Fifth Avenue, Ste. 1205, New York, NY 10036 (tel.: 212-869-9792). By subscription: $175 per year (a bimonthly option is also available for $135 per year). Provides wholesale pricing information and auction results.

## Online Sources of Information

There are many sources of online information, but there is not yet any screening mechanism to separate reliable from unreliable information. You must consider the source of the information and be wary of information provided by sellers of gems or jewelry. The following sites may provide helpful information:

- www.auctionmarketresource.com (provides selected gem and jewelry data for items sold at national and international auctions. Categorizes by type of piece and includes measurements, estimated weights, clarity and color grades of diamonds and colored gemstones, condition reports, color photographs, and enlarged actual signatures [where possible]. Presale estimates and hammer prices (including the buyer's premium) are given for every jewelry item. Each piece has been personally inspected and described by the Auction Market Resource's trained staff of gemologist-appraisers.)
- www.ftc.gov (Federal Trade Commission)
- www.jewelryinfo.org (Jewelry Information Center)
- www.gia.edu (Gemological Institute of America educational site)
- www.diamondregistry.com (diamond industry newsletter with consumer information)
- www.ags.org (American Gem Society)
- www.gem.net (colored gemstone information site)
- www.pearlinfo.com (Cultured Pearl Information Center)
- www.AuctionBytes.com

# CREDITS

## BLACK AND WHITE EXHIBITS AND COLOR PLATES

### Credits for Charts

All the charts and the tables that appear here were especially designed and executed for GemStone Press; however, some from other publications were used as inspiration and reference. Grateful acknowledgment is given to the following for use of their charts as references:

The chart on page 88, "Sizes and Weights of Various Diamond Cuts," with permission of the Gemological Institute of America, from its book *The Jewelers' Manual.*

The chart on page 142, "Comparison of Diamonds and Diamond Look-Alikes," with permission of the Gemological Institute of America, from its publication *Diamond Assignment No. 36,* page 27.

### Credits for Black and White Illustrations and Photographs

All illustrations by Kathleen Robinson.

12: Art Deco brooch courtesy of Christie's Images, NY.

12: Gold and gemstone ring from Sotheby's (online site).

12: Retro brooch courtesy of Christie's Images, NY.

12: Belle Epoque brooch from Christie's.

12: Diamond and sapphire floral brooch from Weschler's.

13: La Pelegrina from Christie's.

13: Mauboussin necklace from Antiquorum Auctioneers.

14: Amalfi watch from Antiquorum Auctioneers.

14: Ladies Retro watch courtesy of Christie's Images, NY.

15: Rockefeller sapphire from Christie's.

15: Bob Hope's watch from Antiquorum Auctioneers.

57: Sotheby's jewelry from Sotheby's (online site).

60: Yahoo! website from Yahoo.com.

102: Old Asscher from Jonathan Birnbach for J.B. International.

102: Old cushion cut from Antiquorum Auctioneers.

103: Trapezoids and half-moons from Doron Isaak.

103: Briolette from Rough and Ready Gems (photo/Azad).

186: Cabochon and faceted rings from Jack Abraham, President of Precious Gem Resources.

241: Pearl cross sections from K. Scarratt, AIGS.

244: Empress Eugénie pearl necklace from Antoinette Matlins.

246: Cross section of cultured pearl from K. Scarratt, AIGS.

250: Natural pearl earrings from Christie's.

252: Black Tahitian pearl necklace from Christie's.

252: Florence Gould necklace from Christie's.

252: Button pearl earclips from Sotheby's.

264: Retro gold bracelet courtesy of Christie's Images, NY.

264: Antique gold filigree ear pendants courtesy of Christie's Images, NY.

268: Georgian brooch courtesy of Christie's Images, NY.

269: Victorian bracelet courtesy of Christie's Images, NY.

270: Georg Jensen necklace from Skinner, Auctioneers and Appraisers of Antiques and Fine Art (Boston and Bolton, Mass.).

271: Lucien Gaillard choker from Christie's.

272: Edwardian pendant from Skinner, Auctioneers and Appraisers of Antiques and Fine Art (Boston and Bolton, Mass.).

272: Belle Epoque choker courtesy of Christie's Images, NY.

273: J.E. Caldwell bracelet from Weschler's.

273: Art Deco pin courtesy of Christie's Images, NY.

274: Retro bracelet and earrings courtesy of Christie's Images, NY.

275: Merle Oberon necklace from Antiquorum Auctioneers.

## Credits for Color Photographs

Page 1: Peacock from Robert Haack Diamonds (photo/Sky Hall); floral brooch from Sotheby's; blue briolette and red radiant from Phillips; vivid yellow emerald-cut diamond courtesy of Sotheby's; vivid yellow ring from Weschler's; intense yellow emerald-cut diamond ring from Butterfields.

Page 2: Emerald cut from Phillips; round, pear, and oval courtesy of Christie's Images, NY; marquise from Sotheby's.

Page 3: Quadrillion™ from Ambar Diamonds; radiant and trilliant from Eugene Biro Corp.; Royal Asscher® from Royal Asscher Diamond Company Ltd.; EightStar® from EightStar Diamond Company (photo/Richard von Sternberg); Gabrielle® heart from Suberi Brothers (photo/Peter Hurst); briolette and rondelles from Manak Jewels, Inc.; earrings, half-moons, and trapezoids from Doron Isaak; Crisscut® baguettes from Christopher Designs (photo/Christony Inc.).

Page 4: Heart-shaped diamond ring from Dicker & Dicker Auctions (www.dickeranddicker.com); platinum and diamond rings and marquise-cut diamond ring courtesy of Sotheby's (www.sothebys.com); emerald-cut diamond ring from Phillips; pear-shaped diamond and oval diamond ring courtesy of Christie's.

Page 5: Gold, pink tourmaline, and tsavorite ring, gold, green chalcedony, and coral pendant/brooch, platinum, aquamarine, and diamond brooch courtesy of Sotheby's; diamond and gold heart pendant from ice.com; modern peridot, diamond, and enamel brooch and earrings from Weschler's; French enamel and gold locket and necklace from Butterfields; white gold, diamond and colored stone flag brooch from Sotheby's Arcade Jewelry; Tomasino Saulini carved cameo, yellow gold and enamel bracelet from Joseph DuMouchelle International Auctioneers; antique gold-framed shell cameo from Dicker & Dicker Auctions (www.dickeranddicker.com).

Page 6: Star ruby from International Colored Gemstone Association (ICA) (photo/Bart Curran); selection of red and pink gemstones and rhodochrosites from Pala International, Inc.(photo/Sky Hall); red beryl from Rex Harris (photo/Sky Hall).

Page 7: Star sapphire and moonstones from International Colored Gemstone Association (ICA) (photos/Bart Curran); selection of blue gemstones from Pala International, Inc. (photo/Sky Hall); chrysocolla from American Gem Trade Association (AGTA), cut by Glenn Lehrer, AGTA Cutting Edge competition winner (photo/Sky Hall); blue Paraiba tourmaline from Cynthia Renee Co. (photo/Robert Weldon).

Page 8: Selection of yellow and orange gemstones from Pala International, Inc. (photo/Sky Hall); topaz from American Gem Trade Association (AGTA) (photo/Natural Arts, Inc.); sunstone from Ponderosa Mine, Inc. (photo/Bart Curran); sapphire, andalusite, and cat's-eye chrysoberyl from Krementz Gemstones (photo/Sky Hall); fancy-cut citrine with concave facets from American Gem Trade Association (AGTA), cut by Cutting Edge winner Richard Homer, American Lapidary Artists (photo/Sky Hall); yellow beryl from AGTA, cut by Cutting Edge winner Karl Egan Wilde (photos/Sky Hall).

Page 9: Selection of green gemstones and tsavorite garnet from Pala International, Inc. (photos/Sky Hall); emerald-cut emerald from International Colored Gemstone Association (ICA) (photo/Sky Hall); Paraiba tourmaline from Cynthia Renee Co. (photo/Robert Weldon); Laboratory-grown synthetic stones from Chatham Created Gemstones; period Art Deco jadeite brooch from Christie's.

Page 10: Briolettes from Rough and Ready Gems (photos/Azad); trilliant from David Brackna (photo/Robert Weldon); oval, round, cushion, and emerald cut from John Parrish Photography; marquise and pear shape photos by Sky Hall; princess from Lucent Diamonds™ (photo/Tino Hammid); cabochons from James Alger (photo/Van Pelt).

Page 11: Rockefeller sapphire from Christie's; Burmese ruby and half-moon diamond ring, sugarloaf cabochon natural sapphire with triangular diamonds in a ring, and Kashmir sapphire courtesy of Sotheby's; Ceylon sapphire, Colombian emerald, and octagonal-cut Burmese ruby from Phillips; padparadscha sapphire from Antiquorum Auctioneers; fancy-color sapphire and diamond necklace from Butterfields.

Page 12: *En tremblant* brooches from Phillips; multicolored natural pearl necklace, natural pearl watch and calendar bracelets, and aquamarine brooch and earrings courtesy of Christie's Images, NY; sunburst pin courtesy of Sotheby's (www.sotheby's.com); moonstone, diamond and sapphire cherub brooch from Butterfields.

Page 13: "Egyptian Revival" jewelry from Antiquorum Auctioneers; Art Nouveau necklace, Retro brooch, Belle Epoque necklace, and Retro bracelet courtesy of Christie's Images, NY; Art Deco ring from Phillips; Art Deco Burmese sapphire and diamond brooch from Joseph DuMouchelle International Auctioneers; sapphire and diamond bracelet from Butterfields.

Page 14: Merle Oberon and Mauboussin necklaces from Antiquorum Auctioneers; Art Deco clip brooch and Ghiso bracelet courtesy of Sotheby's; enamel lapel watch from Weschler's; René Lalique ring courtesy of Christie's Images, NY.

Page 15: Van Cleef & Arpels and Art Nouveau brooches courtesy of Christie's Images, NY; sapphire bracelet, Boivin brooches, Oscar Heyman & Brothers brooch, and Boucheron watch from Phillips; Buccellati brooch and David Webb bracelet from Sotheby's.

Page 16: "Couscous" watch courtesy of Sotheby's; Retro watch courtesy of Christie's Images, NY; Brequet and Patek Philippe watches from Antiquorum Auctioneers; Patek Philippe wristwatch from Butterfields.

# Index

*Notes*

*Notes*

*Notes*

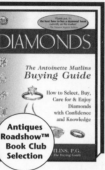

# DIAMONDS: THE ANTOINETTE MATLINS BUYING GUIDE

*How to Select, Buy, Care for & Enjoy Diamonds with Confidence and Knowledge*

*by* Antoinette Matlins, P.G.

Practical, comprehensive, and easy to understand, this book includes price guides for old and new cuts and for fancy-color, treated, and synthetic diamonds. **Explains in detail** how to read diamond grading reports and offers important advice for after buying a diamond. **The "unofficial bible" for all diamond buyers who want to get the most for their money.**

6" x 9", 220 pp., 12 full-color pages & many b/w illustrations and photos; index
Quality Paperback Original, ISBN 0-943763-32-0 **$16.95**

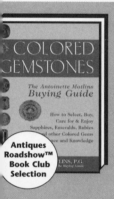

# COLORED GEMSTONES:
## THE ANTOINETTE MATLINS BUYING GUIDE

*How to Select, Buy, Care for & Enjoy Sapphires, Emeralds, Rubies and Other Colored Gems with Confidence and Knowledge*

*by* Antoinette Matlins, P.G.

This practical, comprehensive, easy-to-understand guide **provides in depth** all the information you need to buy colored gems with confidence. Includes price guides for popular gems, opals, and synthetic stones. Provides examples of gemstone grading reports and offers important advice for after buying a gemstone. **Shows anyone shopping for colored gemstones how to get the most for their money.**

6" x 9", 224 pp., 16 full-color pages & many b/w illustrations and photos; index
Quality Paperback Original, ISBN 0-943763-33-9 **$16.95**

# THE PEARL BOOK, 2ND EDITION:
## THE DEFINITIVE BUYING GUIDE

*How to Select, Buy, Care for & Enjoy Pearls*
*by* Antoinette Matlins, P.G.

### COMPREHENSIVE • EASY TO READ • PRACTICAL

This comprehensive, authoritative guide tells readers everything they need to know about pearls to fully understand and appreciate them, and avoid any unexpected—and costly—disappointments, now and in future generations.

- A journey into the rich history and romance surrounding pearls.
- The five factors that determine pearl value & judging pearl quality.
- What to look for, what to look out for: How to spot fakes. Treatments.
- Differences between natural, cultured and imitation pearls, and ways to separate them.
- Comparisons of all types of pearls, in every size and color, from every pearl-producing country.

6" x 9", 232 pp., 16 full-color pages & over 250 color and b/w illustrations and photos; index
Quality Paperback, ISBN 0-943763-28-2 **$19.95**

---

**FOR CREDIT CARD ORDERS CALL 800-962-4544**
*Available from your bookstore or directly from the publisher.* **TRY YOUR BOOKSTORE FIRST.**

# The "Unofficial Bible" for the Gem & Jewelry Buye

## JEWELRY & GEMS:
### THE BUYING GUIDE, 5TH EDITION

*How to Buy Diamonds, Pearls, Colored Gemstones, Gold & Jewelry with Confidence and Knowledge*
by Antoinette Matlins, P.G., *and* A. C. Bonanno, F.G.A., P.G., A.S.A.
—*over 250,000 copies in print*—

**Antiques Roadshow™ Book Club Selection**

*( NEW Retail Price Guides )*

**Learn the tricks of the trade from** *insiders:* How to buy diamonds, pearls, precious and other popular colored gems with confidence and knowledge. More than just a buying guide . . . discover what's available and what choices you have, what determines quality as well as cost, what questions to ask before you buy and what to get in writing. Easy to read and understand. Excellent for staff training.

6" x 9", 320 pp., 16 full-color pages & over 200 color and b/w illustrations and photos; index
Quality Paperback, ISBN 0-943763-31-2 **$18.95**
Hardcover, ISBN 0-943763-30-4 **$24.95**

---

## • COMPREHENSIVE • EASY TO READ • PRACTICAL •
### ENGAGEMENT & WEDDING RINGS, 2ND EDITION
by Antoinette Matlins, P.G., *and* A. C. Bonanno, F.G.A., A.S.A., M.G.A.

Tells **everything you need to know to design, select, buy and enjoy that "perfect" ring** and to truly experience the wonder and excitement that should be part of it.

Updated, expanded, filled with valuable information.

*Engagement & Wedding Rings*, 2nd Ed., will help you make the *right* choice. You will discover romantic traditions behind engagement and wedding rings, how to select the right style and design for *you*, tricks to get what you want on a budget, ways to add new life to an "heirloom," what to do to protect yourself against fraud, and much more.

Dazzling 16-page color section of rings showing antique to contemporary designs.
Over 400 illustrations and photographs. Index.
6" x 9", 304 pp., Quality Paperback, ISBN 0-943763-20-7 **$16.95**

---

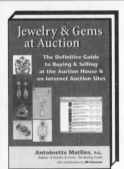

## JEWELRY & GEMS AT AUCTION
*The Definitive Guide to Buying & Selling at the Auction House & on Internet Auction Sites*
by Antoinette Matlins, P.G.
*with contributions by* Jill Newman

As buying and selling at auctions—both traditional auction houses and "virtual" Internet auctions—moves into the mainstream, **consumers need to know how to "play the game."** There are treasures to be had and money to be saved and made, but buying and selling at auction offers unique risks as well as unique opportunities. This book makes available—for the first time—detailed information on how to buy and sell jewelry and gems at auction without making costly mistakes.

6" x 9", 352 pp., fully illustrated
Quality Paperback Original, ISBN 0-943763-29-0 **$19.95**

0?

## CAMEOS OLD & NEW, 2ND EDITION
*by* Anna M. Miller, G.G.

Newly revised and expanded, *Cameos Old & New,* 2nd Ed., is a **concise, easy-to-understand guide** enabling anyone—from beginner to antique dealer—to recognize and evaluate quality and value in cameos, and avoid the pitfalls of purchasing mediocre pieces, fakes and forgeries.

6" x 9", 304 pp., over 300 photographs and illustrations, 130 in full color; index
Quality Paperback, ISBN 0-943763-17-7 **$19.95**

## ILLUSTRATED GUIDE TO JEWELRY APPRAISING,
### 2ND EDITION • *Antique, Period, Modern*
*by* Anna M. Miller, G.G., M.G.A., R.M.V.

This beautifully illustrated guide **provides step-by-step instruction** in jewelry identification and dating, reviews the responsibilities of the appraiser, and describes in detail virtually every style of antique and period jewelry for the hobbyist and serious collector alike.

8½" x 11", 216 pp., over 150 photographs and illustrations; index
Hardcover, ISBN 0-943763-23-1 **$39.95**

## GEMS & JEWELRY APPRAISING, 2ND EDITION
*Techniques of Professional Practice*
*by* Anna M. Miller, G.G., M.G.A., R.M.V.

The **premier guide to the standards, procedures and ethics of appraising gems, jewelry and other valuables.** *Gems & Jewelry Appraising* offers all the information that jewelers, gemologists and students will need to establish an appraisal business, handle various kinds of appraisals and provide an accurate, verifiable estimate of value.

8½" x 11", 256 pp., over 130 photographs and illustrations; index
Hardcover, ISBN 0-943763-10-X **$39.95**

# TREASURE HUNTER'S GEM & MINERAL GUIDES TO THE U.S.A.
*Where & How to Dig, Pan and Mine Your Own Gems & Minerals*
### —IN 4 REGIONAL VOLUMES—

by Kathy J. Rygle and Stephen F. Pedersen • *Preface by* Antoinette Matlins, P.G., *author of* Gem Identification Made Easy

From rubies, opals and gold, to emeralds, aquamarine and diamonds, each guide offers **state-by-state details on more than 250 gems and minerals** and the affordable "fee dig" sites where they can be found. Each guide covers:

- **Equipment & Clothing:** What you need and where to find it.
- **Mining Techniques:** Step-by-step instructions.
- **Gem and Mineral Sites:** Directions & maps, hours, fees, and more.
- **Museums and Mine Tours**

All guides: 6" x 9", Quality Paperback Original, Illustrations, maps & photos, indexes. **$14.95 each**
**Northeast** (CT, DC, DE, IL, IN, MA, MD, ME, MI, NH, NJ, NY, OH, PA, RI, VT, WI)
208 pp., ISBN 0-943763-27-4
**Northwest** (AK, IA, ID, MN, MT, ND, NE, OR, SD, WA, WY)
176 pp., ISBN 0-943763-24-X
**Southeast** (AL, AR, FL, GA, KY, LA, MO, MS, NC, SC, TN, VA, WV)
192 pp., ISBN 0-943763-26-6
**Southwest** (AZ, CA, CO, HI, KS, NM, NV, OK, TX, UT)
208 pp., ISBN 0-943763-25-8

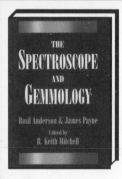

# Buy Your *"Tools of the Trade"*...

## Gem Identification Instruments directly from *GemStone Press*

Whatever instrument you need, GemStone Press can help.
Use our convenient order form, or contact us directly for assistance.

### Complete Pocket Instrument Set
# SPECIAL SAVINGS!
## BUY THIS ESSENTIAL TRIO AND SAVE 12%

Used together, you can identify 85% of all gems with these three
portable, pocket-sized instruments—the essential trio.
10X Triplet Loupe • Chelsea Filter • Calcite Dichroscope

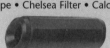

**Pocket Instrument Set:**

**Standard:** With Standard 10X Loupe • OPL Dichroscope • Chelsea Filter    **only $144.95**
**Deluxe:** With Bausch & Lomb 10X Loupe • EZVIEW Dichroscope • Chelsea Filter    **only $179.95**

| ITEM / QUANTITY | PRICE EA.* | TOTAL $ |
|---|---|---|
| **Pocket Instrument Sets** | | |
| **Standard:** With Standard 10X Loupe • OPL Dichroscope • Chelsea Filter | $144.95 | $ _____ |
| **Deluxe:** With Bausch & Lomb 10X Loupe • EZVIEW Dichroscope • Chelsea Filter | $179.95 | _____ |
| **Loupes—Professional Jeweler's 10X Triplet Loupes** | | |
| Bausch & Lomb 10X Triplet Loupe | $44.00 | _____ |
| Standard 10X Triplet Loupe | $29.00 | _____ |
| Darkfield Diamond View | $58.95 | _____ |
| • Spot filled diamonds, other enhancements and zoning instantly. Operates with large maglite (optional). | | |
| **Analyzer** | | |
| Gem Analyzer | $285.00 | _____ |
| • Combines Darkfield Loupe, Polariscope, and Immersion Cell | | |
| **Calcite Dichroscopes** | | |
| Dichroscope (EZVIEW) | $115.00 | _____ |
| Dichroscope (OPL) | $89.95 | _____ |
| **Color Filters** | | |
| Chelsea Filter | $44.95 | _____ |
| Synthetic Emerald Filter Set (Hanneman) | $32.00 | _____ |
| Tanzanite Filter (Hanneman) | $28.00 | _____ |
| Bead Buyer's & Parcel Picker's Filter Set (Hanneman) | $24.00 | _____ |
| **Diamond Testers and Tweezers** | | |
| Type II-a Diamond Spotter | $150.00 | _____ |
| SSEF Shortwave Lamp | $499.00 | _____ |
| Diamondnite Dual Tester | $269.00 | _____ |
| Diamond Tweezers/Locking | $10.65 | _____ |
| Diamond Tweezers/Non-Locking | $7.80 | _____ |
| **Jewelry Cleaners** | | |
| Ionic Cleaner—Home size model | $69.95 | _____ |
| Ionic Solution—16 oz. bottle | $20.00 | _____ |

**See Over for More Instruments**

# Buy Your *"Tools of the Trade..."*

## Gem Identification Instruments directly from *GemStone Press*

Whatever instrument you need, GemStone Press can help.
Use our convenient order form, or contact us directly for assistance.

| ITEM / QUANTITY | PRICE EA.* | TOTAL $ |
|---|---|---|
| **Lamps—Ultraviolet & High Intensity** | | |
| _____ Small LW/SW (UVP) | $71.00 | _____ |
| _____ Large LW/SW (UVP) | $189.00 | _____ |
| _____ Viewing Cabinet for Large Lamp (UVP) | $147.00 | _____ |
| _____ **Purchase Large Lamp & Cabinet together** | $299.00 | _____ |
| **for $299 and save $37.00** | | |
| _____ Dialite Flip Lamp (Eickhorst) | $64.95 | _____ |
| **Other Light Sources** | | |
| _____ Large Maglite | $15.00 | _____ |
| _____ Flex Light | $29.95 | _____ |
| **Refractometers** | | |
| _____ Standard Refractometer (Eickhorst) | $625.00 | _____ |
| _____ Pocket Refractometer (Eickhorst) | $495.00 | _____ |
| _____ Refractive Index Liquid—10 gram | $42.50 | _____ |
| **Spectroscopes** | | |
| _____ Spectroscope—Pocket-sized model (OPL) | $89.00 | _____ |
| _____ Spectroscope—Desk model w/stand (OPL) | $225.00 | _____ |

**Shipping/Insurance per order in the U.S.: $4.95 first item,** SHIPPING/INS. $_____
**$3.00 each add'l item; $7.95 total for pocket instrument set.**

Outside the U.S.: Please specify *insured* shipping method you prefer
and provide a credit card number for payment. **TOTAL $ _____** **

---

Check enclosed for $ _____ (Payable to: GEMSTONE PRESS)
Charge my credit card: ❏ Visa ❏ MasterCard
Name on Card _____
Cardholder Address: Street _____
City/State/Zip _____
Credit Card # _____ Exp. Date _____
Signature _____ Phone (_____)_____
*Please send to:* ❏ Same as Above ❏ Address Below
Name _____
Street _____
City/State/Zip _____ Phone (_____)_____

*Phone, mail, fax, or e-mail orders to:*
**GEMSTONE PRESS, P.O. Box 237, Woodstock, VT 05091**
*Tel: (802) 457-4000 • Fax: (802) 457-4004 • Credit Card Orders: (800) 962-4544*
**www.gemstonepress.com**
**Generous Discounts on Quantity Orders**

## See Over for More Instruments

**TOTAL SATISFACTION GUARANTEE**
If for any reason you're not completely delighted
with your purchase, return it in resellable condition
within 30 days for a full refund.

*Prices, manufacturing specifications, and terms subject to change
without notice. Orders accepted subject to availability.

**All orders must be prepaid by credit card, money order or check
in U.S. funds drawn on a U.S. bank.

01

*Please send me:*

**CAMEOS OLD & NEW, 2ND EDITION**
_____ copies at $19.95 (Quality Paperback) *plus s/h\**

**COLORED GEMSTONES: THE ANTOINETTE MATLINS BUYING GUIDE**
_____ copies at $16.95 (Quality Paperback) *plus s/h\**

**DIAMONDS: THE ANTOINETTE MATLINS BUYING GUIDE**
_____ copies at $16.95 (Quality Paperback) *plus s/h\**

**ENGAGEMENT & WEDDING RINGS: THE DEFINITIVE BUYING GUIDE, 2ND EDITION**
_____ copies at $16.95 (Quality Paperback) *plus s/h\**

**GEM IDENTIFICATION MADE EASY, 2ND EDITION:**
**A HANDS-ON GUIDE TO MORE CONFIDENT BUYING & SELLING**
_____ copies at $34.95 (Hardcover) *plus s/h\**

**GEMS & JEWELRY APPRAISING, 2ND EDITION**
_____ copies at $39.95 (Hardcover) *plus s/h\**

**ILLUSTRATED GUIDE TO JEWELRY APPRAISING, 2ND EDITION**
_____ copies at $39.95 (Hardcover) *plus s/h\**

**JEWELRY & GEMS AT AUCTION: THE DEFINITIVE GUIDE TO BUYING & SELLING**
**AT THE AUCTION HOUSE & ON INTERNET AUCTION SITES**
_____ copies at $19.95 (Quality Paperback) *plus s/h\**

**JEWELRY & GEMS: THE BUYING GUIDE, 5TH EDITION**
_____ copies at $18.95 (Quality Paperback) *plus s/h\**
_____ copies at $24.95 (Hardcover) *plus s/h\**

**THE PEARL BOOK, 2ND EDITION: THE DEFINITIVE BUYING GUIDE**
_____ copies at $19.95 (Quality Paperback) *plus s/h\**

**THE SPECTROSCOPE AND GEMMOLOGY**
_____ copies at $60.00 (Hardcover) *plus s/h\**

**TREASURE HUNTER'S GEM & MINERAL GUIDES TO THE U.S.A.:**
**WHERE & HOW TO DIG, PAN AND MINE YOUR OWN GEMS & MINERALS—**
**IN 4 REGIONAL VOLUMES** $14.95 per copy (Quality Paperback) *plus s/h\**
_____ copies of NE States _____ copies of SE States _____ copies of NW States _____ copies of SW States

\* In U.S.: Shipping/Handling: $3.75 for 1st book, $2.00 each additional book.
  Outside U.S.: Specify shipping method (insured) and provide a credit card number for payment.

---------------------------------------------------------------------------------

Check enclosed for $_____ (Payable to: GEMSTONE Press)
Charge my credit card: ❑ Visa ❑ MasterCard
Name on Card (PRINT) _____
Cardholder Address: Street _____
City/State/Zip _____
Credit Card # _____ Exp. Date _____
Signature _____ Phone (____)_____
*Please send to:* ❑ Same as Above ❑ Address Below
Name (PRINT) _____
Street _____
City/State/Zip _____ Phone (____)_____

| TOTAL SATISFACTION GUARANTEE |
|---|
| If for any reason you're not completely delighted with your purchase, return it in resellable condition within 30 days for a full refund. |

*Phone, mail, fax, or e-mail orders to:*
**GEMSTONE PRESS,** Sunset Farm Offices,
Rte. 4, P.O. Box 237, Woodstock, VT 05091
*Tel:* **(802) 457-4000** • *Fax:* **(802) 457-4004**
*Credit Card Orders:* **(800) 962-4544**
**www.gemstonepress.com**
**Generous Discounts on Quantity Orders**

Prices subject
to change

## Try Your Bookstore First